W9-AGM-503

Global Anarchy in the Third Millennium?

Race, Place and Power at the End of the Modern Age

Joseph Wayne Smith

Graham Lyons

and

Evonne Moore

First published in Great Britain 2000 by
MACMILLAN PRESS LTD
Houndmills, Basingstoke, Hampshire RG21 6XS and London
Companies and representatives throughout the world

A catalogue record for this book is available from the British Library.

ISBN 0–333–68143–6

First published in the United States of America 2000 by
ST. MARTIN'S PRESS, INC.,
Scholarly and Reference Division,
175 Fifth Avenue, New York, N.Y. 10010

ISBN 0–312–22908–9

Library of Congress Cataloging-in-Publication Data
Smith, Joseph Wayne.
Global anarchy in the third millennium? : race, place and power
at the end of the modern age / Joseph Wayne Smith, Graham Lyons and
Evonne Moore.
p.   cm.
Includes bibliographical references and index.
ISBN 0–312–22908–9 (cloth)
1. Sustainable development.   2. Environmentalism.
3. International economic relations.   4. Social problems.
5. Civilization, Modern—1950–   I. Lyons, Graham, 1954–
II. Moore, Evonne.   III. Title.
HC79.E5S5356   1999
363.9'1—dc21
99–41294
CIP

This book is printed on paper suitable for recycling and made from fully managed and sustained
forest sources.

10   9   8   7   6   5   4   3   2   1
09   08   07   06   05   04   03   02   01   00

Printed and bound in Great Britain by
Antony Rowe Ltd, Chippenham, Wiltshire

Contents

1 Ragnarok! Race, Place and Global Anarchy at the End of the Modern Age

Much evidence exists in the 1990s for the relevance of the "sheer chaos" paradigm of world affairs: a global breakdown of law and order, failed states and increasing anarchy in many parts of the world, a global crime wave, transnational mafias and drug cartels, increasing drug addiction in many societies, a general weakening of the family, a decline in trust and social solidarity in many countries, ethnic, religious, and civilizational violence and rule by the gun prevalent in much of the world. In city after city – Moscow, Rio de Janeiro, Bangkok, Shanghai, London, Rome, Warsaw, Tokyo, Johannesburg, Delhi, Karachi, Cairo, Bogota, Washington – crime seems to be soaring and basic elements of Civilization fading away. People speak of a global crisis in governance. The rise of transnational corporations producing economic goods is increasingly matched by the rise of transnational crime mafias, drug cartels, and terrorist gangs violently assaulting Civilization. Law and order is the first prerequisite of Civilization and in much of the world – Africa, Latin America, the former Soviet Union, South Asia, the Middle East – it appears to be evaporating, while also under serious assault in China, Japan, and the West. On a worldwide basis Civilization seems in many respects to be yielding to barbarism, generating the image of an unprecedented phenomenon, a global Dark Ages, possibly descending on humanity. (Huntington, 1996, 321)

I think there are good reasons for suggesting that the modern age has ended. Today, many things indicate that we are going through a transitional period, when it seems that something is on the way out and something else is painfully being born. It is as if something were crumbling, decaying and exhausting itself, while something else, still indistinct, were arising from the rubble.

> – Václav Havel, President of the Czech Republic.
> (quoted from Korten, 1995, 1)

The substitution of intellectual for physical strife is necessary to an expansion of the consciousness of kind because only through the diminution of physical conflict can sympathy grow, and because also the wider consciousness of kind involves a wider understanding. But this is not all. Intellectual strife directly and positively diminishes physical strife, with all its wastefulness and misery. This it does because all intellectual activity is in its very nature deliberative. It inhibits impulse, it hinders action, it restrains motor discharge.

It is not then a duty for men and women to suppress their intellectual convictions, to yield tamely their independently thought-out views of truth, and right, and policy, in the mistaken notion that intellectual contention is disreputable, or unmannerly, or unkind, as are the forms of physical strife. The precise opposite is our true obligation. Intellectual strife makes for rational, and ultimately for ethical, like-mindedness; it makes for peace, prosperity, and happiness. The highest duty of every rational being is to engage with sincere and disinterested earnestness in the fruitful contests of intellectual strife.

— Franklin H. Giddings (1906, 324–5)

Ragnarok: Norse mythology, the ultimate destruction of the gods and man in a cataclysmic battle against the forces of evil, out of which a new world will arise.

(A Standard Dictionary Definition)

GLOBAL ANARCHY AND THE COMING DARK AGES

What happens when an irresistible force meets an immovable object? An irresistible force is, by definition, a force which is capable of moving *any* object. An immovable object is by definition an object incapable of being moved by *any* force. So what happens when these two ontologically strange entities meet? Clearly we have a contradiction; logically the immovable object both moves and does not move. According to a standard view of logic (which we will have more to say about in chapter 3) there can be no irresistible forces and immovable objects. Yet taken individually, there does not *prima facie* seem to be anything wrong with either the idea of an irresistible force or an immovable object. However if there were such things (and observe that an irresistible force opposing another irresistible force makes either force, in effect, an "immovable object") they would annihilate each other: the seeds of their destruction lie within their own being.

Here we are concerned with the clash of forces which in a human rather than a metaphysical sense are seemingly "irresistible" and with objects which for all effective purposes are "immovable", both in the empirical world and the world of thought and ideas. In both realms of being, we are concerned with contradictions or antinomies that cannot be resolved in conventional and orthodox ways – unless one calls annihilation and destruction an "orthodox way". This book is a development of our previous books, including *The Bankruptcy of Economics* (Smith et al., 1998a), *Global Meltdown* (Smith et al., 1998b), *The Unreasonable Silence of the World* (Sauer-Thompson and Smith, 1997) and *Healing a Wounded World* (Smith et al., 1997).[1] These books have examined the prospects of the survival of modern civilization in the face of the "irresistible force" of economic globalization and the "immovable objects" of ecological scarcity, the environmental crisis and the limits to growth. We have argued that this conflict cannot be resolved and that human civilization, and perhaps the human species itself, will be destroyed between the Scylla of the global economy and the Charybdis of the Earth's ecology, with the result of global anarchy – the breakdown of modern civilized order and the rise of a new barbarism (Geyer, 1985; Kaplan, 1997; Robins and Pye-Smith, 1997). Robert Kaplan's *The Ends of the Earth* (Kaplan, 1997) has greatly influenced us. Kaplan presents essentially a travel guide of a number of "hot spots" in the world where social order and civilized values have broken down, but he also presents a journey in time, where the future – a world of bleakness, ecological devastation and ruin (Kennedy, 1993) – is understood in terms of the present. However Kaplan's book is theoretically weak and lacks a cogent philosophical basis, which we have tried to supply elsewhere (Smith et al., 1998b). This book examines in more detail a theme that has been lying half buried in our other works: the conflict over race and place and the contribution which this conflict makes to the new world disorder. Benjamin Barber, for example, has described the world as caught between W.B. Yeats', two eternities of "race" and "soul", "race reflecting the tribal past, that of soul anticipating the cosmopolitan future" (Barber, 1995, 4). Both "race" and "soul" according to Barber offer us a bleak undemocratic future:

> The first scenario rooted in race holds out the grim prospect of a retribalization of large swaths of humankind by war and bloodshed: a threatened balkanization of nation-states in which culture is pitted against culture, people against people, tribe against tribe, a Jihad in the name of a hundred narrowly conceived faiths against every kind of interdependence, every kind of artificial social cooperation and mutuality: against technology, against pop culture, and against integrated markets; against modernity itself as well as the future in which modernity issues. The second paints that future in shimmering pastels, a busy portrait of onrushing economic, technological, and ecological forces that

demand integration and uniformity . . . one McWorld tied together by communications, information, entertainment, and commerce. Caught between Babel and Disneyland, the planet is falling precipitously apart and coming reluctantly together at the very same moment. (Barber, 1995, 4)

Contrary to Barber we see hope for the survival of humanity tied to the survival of "race" or "community" and a "sense of place" (Roberts, 1989) and this position is defended in this book.

James Dale Davidson and William Rees-Mogg are right in our opinion to observe in their book *The Great Reckoning: How the World Will Change Before the Year 2000* that "We are again living in a period which has the authentic feeling that the world could come to an end, or at least that some immense change could occur" (Davidson and Rees-Mogg, 1994, xi). Further, these writers observe, "almost everyone assumes that existing trends will continue, until the plane crashes, the business goes bankrupt, the government falls or the regime is overthrown" (Davidson and Rees-Mogg, 1994, xiv).

The modern world is coming to an end and the global chaos, anarchy and social dislocation observed by Kaplan and others is matched only by the intellectual and metaphysical *angst* that characterizes our time of crisis. This book is an attempt to explore the philosophical ramifications of the idea of the end of modernity – the end of the modern age – and in particular to develop a critique at the deepest level of the reigning religions of modernity – globalism, cosmopolitanism, internationalism and liberalism itself. John Gray, in an article commenting on the strong showing of the radical Islamic party *Refah* on Christmas Eve 1995 in Turkey's parliamentary elections, said that

It is difficult to assess the impact on Western societies of the dawning realisation that the epoch in which they were governor and tutor of the entire world has come to an end. We can be sure, though, that it will be incalculably large, and accompanied by enormous disorientation and denial . . . The deeper lesson of Islamist advance in Turkey is that the conflicts by which the world will be riven in the coming century will not be between different Western ideologies. They will be conflicts fuelled by militant religions, resurgent ethnicities and – not least – by the pressures of expanding populations on scarce natural resources. In such a world we should not expect liberal values to spread. A sufficiently demanding objective for liberal cultures will be survival. (Gray, 1996, 13)

It is the view of the present authors that liberal culture and any world order founded upon liberal principles is unsustainable; Thomas Fleming is right to see liberalism as a "denatured Christianity", a "radioactive poison that rots out all peculiarities, reducing individual men and women to ciphers, erasing national frontiers, and destroying all distinctive institutions that reflect and transmit differences of culture, religion, and – for want of a better word – formation" (Fleming, 1997, 10). Liberal ideology and liberal society will be swept away in the deluge that is to come.

For most of us such thoughts of apocalyptic pessimism seem extreme and poisonous, a paranoid vision that has no connection to reality. It is worthwhile then to develop our eschatology with considerable scene-setting. The idea that our comfortable world – be it our nation, the global economy, modern civilization or even ourselves – could come to an end and be extinguished – is difficult to accept. Yet nations, economies and civilizations have risen and fallen as surely as individuals have been born and died. Arnold J. Toynbee's *A Study of History* (1960) is still insightful for those seeking some theoretical explanation of the rise and fall of civilizations and the fate of the West. Toynbee examined 28 civilizations in his massive work, 18 of which had died and nine of the 10 remaining were shown to have already broken down. The one remaining unbroken, at the time of this writing, was Western civilization. What caused civilizations to break down? Toynbee summarized his answer in three points: "a failure of creative power in the creative minority, which henceforth becomes a merely 'dominant' minority; an answering withdrawal of allegiance and mimesis on the part of the majority; a consequent loss of social unity in the society as a whole" (Toynbee, 1960, 924). Toynbee disagreed with Spengler, who believed that societies are organisms with natural passages from birth, to youth, to maturity, to decay. Nor does geographical contraction caused by military aggression necessarily lead to social decay in Toynbee's opinion. The decay of technical achievement is a result, not the cause, of social breakdown. Gibbon's thesis that barbarism and religion (e.g. Christianity) cause social breakdown is rejected by Toynbee on the grounds that Gibbon does not take his analysis back far enough; successful aggression against societies occurs after social breakdown has occurred. Societies which are still growing may be stimulated to further growth by external aggression and even societies in decline may be given a new lease of life by such aggression. Toynbee's alternative explanation of the breakdown of civilizations is as follows. The only way in which the "uncreative majority" can follow the leadership of the "creative minority" is by mimesis, by mechanical imitation and drill. If the "creative minority" become infected with the mechanicalness of their followers or if the leaders exchange persuasion for compulsion, then the society loses its capacity for self-determination and begins to disintegrate.

According to Toynbee the disintegration of civilizations occurs through a schism in the body social into three factions: the dominant minority, internal proletariat and external proletariat. These are each responsible for a particular creation: the dominant minority, a universal state; the internal proletariat, a universal church, and the external proletariat, barbarian warbands, waiting their chance to storm the gates of the society and plunder its remaining riches. The disintegration of a civilization is accompanied by a "schism in the soul", with the various ways of life being replaced by negative substitutes – abandonment for creativity, promiscuity for a "sense of style" – so that the once creative minority becomes ultimately as vulgar in its way of life in the final stage of dissolution as the external barbarians.

The "schism in the soul" of modernity is deep. Even theorists generally sympathetic to the global capitalist order recognize this. For example, Lester Thurow in his book *The Future of Capitalism* (1996) says that the "fault lines of financial instability are real" (Thurow, 1996, 231). The "social volcanos" of religious fundamentalism and ethnic separatism are again erupting so that, for example, "Today northern Italians are free to tell southern Italians what they think of them. Italy is no longer held together by the glue of the cold war" (Thurow, 1996, 238). The nation-state no longer has a dominant ideology to supply a social glue for the modern world, so we are seeing, Thurow observes, the nation breaking-up into warring ethnic and racial groups. Paradoxically, the global economy is allowing ethnic and racial separatism to grow:

> Why not break up into tribal ethnic groups and fight it out? Such sentiments are legitimated by today's world economy. Everyone now understands that one does not have to be a big economy with a big internal market to succeed. City-states like Hong Kong or Singapore can succeed. It used to be that everyone thought that breaking up a country into smaller pieces meant a lower standard of living; today everyone knows that this isn't true. As a result, one can go it alone and does not have to cooperate with other ethnic groups to have a high standard of living. With this knowledge goes one of the previously existing impediments to ethnic feuding. (Thurow, 1996, 241)

Thurow goes on to compare today's society with the fall of Rome and the coming of the Dark Ages: "Immigrants are flooding into the industrial world but no one is willing to incur the costs that will make them into first-world citizens. Both the Soviet empire and the American alliances have broken apart. Weak nations are succumbing to feudal lords . . . and even strong ones are giving up their powers to local leaders" (Thurow, 1996, 263). Literacy fell during ancient Rome's fall to the point that at the depth of the Dark Ages only a few monks could read. Functional illiteracy is rising in the United States and other countries (Thurow, 1996, 263). Standards of living plummeted during the Dark Ages; today, although total productivity is still rising, 80 percent of the US population is experiencing a fall in real wages (Douthwaite, 1992). Falling wages, especially for black Americans, constitutes a "declaration of economic war" (Thurow, 1996, 269) and if capitalism and democracy do not deliver a bigger share of the pie, Thurow notes, they will be discredited for a substantial portion of the American population (Thurow, 1996, 268). In the Dark Ages, banditry was widespread and countered by walled cities; today guarded communities, "walled" by electronic protection devices and armed guards, are on the rise (Thurow, 1996, 264). Further, the fall of Rome saw the private squeezing out the public sector until the public sector virtually disappeared. The seeds of feudalism were thus present in the disintegration of Rome because, "Almost by definition feudalism is public power in private hands. Those who had been free citizens gradually sold themselves into serfdom to gain safety from roving gangs and essential services that only a feudal master could provide" (Thurow, 1996, 265).

James Dale Davidson and William Rees-Mogg in their book *The Great Reckoning*, predict that a "financial armageddon" will occur (Davidson and Rees-Mogg, 1994, 25–9). The end, they observe, "will not only reveal the insolvency of many individuals and corporations, it may also bring bankruptcy to the welfare state and widespread breakdown of authority within political economies. . . . More than you may now imagine, you are vulnerable to financial, economic, and political collapse" (Davidson and Rees-Mogg, 1994, 25). Global depression will arise from a number of factors including compounding debt; the insolvency of many major financial institutions; the collapse of state-dominated economies in the former Soviet Union, Eastern Europe, parts of Latin America and much of Africa; the crash of the Asian stock markets; the end of the Cold War; a saturation of markets for most products of the post-war boom and the rise of "subversive" technologies such as information technology which destabilize society through the creation of technological-structural unemployment. They also believe that it is time for a downturn in the long term Kondratieff-cycle or business-cycle, predicting another 1929-style stock market crash, probably before the year 2000. Although this prediction may be premature, Davidson and Rees-Mogg predicted the 1987 stockmarket crash, the fall of Communism, the breakup of the multi-ethnic Soviet Empire and the bankruptcies of the United States savings and loans institutions. Their prediction of an economic implosion of many South East Asian economies was also borne out in 1997 and 1998 (Baker, 1997). We will have more to say about the coming financial meltdown of the global economy in the final chapter of this book.

    While some theorists believe that a globalized economy does not yet exist (Hirst and Thompson, 1992), others believe that the globalized economy (or approximately "globalized" economy) and the retreat of the nation-state in the face of "turbo-charged capitalism" (Luttwak et al., 1996) is bringing forth social and ecological disaster (Smith, 1994b; Douthwaite, 1996; Mander and Goldsmith eds, 1996; Marquard, 1997). *Rolling Stone* magazine national editor, William Greider, author of *One World, Ready or Not: The Manic Logic of Global Capitalism* (Greider, 1997), sees modern global capitalism as an "awesome machine running over terrain and ignoring familiar boundaries. . . . As it goes, the machine throws off enormous mows of wealth and bounty while it leaves behind great furrows of wreckage" (Greider, 1997, 11). This juggernaut has no central control, being guided by its own momentum: "The wondrous machine of global revolution is oscillating out of control, widening the arcs of social and economic instabilities in its wake. The destructive pressures building up within the global system are leading toward an unbearable chaos that, even without a dramatic collapse, will likely provoke the harsh, reactionary politics that can shut down the system" (Greider, 1997, 316). Global finance "is in a reckless footrace with history, plunging toward some sort of dreadful reckoning with its own contradictions, pulling everyone else along with it" (Greider, 1997, 316). Greider is also author of *Secrets of the Temple: How the Federal Reserve Runs the Country* (1987) – it is therefore odd to find Greider proposing that the global economy can be redirected onto a beneficial path by the reregulation of financial capital, controls implemented through the nation-state (Greider, 1997, 317), because the process of economic globalization almost by definition is destroying this method of control. In fact later in his book Greider does recognize that the weakness of political leaders will make his proposed solution "quite difficult, if not impossible" (Greider, 1997, 472). The God of the self-regulating market will fail: "the global system will, indeed, probably experience a series of terrible events – wrenching calamities that are economic or social or environmental in nature – before common sense can prevail" (Greider, 1997, 473). Common sense has not prevailed to date, so why should it prevail in the future, however horrible it will be? Greider recognizes early in his book (Greider, 1997, 12) that while new technologies have helped the "poor" (when the "poor" can afford them (Douthwaite, 1996)) at the same time the new technologies have unleashed the barbarian capacity for the strong to exploit the weak, a technological version of the survival of the fittest, the law of the jungle and might is right. On the basis of Greider's premises, this is a more logical conclusion to accept: the weak will be crushed by the strong.

    David Korten in his book, *When Corporations Rule the World* (1995), argues that global capitalism is a threat to the long term sustainability of human societies. The root of the crisis of civilization, poverty, social disintegration and environmental destruction is a social system concerned with nothing beyond short term economic gain and a growth-centered development philosophy. This has resulted in metaphysical and spiritual alienation, an existential dark night of the soul because the manic pursuit of money ("a useful but wholly substanceless and intrinsically valueless human artifact" (Korten, 1995, 6)) cannot provide a sound basis for a meaningful and sustainable world. Consequently:

> we are experiencing accelerating social and environmental disintegration in nearly every country of the world – as revealed by a rise in poverty, unemployment, inequality, violent crime, failing families, and environmental degradation. These problems stem in part from a fivefold increase in economic output since 1950 that has pushed human demands on the ecosystem beyond what the planet is capable of sustaining. The continued quest for economic growth as the organizing principle of public policy is accelerating the breakdown of the ecosystem's regenerative capacities and the social fabric that sustains human community; at the same time, it is intensifying the competition for resources between rich and poor – a competition that the poor invariably lose. (Korten, 1995, 11)

To build a sustainable society, Korten says, means that

> we must break free of the illusions of the world of money, rediscover spiritual meaning in our lives, and root our economic institutions in place and community so that they are integrally connected to people and life. Consequently, we concluded that the task of people-centered development in its fullest sense must be the creation of life-centered societies in which the economy is but one of the instruments of good living – not the purpose of human existence. (Korten, 1995, 11)

These are noble and heart-warming sentiments, but they are sentiments, we will show, which are unlikely to be realized.

Modern civilization faces threats far greater than those mentioned by all of the authorities quoted above, with the exception of Korten. An excellent account of the physical and technological dangers which humanity faces and which are likely to doom us to extinction as a species has been given by John Leslie in his book *The End of the World: The Science and Ethics of Human Extinction* (1996). We have also discussed many of the physical, technological and ecological threats confronting humanity in our other works (Smith et al., 1997; Smith et al., 1998 a, b) so we will be brief in the account which now follows. Perhaps the seriousness of the global environmental crisis can be judged by two important statements. The first statement is by the Union of Concerned Scientists in their *World Scientists' Warning to Humanity* made in 1992 (an organization comprising scores of Nobel Prize winners):

> Human beings and the natural world are on a collision course. . . . The Earth's ability to provide for growing numbers of people is finite; . . . and we are fast approaching many of the Earth's limits. Pressures resulting from unrestrained population growth put demands on the natural world that can overwhelm any efforts to achieve a sustainable future. . . . No more than one or a few decades remain before the chance to avert the threats we now confront will be lost and the prospect for humanity [and Nature] immeasurably diminished (quoted from Myers, 1993, 205).

Our second statement is from a joint statement issued by the US National Academy of Sciences and the British Royal Society, *Population Growth, Resource Consumption, and a Sustainable World,* also issued in 1992:

> If current predictions of population growth prove accurate and patterns of human activity on the planet remain unchanged, science and technology may not be able to prevent either irreversible degradation of the environment or continued poverty for much of the world. . . . Some of the environmental changes may produce irreversible damage to the Earth's capacity to sustain life. The overall pace of environmental change has unquestionably been accelerated by the recent expansion of the human population. . . . The future of our planet is in the balance (quoted from (Myers, 1993, 205)).

A lively debate exists about the nature of the limits of economic growth and human population expansion (Mikesell, 1995; Smith, 1995; Bronner, 1997; Fodor, 1997). Even a cautious scholar such as Joel E. Cohen recognizes that "the possibility must be considered seriously that the number of people on Earth has reached, or will reach within half a century, the maximum number the Earth can support in modes of life that we and our children and their children will choose to want" (Cohen, 1995, 367). There is of course great uncertainty about the time-frame in which the drama of the Earth's environmental crisis is being enacted. Consider for example global warming produced by the enhanced greenhouse effect. Jane Francis, an ancient climate systems expert at Leeds University, believes that in geological terms the warming of the Earth through greenhouse gases is merely a "blip" as the Earth itself is in an unusual warm spell, a statistical irregularity, in an ice age that began 30 million years ago (*Herald Sun*, 1997).

Over a period of hundreds of millions of years it is quite likely that a killer asteroid of 10 kilometers or greater in diameter could strike the Earth and annihilate most life – the mass extinctions seen in the fossil record (e.g. 250 million years ago 90 percent of species abruptly vanished) are thought by some theorists to be the result of asteroid impact. The debate about the environmental crisis and the limits to growth, to be meaningful, must be isolated to a specific time frame (Mikesell, 1995). If technological sophistication continues for hundreds of millions of years, then anything which is physically possible may become technically possible and all of humanity's biophysical and ecological problems could be solved. Humanity may pass the evolutionary baton to superior thinking machines who leave a dying solar system to explore the infinite cosmos. Our bigoted concern is with human survival in the short term – no longer than the next century. Futurology turns to science fiction after that.

The technological optimists believe that technology will ultimately solve humanity's problems and resolve short-term limits (Simon ed., 1995). We doubt whether this is so. There are a number of reasons for this. One argument which will be developed in some depth in chapter 3 of this book is that there are cognitive limits to science such that a point is reached when incoherence arises. This view has been recently advocated by John Horgan in his book *The End of Science: Facing the Limits of Knowledge in the Twilight of the Scientific Age* (1996), but also earlier by Stent (1969, 1978). According to this position, pure science "has already entered an era of diminishing returns" (Horgan, 1996, 16). He quotes the materialist philosopher Daniel Dennett (who believes that consciousness and our sense of a unified self is an illusion) who surprisingly enough has observed that science has an inherent limitation built into its very possibility of success:

There's a curious paradox looming [in modern science]. One of the very trends that makes science proceed so rapidly these days is a trend that leads science away from human understanding. When you switch from trying to model things with elegant equations to doing massive computer simulations . . . you may end up with a model that exquisitely models nature, the phenomena you're interested in, but you don't understand the model. That is, you don't understand it the way you understood models in the old days. . . . Software systems are already at the very edge of human comprehensibility . . . Even a system like the Internet is absolutely trivial compared to a brain, and yet it's been patched and built on so much that nobody really understands how it works or whether it will go on working. And thus, as you start using software-writing programs and software-debugging programs and codes that heal themselves, you create new artifacts that have a life of

their own. And they become objects that are no longer within the epistemological hegemony of their makers. And so that's going to be sort
of like the speed of light. It's going to be a barrier against which science is going to keep butting its head forever. (quoted from Horgan,
1996, 179–80)

Scientific progress is dependent upon a range of social, political and historical factors, so viewed historically "the modern era of rapid scientific
and technological progress appears to be not a permanent feature of reality
but an aberration, a fluke, a product of a singular convergence of social,
intellectual, and political factors" (Horgan, 1996, 21). In support of his
position Horgan quotes University of Chicago physicist Leo Kadanoff who
predicts "hard times" for physics, manifested in a decline in the number of
physicists as well as social support for physics. This is due to the conditions of the late twentieth century such as the end of the Cold War and the
challenge posed to the pro-science faiths of rationalism and Enlightenment
values ("Enlightenmentism") by anti-science forces. We will discuss this
further in chapter 3.

Technological advancements often create further social problems
(Ellul, 1990). For example, according to computer expert Peter de Jager,
the Y2K problem or millennium bug if not fixed could cause a global depression as many important computer systems, if uncorrected, will crash on
January 1, 2000 (Lynch, 1997). The problem arises because of software
that allows only two digits in the date field for the year. Pessimists such as
Dr. Gary North (who is regarded in the computer world as an "apocalyptic
fanatic"; web address www.garynorth.com) believes that Y2K is unlikely
to be fixed in time so a global economic collapse will occur as of January
1, 2000. The world's mainframe computers crashing or ceasing to function
correctly will affect banks, Social Security, Medicare, transport, communications networks and possibly many national defense systems. We do not
have the competence in computer programming to be able to assess
whether pessimists such as North are correct and nor is it necessary for this
example to illustrate our point. A globally connected computer linked
world is an increasingly vulnerable world; *ergo* it is false to suppose that
technology will magically solve our social and environmental problems.

Indeed, with the breakup of the Soviet Union, nuclear annihilation may
be more likely than in the Cold War. Organized crime in Russia has been
seeking control of 15,000 tactical nuclear warheads as a way to "hijack the
State" (Hersh, 1994) and fuel global nuclear terrorism (Gurr, 1997). Apart
from the terrorist threat, one scenario sees the growing social chaos and
starvation in North Korea leading to Kim Jong IL, North Korea's present
leader "going down in flames" by launching a missile attack on South Korea and even Japan. Defecting official, Hwang Jang-yop, stated in April

1997 that North Korea was preparing for war. In an intelligence report prepared in August 1997 this top northern defector said, "The North can turn the South into a sea of flame and annihilate it by using nuclear and chemical weapons and rockets. . . . The North believes it will win a war and plans to annihilate Japan . . . if the United States meddles in it". As well: "It is clear without any doubt that a historic tragedy is approaching our people" (Reuter, Associated Press, 1997, A13). International aid organizations believe that almost one fifth of the North Korean population will die of starvation without foreign food aid (Associated Press, 1997, 11). Such a climate of social misery could condition the North Koreans to accept the inevitability of a nuclear and chemical inferno.

In summary then, it is naive to believe that the technological sophistication of modern society will shield it from the forces of global anarchy generated by the clash between the forces of money, ecology and "race". In the short term, technology has a major part to play in the breakdown of civilization and in the longer term, the possible extinction of the human race (Leslie, 1996). Further, even if technology were a *deus ex machina*, a flourishing technological base to society ultimately requires a flourishing scientific infrastructure and this in turn presupposes that a high degree of social cohesion and order exists in society. The idea of global anarchy challenges the possibility of this necessary social stability being sustainable into the indefinite future.

In this section we have introduced the idea of the end of the modern age, the breakdown of civilized order and the coming of a new Dark Age. The central focus in this book is upon the clash occurring over "race" and "place", "blood" and "money", the particular and the universal and the ensuing identity-war that inevitably unfolds when the unmixable are forced to mix. As a backdrop to this conflict we have sketched, using the works of a number of authorities, a multitude of other crises that are each in turn acting to destroy civilized order and produce global anarchy. Our challenge to the optimist is to show how not one, but all of these problems which appear to be interacting in complex non-linear ways (Smith et al., 1997) can be *systematically* dealt with. We do not believe that any of these problems, which constitute a "crisis of civilization" (Lyons et al., 1995), can be "solved" in any way that preserves modernity and the ideologies that legitimize the modern age. The failure and ultimate collapse of modernity is best seen through a "vectorial" analysis (what are the forces and what are their directions) of the forces of race and place.[2]

RACE, PLACE AND THE CLASH OF CIVILIZATIONS

According to Samuel P. Huntington, "History has not ended. The world is not one. Civilizations unite and divide humankind" (Huntington, 1993, 194). People do not give ultimate significance to economic interest or political ideology, "Faith and family, blood and belief, are what people identify with and what they will fight and die for" (Huntington, 1993, 194). Consider for example the present geopolitics of Australia. Since the end of the Cold War, the foreign policy of Australia has been shaped by two assumptions: (1) economic considerations trump all other considerations and (2) Australia's future lies with Asia (Harries, 1993). Proposition (1) is the fashionable view that geo-economics has replaced geo-politics as the decisive decision mechanism in world affairs. Proposition (2) has many components as Owen Harries, editor of *The National Interest* notes, including "the changed pattern of Australia's trade; admiration for the fantastic economic progress made by much of Asia; a sense of freedom from Cold War dependence on the United States; resentment of Europe's exclusionary policies and of abandonment by Britain; and, not least, a need to demonstrate national independence and renewal by breaking with established historical patterns and striking out in new directions" (Harries, 1993, 19). Samuel Huntington's *The Clash of Civilizations and the Remaking of World Order* (1996) has advanced a thesis which essentially challenges both assumptions. Huntington argues that the fundamental source of conflict in the new post-Cold War world will not be ideological or economic, but *cultural*, a "clash of civilizations" such that "the fault lines between civilizations will constitute the principal battle lines" (Harries, 1993, 19). Huntington looks critically at the position championed by former Prime Minister Paul Keating that Australia is part of Asia. The argument is, absurdly, that Australia should "enmesh" with Asia, become a republic and break away from Britain, so that the country could become independent – and for some reason becoming "enmeshed" with Asia would not mean any lack of independence. For Keating, Australia must shake off its "anglophilia" at all costs if it is to engage economically with Asia. Huntington observes that the Keating position is based on the view that economics overrides culture, that economic might makes right. Rightly, Huntington views the Asianization ploy with skepticism, noting that the elites and the general public are in conflict on this issue. More importantly, the decision to change a nation to suit economic trends could well become "a major marker in the decline of the West" (Huntington, 1996, 153). This choice though will not eliminate Australia's Western heritage; Australia "will be a permanently torn country, both the "branch office of empire" which Paul Keating decried, and the "new [sic. *poor*] white trash of Asia", which Lee Kuan Yew contemptuously termed it" (Huntington, 1996, 153).

Australia is the first Western society in history where the elites advocate transformation into a non-Western society.[3] Australia and New Zealand are the most isolated parts of the West and the most vulnerable to civilizational conflicts (Harries, 1993).

Huntington divides mankind into various often overlapping civilizations including the West, Confucian or Sinic, Japanese, Buddhist countries from Thailand to Mongolia, Islamic, Hindu, Slavic-Orthodox, Latin American and African. There is considerable overlap between Huntington's civilizations and in some cases it is not clear why a particular civilization is considered as "distinct". Latin American civilization seems to be part of the West insofar as the West is identified with this combination of factors: (1) a classical legacy including Greek philosophy and rationalism, Roman law, Latin and Christianity; (2) Western Christianity; (3) European languages; (4) the separation of Church and State; (5) the rule of law; (6) social pluralism and civil society; (7) representative bodies and (8) individualism. For our purposes though this is an adequate conceptual basis to distinguish Western civilization from other civilizations such as the Islamic. We accept as well that there is considerable vagueness to the idea of a civilization, but for our purposes this is not a major problem. Also on this basis, Westernization must be distinguished from modernization. Modernization typically involves industrialization and urbanization. Huntington's thesis is that modernization, while breaking down local and social identities is creating a vacuum that is being filled by culture and religion, especially religious fundamentalism in Islam, Hindu India, Latin America and the West. The West, especially American popular culture, is threatening the autonomy of other cultures, thus producing an anti-Western backlash in other civilizations in Asia and the Middle East. This revolt against the West is also seen in anti-Western cooperation between Confucian and Islamic civilizations such as China's readiness to supply weapons and technology to Libya and Iraq, nuclear technology for Iran and help in building a nuclear reactor for Algeria. The possibility does exist for it to be "the rest against the West" (Connelly and Kennedy, 1994; Smith et al., 1998b).

Huntington grants that not all future conflicts will occur between different civilizations as some conflicts will take place between nation-states and groups comprising one or more civilizations. Huntington mentions that there will also be a global "real clash", a clash between Civilization in general and barbarism or global anarchy and here all of the great civilizations of the world will hang together or hang separately (Huntington, 1996, 321). Our point of departure from writers such as Huntington, Kennedy (1993) and Kaplan (1997) is that the major force threatening "Civilization", and especially Western civilization, is *internal* and is primarily a lack of identity and social cohesion brought about by a weakening of the nation-state by economic globalization and a creation of (with qualification[4]) multicultural, multiracial societies in Australia, New Zealand, Canada, Britain, Europe, and the United States, largely by policies of mass immigration in the post World War II period. Majorities soon become minorities and Huntington's "clash of civilizations" is played out within the West, within each nation-state of the West and in every city and suburb. The fault lines of *race* and *place*, the battle between nationalism and internationalism will be a major cause of the breakdown of Civilization and the ushering in of an era of global anarchy.[5]

In a book of this scope we cannot support our thesis by a detailed empirical country-by-country examination, although we have made a small contribution in this direction elsewhere (Smith et al., 1998b). Our basic evidence and mode of argument must be on the meta-empirical level, theoretical and interpretive, attempting to fit important books and articles written from a wide range of political and philosophical perspectives into a coherent whole. Readers with a philosophical background will see that this method presupposes a coherence or systemic *criterion* of truth (Rescher, 1973, 1979). As this is a work primarily in social and political affairs we will not attempt to justify plausible presuppositions in the actual structure of our argument. We have assumed that the authorities which we quote in this book have got their basic empirical spade work right. What we shall attempt to do is try and fit the conceptual pieces of their work into a meaningfully designed tapestry. Intellectual controversies are often a reflection of wider social and political realities. This seems, to Australian outsiders, to be particularly true of American society and American intellectual life.

Robert Hughes, an expatriate Australian writer now living in America, observes in his recent book, *American Visions* (1997a), a history of America through a history of its art, that America "has been riven by inequality and social tension to the point of fatigue, resentment, fanaticism; and for the first time in its history, the future looks worse than the past to a large and growing number of its citizens. With the millennium at hand, in a society founded on messianic optimism, more imps and goblins will appear than ever before; the sleep of reason will produce its monsters" (Hughes, 1997a, 620). Elsewhere Hughes says that "America at the end of the millennium is exhausted of ideas and defeated by unrealized expectations. . . . America's immigrant roots have led to an obsession with identity and newness" (Hughes, 1997b, 3). America is beginning to unravel, Hughes observes elsewhere (Hughes, 1992, 1993). L. and O. Handlin also observe a "pervasive sense of unhappiness" in the United States (Handlin and Handlin, 1995, 15).

The cultural and identity wars in the United States are strong evidence of the fragmentation of American life and culture, and arguably of "disintegration at the moral core of civilization" (Ryn, 1993). This has occurred as a once group-oriented society with a sense of national cohesion became increasingly individual-oriented as a product of the development of the global consumer society. Multiculturalism, as David Rieff has argued (Rieff, 1993), is itself a product of the globalized consumer society, an attempt to accommodate people to the freer movement of people and capital around the world. Rieff notes that, "The market economy, now global in scale, is by its nature corrosive of all established hierarchies and certainties, up to and including – in a world now more than 50 percent non-white and in which the most promising markets lie in Asia – white racism and male domination. If any group has embraced the rallying cry "Hey, hey, ho, ho, Western culture's got to go", it is the world business elite" (Rieff, 1993, 69). Non-discriminatory immigration in the post-1965 period has led to an explosion of ethnic, racial and cultural diversity in the United States (and Australia (from 1975), Canada and Britain as well) to such a degree that America is set to become a completely multiracial, multicultural society without an ethnic or racial majority, "in which", in the words of Nathan Glazer, "no cultural theme linked to any racial or ethnic group has priority, and in which American culture is seen as the product of a complex intermingling of themes from every minority ethnic and racial group, and from indeed the whole world" (Glazer, 1997, 11). Multiculturalism thus has a universalistic demand to recognize all groups, although it has not yet recognized ethnic European groups (Glazer, 1997, 14). Glazer offers no explanation of this strange neglect, but in the light of Rieff's thesis it is clear why this is so. Nations which were predominantly European, and once even Anglo Saxon in ethnicity, must be open for the deep penetration of the global economy, and the idea of nationhood based around race and ethnicity (Isaacs, 1989; Connor, 1994), "as a family, to which outsiders may indeed be admitted, but only under very special circumstances and with great care" (Brimelow, 1993, 19), is anathema to the global elites. The Asianization of Australia is an excellent example of how a former national culture can be delegitimated and dissolved so that it can be remade; the push by Australia's elites for a republic is another example.[6]

Critics, predictably, are likely to dismiss any such arguments with the debate stopping terms of abuse "Racist!", "Conspiracy!" But we do not need to delve very deep into the literature of multiculturalism itself to find support for David Rieff's position. Stephen Castles, Mary Kalantzis, Bill Cope and Michael Morrissey's book *Mistaken Identity: Multiculturalism and the Demise of Nationalism in Australia* (1988) is a good example of a text arguing (albeit in an Australian context) that multiculturalism poses a challenge to the traditional concept of the nation-state. This book, which was a product (at the time) of four members of the Centre for Multicultural Studies at the University of Wollongong, traces the demise of traditional forms of nationalism in Australia and maps the rise of multiculturalism. In the course of doing this, the authors raise and try (unsuccessfully) to deal with some important but neglected questions in the multiculturalism debate. If Australia is to move away from "racist" and "nationalistic" models of a nation, and is to build a society where cultural diversity is celebrated, then how is the tension between ethnic pluralism and social cohesiveness to be dealt with? If the definition of a "nation" in terms of shared history, traditions and culture is no longer acceptable, then how can a "nation" be defined? With the erosion of the dominance of Anglo-Australian culture and values, how are core values and meaning for Australian society constructed? Can multiculturalism be used to define the Australian nature or are political scientists deluded in believing that multiculturalism has shaken the foundations of the ethnocentric structures so deeply entrenched in Australian history?

In the last three chapters the authors address these questions. They maintain that ". . . the project of imagining communality, imagining the shared mission of the nation, imagining our domestic progress as all of us move simultaneously through history, is torn apart by a new emphasis on cultural differences" (Castles et al., 1988, 116). Nevertheless, whilst there has been a revived emphasis on difference both in the expression of individual life-styles and also of "national uniqueness", technological change, especially in communications and the integration of the world market, have made the world both smaller and also more homogeneous. As they put it, "even the most committed 'Greenie' critic of modern culture flies by jet to protest conventions, and returns home to listen to 1960s 'hippie' rock on a compact disc player" (Castles, et al., 1988, 140). Homogenization has made cultural differentiation possible, but it has also made it a meaningless epiphenomenon, a shadowy singularity in the great ether of the international industrial structure. They maintain that multiculturalism has a contradictory and limited vision, failing to address the root causes of inequality in Australian society. Continuing their argument, they maintain that the answer lies not in abandoning multiculturalism, but in addressing social inequalities and supporting and augmenting the values of cultural self-determination and cosmopolitan identity. Along with this must also come specific strategies to aid groups which are discriminated against, and disadvantaged groups. A sense of community needs to be developed without the ideology of nationhood. How this is to be done, we are not told. What is most likely however, in their opinion, is an extrapolation of existing trends, for the decisions that matter socially will be made by international corporate bureaucracies, while increasingly more people retreat into alienation, hopelessness, drug abuse and violence. The "iron cage" of capitalism will be firmly in place around us.

At the cultural level in America, the most extreme manifestations of multiculturalism have centered around Afrocentrism and the controversial works of a number of Afro-American scholars who believe that a Eurocentric bias has led to a conspiracy of neglect of the achievements of Africans (Bernal, 1987; Lefkowitz and MacLean Rogers eds, 1996). In particular, classical civilization is alleged to have African roots. The controversial "Portland Baseline Essays", originally commissioned for use in Portland Oregon public schools, were to form the basis of the Afrocentric curricula. Among its historical insights: Egyptians were a "black" people who had the technological capacity to fly.[7] As well, Beethoven and Robert Browning were also black. There are also reports of Milwaukee schools introducing children to the ideas of African cults including genital mutilation and the use of cocaine for communion, according to a note in the March 1997 edition of *Chronicles* (pages 6–7). Leon Todd, a black member of Milwaukee's School Board, led a fight to eliminate such Afrocentric teachings from the schools. The result: his house was set alight by a Molotov cocktail. As another example, *Santeria*, an Afro-American religion that is a mixture of Christian symbolism as well as pagan and voodoo practices such as animal sacrifices, has become quite popular in immigrant communities in Miami, New York and Washington D.C. In 1989, according to another note in *Chronicles* (March, 1997, page 9), the Smithsonian Institute sponsored Santeria rituals at its annual Folklife Festival.

An enormous body of literature has been published in recent times attacking both multiculturalism and political correctness, generally written by cosmopolitan conservatives and backed in whole or in part by conservative foundations (Wilson, 1995). The critical fire of these writers, representing some of the best public policy writers in America, has been directed against the fundamental idea of multiculturalism that ethnicity, race, gender, social class and sexual orientation significantly influence not only one's sense of self-identity, but also cognition (Yates, 1992, 435) so that "members of other races and religions are not trivially different . . . but fundamentally so" (Yates, 1992, 435; Watson, 1996, 16; Goldberg ed., 1994). The implications of this view, seen at its most extreme in the case of Afrocentrism, have been explored and criticized by Allan Bloom's *The Closing of the American Mind* (1987); Charles J. Sykes' *Profscam* (1988) and *The Hollow Men* (1990); Peter Shaw's *The War Against the Intellect* (1989); Roger Kimball's *Tenured Radicals* (1990); Page Smith's *Killing the Spirit* (1990); Dinesh D'Souza in *Illiberal Education* (1991) and *The End of Racism* (1995); William J. Bennett's *The De-Valuing of America* (1992); Martin Anderson's *Imposters in the Temple* (1992); Richard Bernstein's *Dictatorship of Virtue* (1994); Robert Hughes' *Culture of Complaint* (1993); George Roche's *The Fall of the Ivory Tower* (1994); Bill Readings' *The University in Ruins* (1996) and Susan Huck's *Why Do*

We Americans Submit to This? (1997) (cf also (Hook, 1989; de Lacey and Moens, 1990; Searle, 1990; Taylor, 1991; Bell, 1992; Berman, ed., 1992; Francis, 1993). The central thesis of all of these works is well summarized by Bill Readings: "The University . . . no longer participates in the historical project for humanity that was the legacy of the Enlightenment: the historical project of culture" (Readings, 1996, 5). The acceptance of multiculturalism is a betrayal of liberal internationalism and cosmopolitan ideas, it is a surrender to particularism, tribalism, ethnocentrism and ultimately racism (O'Brien, 1995). Many other claims are made by these writers, but we are concerned here with core issues.

The response to these critics by John Wilson in *The Myth of Political Correctness* (1995) is to contest the accuracy of specific episodes of intellectual suppression, to isolate inaccuracies in the various books cited above and to argue that the right, especially with respect to economic doctrines, can be just as oppressive as the left. Interestingly enough Wilson does grant that there has been a suppression of some thought and research on United States campuses, especially regarding racial research (Wilson, 1995, 53–6). However Wilson does not go to the heart of the matter in his book. As Menand recognizes "it is absurd to insist that the famous great books that served young middle-class white men can serve the same function now that the audience is more diverse" (Menand, 1991, 51). Lawrence W. Levine recognizes that the changing demographics of America lies behind the present identity debates (Levine, 1996). Levine notes that at the University of California at Berkeley (where he spent most of his teaching career) the percentage of white undergraduate students fell from 68.6 percent in 1974 to 32.4 percent in 1994. Asians increased from 15.8 percent to 39.4 percent, Hispanics from 3.2 percent to 13.8 percent, African Americans from 4.4 percent to 5.5 percent and Native Americans from 0.5 percent to 1.1 percent (Levine, 1996, xviii). Further:

> Berkeley's experience is an indication of the transformation the entire nation will experience in the near future. While Whites constituted about three-quarters of the United States population in 1995, the Census Bureau estimates that by 2050 they will have declined to barely half of the population with Hispanics comprising almost 25 percent, Black about 15 percent, and Asians nearly 10 percent. (Levine, 1996, xviii)

Universities are at the "sharp end" of the cultural and ethnic transformation, which is why the cultural war and identity debate in the United States has focused on the campus. The campus debate though is a symbol of wider social transformations:

The "traditional" curriculum that prevailed so widely in the decades between the World Wars, and whose decline is lamented with such fervor by the conservative critics, ignored most of the groups that compose the American population whether they were from Africa, Europe, Asia, Central and South America, or from indigenous North American peoples. The primary and often exclusive focus was upon a narrow stratum of those who came from a few Northern and Western European countries whose cultures and mores supposedly became the archetype for those of all Americans in spite of the fact that in reality American culture was forged out of a much larger and more diverse complex of peoples and societies. In addition, this curriculum did not merely teach Western ideas and culture, it taught the *superiority* of Western ideas and culture; it equated Western ways and thought with "Civilization" itself. This tendency is still being championed by contemporary critics of the university. (Levine, 1996, 20–1)

Thus, the alleged universalism of the West betrays its own particularistic source. As we will argue later in this book, there is nothing *particularly* wrong with this, but for a holder of Enlightenment values of objectivity, non-discriminationism and cosmopolitan impartiality, this confession would be fatal. Conservative cosmopolitan critics of multiculturalism have been conceptually shipwrecked on the reef of racial conflict. For example Dinesh D'Souza in *The End of Racism* (1995), argues that racial tensions in American society are a passing phase of human life and that the creation of a multiracial color-blind society is achievable. This will involve American blacks taking responsibility for themselves, embracing mainstream culture and abandoning cultural relativism. For D'Souza cultural relativism is at fault because it erases the distinction between barbarism and civilization: "the most formidable ideological barrier facing blacks is not racism but antiracism" (D'Souza, 1995, 528). There are many books presenting detailed arguments indicating that D'Souza's position is overly simplistic and fatally flawed. Nathan Glazer in *We are All Multiculturalists Now* (1997) points out that the degree of separation between blacks and whites today could not be predicted at the time of the passage of the Civil Rights Act in 1964 (Glazer, 1997, 123). Separatism is now a live issue (Glazer and Moynihan, 1970, xxiii; Moynihan, 1993). Andrew Hacker in *Two Nations: Black and White, Separate, Hostile, Unequal* (1992) believes that the United States is in a state of "*de facto* apartheid" and he personally doesn't know where to begin in terms of changing this (Roediger, 1992). Even here Hacker has not fully explored the growing conflict between blacks and other minorities such as Hispanics and Jews (Sleeper, 1990; Boyle, 1995; Friedman, 1995; De Alva et al., 1996). Racial integration in America has been a "tragic failure", Tom Wicker has argued (Wicker,

1996). A growing resentment and criticism of affirmative action and other racially based programs (Lynch and Beer, 1990; Rosen, 1994; Roberts and Stratton, 1995; Carey, 1996; Jenkins, 1996) has the potential to spark a "race war" in the opinion of Carl T. Rowan in *The Coming Race War in America* (1996) and Richard Delgado in *The Coming Race War?* (1996). An end of "racism" is very far away (Segal, 1967; Stone, 1985; Dench, 1986; De Silva and May eds, 1991; Johnson, 1995; Gates and West, 1996; Stix, 1997). A Hobbesian racial war of all against all is a more likely prospect.

STATEMENT OF THE ARGUMENT

Secession and separatism have often been proposed as solutions to seemingly intractable problems to "marriages" facing irreconcilable differences (Wollacott, 1996). The physicist Freeman Dyson in his book *Imagined Worlds* (1997) has taken the idea of separatism to its logical conclusion by proposing that racial differences which are socially divisive on Earth would be harmless when distinct populations occupy distant asteroids (Dyson, 1997, 150, 155; Benford, 1997). Until the happy day when that high tech fix is available, the suffering people constituting humanity must deal with themselves and all of the problems detailed in this chapter. We believe that humanity will deal very poorly with the crises of civilization. Ecological sustainability and the survival of a sense of place and community requires, we and others have argued (Smith et al., 1997; Dyson, 1997, 149), *localism* rather than *globalism* – the development of smaller, self-reliant communities, adopting a *conserver* rather than a *consumer* life-style (Trainer, 1995, 1996). As we have argued in this chapter, and will elaborate upon in chapter 5, the direction of the global economy is in precisely the opposite direction to one necessary for ecological sustainability. Human *hubris* – insolent pride about our technological prowess – will ensure that a remorseless fall, an ecological *nemesis* will occur, probably sometime in the next century (Leslie, 1996). For this reason we believe that a collapse of civilization, a day of Ragnarok, is inevitable. This fear has been used by many environmentalists as an ultimate trump-card resembling the warnings of an Abrahamic prophet: "repent, change your ways, or else!" But people do not in general "repent" and "change their ways" unless necessity grasps them by the throat and forces them to, at ecological gun point. Consequently it is time for one book and one group of authors to begin to explore the "or else" option. This book will begin the exploration of the emerging global anarchy and the final dark age, the twilight of civilization and culture.[8] Secession, separatism and fragmentation are to be the fate of mankind, socially, politically and epistemologically.

Chapter 2 of this book explores the moral, political and philosophical ramifications of the failure of the Enlightenment project – a fully rational justification of morality, politics and science – and begins an attack upon the ideologies of cosmopolitanism and internationalism. Chapter 3 takes this critique further, attacking universalism at the most basic level in mathematical logic and physics. Global anarchy is arising conceptually as well as socially; our best scientific theories about the nature of a physical reality are mutually inconsistent and probably internally inconsistent as well. We will see that in the realm of mathematical logic, even the logical word "all" generates antinomies of reason. The reader who is uninterested in logic and physics does not need to read this chapter to follow the argument of this book. Indeed, we have deliberately structured this book – consistent with our philosophy of fragmentation – so that the remaining chapters have a relative autonomy from each other. Each chapter is a relatively independent elaboration of the theme detailed in this chapter of the coming global anarchy and the breakdown of civilization; each chapter attacks globalism in each of its many forms. Chapter 4 outlines the failure of the "one-world" dream, examining the role of the United Nations in the new world disorder. Finally, Chapter 5 circles back to the themes introduced in this chapter centered around economic globalization and the coming breakdown and break up of the nation-state and world order.

Each chapter of this book could (and should) be expanded into a series of books in their own right. However time and publishing resources are limited. Consequently we have deliberately written this book in a highly condensed, concise, heavily referenced style, which we hope is clearer and more logical than thicker books on the market which explore our theme in a more wordy, discursive and relaxed style. The majority of our readers will probably disagree with most of the contents of this book – that is neither here nor there. We should not buy, read and study books solely to reinforce our pre-established views. As the opening quote in this chapter by that great social theorist F.H. Giddings proposed, we should court controversy and intellectual strife because it *may* (we do not share Giddings' optimism) diminish physical strife. One can only hope.

2 The Failure of the Enlightenment Project: The Balkanization of Everything

We need to learn to love our differences. But in the meantime, and for a long time, we are going to be faced with chaos and political disintegration – both at levels which will make the ideal of democratic capitalism seem laughable. The process has already begun with ethnic violence, unprovoked crime, ruthless regimes and the migration of millions of permanent refugees. Central governments have begun to wither, regional and tribal identities are being revived, and fundamentalism of every stripe is becoming ever more obvious and more strident. Under the pressure of environmental and demographic stress, we are watching the old order crack and fragment into city states, shanty states and ragtag private armies belonging to a whole new generation of local warlords. . . . In evolutionary terms, what we are seeing is the rebirth of warrior societies, the reprivatising of mankind into smaller, more ruthless communities in which the radius of trust is being limited once again to immediate kin and close comrades. We are being retribalized, closing the genetic gates; but with nature breaking down and clean water in dangerously short supply, our biological roots can no longer provide us with the moral nourishment we need. (Watson, 1995, 250–1)

Universities are the most overrated institutions of our age. Of all the calamities that have befallen the 20th century, apart from the two world wars, the expansion of higher education in the 1950s and 1960s was the most enduring. It is a myth that universities are nurseries of reason. They are hothouses for every kind of extremism, irrationality, intolerance and prejudice, where intellectual and social snobbery is almost deliberately instilled and where dons attempt to pass on to their students their own sins of pride.

The wonder is that so many people emerge from these dens still employable, although a significant minority – as we have learned to our cost – go forth well-equipped for a lifetime of public mischief-making. (Johnson, 1991, 21)

ENLIGHTENMENT'S WAKE

John Gray in his book *Enlightenment's Wake: Politics and Culture at the Close of the Modern Age* (Gray, 1995) proclaims that the Enlightenment project – of the rational reconstruction of morality and a foundationalist view of science as providing a litmus test of all purported forms of knowledge – "is affirmed chiefly for fear of the consequences of abandoning it" (Gray, 1995, 144).[1] In particular the "hegemony of liberalism" has come to resemble the Christian apologetic theology of the early modern age, when it was clear that Christianity was no longer "the prime animating force" in the culture of the West, but fear still prevented creative thought about an alternative. Today, in the late modern period, we live in the "dim ruins" of the Enlightenment project, Gray believes, a project which has proved to be self-defeating. As the Enlightenment project was the defining project of the modern period, this means that we are at the end of the modern age.[2] Universalism is coming into question and a "renaissance of particularisms", both ethnic and religious, is occurring. Globalization and the increasing rationalization of the world, the triumph of liberal capitalism over Soviet communism, is not, according to Gray, resulting in the birth of a new universalistic civilization; rather the totalizing effects of economic globalization – the overwhelming domination of the market over all aspects of our lives – is resulting in a world which is "out of control", an alien world, increasingly distant from human culture and communities (Gray 1995, 145). This money power is accountable only to itself. In short: "The legacy of the Enlightenment project – which is also the legacy of Westernization – is a world ruled by calculation and wilfulness which is humanly unintelligible and destructively purposeless" (Gray, 1995, 146; Lasch, 1991; Watson, 1994).

For Gray, Westernization produces a "revolutionary nihilism" that inevitably disrupts "traditional conceptions of the human relationship with the earth . . . [supplanting] them by humanist and Baconian instrumentalist understandings, in which nature is no more than an object of human purposes" (Gray, 1995, 146). The self-undermining nature of the Enlightenment project, in Gray's opinion, results in the collapse of the humanism and universalism of Christianity and the logocentrism of Western philosophy, with no possibility of a return to pre-modern modes of thought as a philosopher such as Alasdair MacIntyre hopes for (MacIntyre, 1981, 1988, 1990). After eating the bitter fruit of the tree of Western Enlightenment, there can be no re-enchantment of the world. On this position, we postmoderns are forced to live in a culture that "has been transformed irreversibly by an Enlightenment project that has shown itself to be self-consuming" (Gray, 1995, 147; Derrida, 1982, 1988; Lyotard, 1988; Harvey, 1989). Although providing an insightful discussion of some of the limitations of the work of Alasdair MacIntyre and Richard Rorty (1989, 1991a, b), Gray fails to show how humanity can live in a "self-consuming" environment, and as he has set this problem up, it is virtually true by definition that he would fail. It is equivalent to asking how a living organism could survive with terminal inoperable cancer. He concludes his book with the suggestion that non-Occidental peoples may be able to escape the nihilism of the Enlightenment and a footnote indicates that he has in mind the spirituality of various Buddhist and Taoist traditions. But these traditions often exist happily side-by-side with a virulent Asian capitalism that is pushing large parts of Asia to the brink of environmental destruction (Smith et al., 1997). Perhaps recognizing the implausibility of his conjecture Gray then immediately says

> . . . it may be that even those non-Occidental cultures which have modernized without wholesale Westernization have nevertheless assimilated too much of the Western nihilist relationship with technology and the earth for a turning in man's relationship with the earth to be any longer a real possibility. If this were to be so, it would be consonant with the sense of releasement invoked in this inquiry, which encompasses an openness to ultimate danger, to the contingency and mortality not only of human cultures and of other living things, but also of the earth itself. (Gray, 1995, 184)

In this chapter and the next we shall explore the theme of the failure of the Enlightenment project in more detail. The next chapter will examine our epistemological crisis and the limits of universalism by looking at the cognitive impasse which modern physical and mathematical science is approaching. Philosophers of science typically approach this subject by examining the issue on philosophical turf: discussing the problems of relativism, skepticism and the incommensurability of theories. We have also done this in the past (Smith et al., 1997), but here we shall take a different approach, viewing the problem of epistemological endism from within the dynamics of the "hard" sciences themselves. First however we shall explore in more detail the failure of the Enlightenment project with respect to the goal of supplying a rational reconstruction of morality and an objective justification of moral maxims. There has been a "renaissance of particularisms", as Gray observes, precisely because at a basic grassroots level many, but not all people have lost faith in universalism and cosmopolitan doctrines. This is a historical process which is occurring as part of the inevitable working through, or "remorseless working of things" (Smith et al., 1997) of modernization and globalization, and will occur no matter how hard philosophers and social theorists stamp their little feet. Therefore we suggest that the inevitable be accepted and *particularism* be openly embraced, that there is no *universal* standard of moral value, and that moral value if it exists is contingent upon the local – the nation, race, ethnic group, class or whatever association it is that the individual is in, and derives a sense of identity and meaning from (Nielsen, 1986; Taylor, 1989a; Rasmussen ed., 1990; Scruton, 1990; Twinning ed., 1991; Almond, 1992). Let us now go back over some arguments which could lead us to reach the conclusions which John Gray has reached, and having done this let us fearlessly explore the foggy world of particularism and the limits of morality.

THE END OF MORALITY

The Enlightenment project, insofar as it was concerned with morality, sought to provide a rational justification for morality (MacIntyre, 1981; O'Brien, 1995). Modern moral philosophy – by contrast to the ethics of many past civilizations (Browne, 1990) – has typically been *universalistic* or *cosmopolitan*, "the status of the ultimate unit of concern attaches to *every* living human being *equally*" (Pogge, 1994, 89; Goodin, 1988). The distinction between the moral agent and others is morally irrelevant (Stocker, 1976; Walker, 1987); all people must be treated with equal and impartial positive consideration with respect to their interests (Gewirth, 1988). Cosmopolitanism, an idea introduced by the Greek Stoics, is the position that "all humans are brothers by virtue of their shared reason" (Maxwell, 1990, 36). "Cosmopolitanism" comes from the Greek *Kosmopolites*, meaning "citizen of the world". "Parochialism" comes from the Latin *parochia*, meaning "parish", a local entity. In the third century B.C., Zeno of Citium, who first promulgated Stoicism, was able to proclaim "I am a citizen of the world" (Hardin, 1985). Stoicism influenced St. Paul in allowing baptism of the Gentiles and influenced Roman law, as Maxwell observes: "Cicero, the interpreter of Greek Stoicism for the Romans, brought in the notion of equality in the first century. By A.D. 212 the Emperor Caracalla proclaimed: 'All those who live within the borders of the Roman Empire are Roman citizens'" (Maxwell, 1990, 36). The Stoics were early rationalists, naturalists and materialists, seeking a "life consistent with nature" and a rationality in tune with natural law. They were skeptical of concepts such as God because of its abstraction from material reality. They should have been more skeptical about other abstractions such as cosmopolitanism. One of the results of this short-sighted cosmopolitanism was imperial over-shoot and ultimately the fall of Rome, a lesson which contemporary North America has not learnt.

Ethical particularism, by contrast, justifies preferential consideration of the interests of some against others, thus justifying discrimination. The universalistic or cosmopolitan foundation of modern moral philosophy usually accepts *individualism*, that the unit of evaluation is the individual person, not tribes, races, communities or nations (Pogge, 1994, 89).[3] Finally, the generality of moral rules have "global force," apply to all humanity and possibly all moral agents across space and time and do not vary according to circumstance (Beitz, 1994). This conception of morality in particular has come under attack by communitarians (Buchanan, 1989; Walzer, 1990; Shapiro, 1995) and post-modernists (see Thompson, 1992). More generally Nietzsche was one of the first modern philosophers to see that the Enlightenment project on morality was doomed to inevitable breakdown and that it would end finally in nihilism. Alasdair MacIntyre in his book *Three Rival Versions of Moral Inquiry: Encyclopaedia, Genealogy and Tradition* (1990) states in concise form the Nietzschean argument that we face an undecidable and incommensurable plurality of moral theories and perspectives:

> . . . whereas it was a tenet of Enlightenment cultures that every point of view, whatever its source, could be brought into rational debate with every other, this tenet had as its counterpart a belief that such rational debate could always, if adequately conducted, have a conclusive outcome. The point and purpose of rational debate was to establish truths and only those methods were acceptable which led to the conclusive refutation of error and vindication of truth. The contrast with contemporary academic practice could not be sharper. For with rare exceptions the outcomes of rational debate on fundamental issues are systematically inconclusive. . . . [To rationally resolve debates would require] appeal to a standard or set of standards such that no adequately rational person could fail to acknowledge its authority. . . . there can be no such standard; any standard adequate to discharge such functions will itself be embedded in, supported by, and articulated in terms of some set of theoretical and conceptual schemes. . . . [and as] each rival theoretical standpoint provides from within itself and in its own terms the standards by which, so its adherents claim, it should be evaluated, rivalry between such contending standpoints includes rivalry over standards. There is no theoretically neutral, pre-theoretical ground from which the adjudication of competing claims can proceed. It is all too easy to conclude further that therefore, when one large-scale theoretical and conceptual standpoint is systematically at odds with another, there can be no rational way of settling the differences between them. And Nietzsche's genealogical heirs do so conclude, for this as well as for other reasons. (MacIntyre, 1990, 172–3; Gray, 1995, 150–1)

There is considerable debate about whether Nietzsche is a relativist, committed to the position that all interpretations of the world are equally valid (or invalid).[4] Ross Poole in his book *Morality and Modernity* (1991) denies that Nietzsche is committed to relativism. For example, Poole claims that Nietzsche wishes to reject the moral interpretation of the world and that is the meaning of Nietzsche's slogan "beyond good and evil". The rejection of the moral point of view if made on the grounds of morality would of course be self-refuting. Nietzsche's perspectivism differs from relativism, Poole observes, because while accepting that all views of the world are products of a particular perspective and there can be no privileged accounts of what the world is like, some perspectives are more "adequate" than others because of various criteria such as comprehensiveness, consistency and aesthetic pleasure (Poole, 1991, 113–14). However, "adequate" cannot mean " rationally adequate" because as we have seen from MacIntyre (1990, 172–3), debate will again arise about the rational justification of these standards and criteria and the specter of relativism will arise again. The problem of the justification of the standards of rationality is an outstanding problem for Western philosophy which has been with it since its inception (Smith, 1988a, b; Radnitzky and Bartley III, eds, 1987), and the problem is still very much a "live" one in the philosophy of science. As Kitcher has noted, "recent work in the history of science and in the sociology of science has offered even more sweeping versions of the original [anti-objectivist] critiques" (Kitcher, 1993, 8). Philosophical pluralism and the existence of perennial philosophical disputes – of unending debates seemingly without hope of solution – calls the Enlightenment faith in the powers of rational argumentation into question. Wilhelm Dilthey (1833–1911) in his *Gesammelte Schriften* believed that "the anarchy of philosophical systems is one of the most powerful supports from which skepticism draws ever-renewed nourishment. A contradiction arises between the historical realization of their boundless multiplicity and the claims of each to universal validity which supports the skeptical spirit more powerfully than any theoretical argumentation" (quoted from Rescher, 1985, 4). Richard Rorty in his book *Consequences of Pragmatism* draws the logical conclusion from this:

> When it turns out that . . . [philosophical] principles are as plentiful as blackberries, nothing changes except the attitude of the rest of culture towards the philosophers. Since the time of Kant, it has become more and more apparent to non-philosophers that a really professional philosopher can supply a philosophical foundation for just about anything. This is one reason why philosophers have, in the course of our century, become increasingly isolated from the rest of culture. Our proposals to

guarantee this and to clarify that have come to strike our fellow intellectuals as merely comic. (Rorty, 1982, 169)

N. Rescher in his *The Strife of Systems* (1985) takes the view that disagreement is "an intrinsic and inevitable aspect of philosophy as an intellectual discipline" (Rescher, 1985, 8). Philosophy "seems to be in the paradoxical position of a subject whose legitimacy is undermined by the course of its own history" (Rescher, 1985, 11). Moreover "a death wish runs like a recurrent leitmotiv throughout the history of philosophy" (Rescher, 1985, 16). In his view, philosophical problems cannot be resolved without "evaluative inputs": "One cannot distance oneself from value commitments without exiling oneself from philosophy." (Rescher, 1985, 114). There is a mode of justification, according to Rescher "whose basis is not entirely objective and impersonal but in some respects personal and subjective" (Rescher, 1985, 115). Rescher's position of orientational pluralism is that doctrinal diversity reflects a diversity of cognitive values. But "conflict regarding values (even merely cognitive values) is ultimately unresolvable on a presupposition-free, objective basis, because disputes about values are themselves inherently evaluative" (Rescher, 1985, 118). This however leads us back to a Nietzschean plurality of ultimately undecidable and incommensurable theories.

A deep form of philosophical pluralism or cosmological multiculturalism has been argued for by Richard Sylvan. Sylvan's pluralistic project, now halted by his tragic death, was that "all time-tested philosophical theories are structurally sound and can be restored" (Sylvan, 1989a, 1). Sylvan believed that modern logic supplied the technology for the rehabilitation of many dilapidated philosophical positions. Indeed, in the next chapter we shall argue that modern logic has in fact intensified our epistemological crisis, supplying a tool for the refutation of many seemingly true positions. Sylvan accepted a doctrine of strong philosophical pluralism on the basis of theoretical underdetermination, that truth or acceptability cannot be uniquely determined by humans, that many theories often fit the observed data, the data itself usually being far from theory-neutral so that there are no "absolutely neutral descriptions or accounts" of the world (Sylvan, 1984, 4). Presumably the previous statement itself, under pain of self-refutation, is not an absolutely neutral description of the world. For Sylvan "*all admissible* (comprehensive, fundamental) *theories are true* pluralistically" (Sylvan, 1984, 19); regarding pluralistic truth "they all have the same non-zero status of validity" (Sylvan, 1984, 19). However this strong pluralism does not collapse into relativism in Sylvan's opinion as positions can still be evaluated: "Nor do all theories other than that picked out as true stand on an equal footing. Some theories are superior in various respects to others, most importantly for present purposes in extent of falsehood and in nearness to truth" (Sylvan, 1984, 20). This claim is itself consistent with the claim that theories have the same non-zero status of validity. However Sylvan's strong pluralism also applies to truth, as truth (on one theory at least) is dependent on the way "the world is". The position now begins its slide towards relativism because the criterion of truth will be dependent upon broad metaphysical world views, and as such there can be no non-circular demonstration of the objective truth of such world views. Likewise Sylvan's criteria for theory-evaluation will also be internal to a metaphysical world view, and we have seen that all such world views stand on an epistemologically equal footing. Sylvan wishes to reject racist ideologies and Islamic fundamentalism as flawed: "Islam shows the damage a manifestly false position (as seen from the 'outside') can inflict" (Sylvan, 1984, 31). Islamic fundamentalism may be viewed as "manifestly false" from the perspective of liberal democracy, but liberal democracy, according to radical pluralism is manifestly false from the perspective of Islamic fundamentalism. Sylvan fails to show how his cosmological multiculturalism escapes the net of cognitive relativism.

Ethics and moral theory are generally, and rightly we believe, regarded as "softer" theories than scientific and metaphysical theories in the sense that the latter theories are more general and comprehensive so that an epistemological crisis in metaphysics and epistemology will immediately infect ethics and moral theory. This is precisely what has occurred, for the "end of philosophy" (Cohen & Dascal eds, 1989; Baynes, et al., 1993) means as well the "end of ethics and moral theory." (Hems, 1971; Hinckfuss, 1987; Kleinberg, 1991; Danielson, 1992, 3).

Conventional ethics and moral theory face problems though, which metaphysics and epistemology do not. Again the fundamental insight is Nietzschean: "evil features are not simply ineliminable but actually necessary if any good features are to be possessed at all" (Nehamas, 1985, 210; Gray, 1995, 162), or as Gray puts it "the goods specified by morality often have among their necessary conditions things specified by morality as evil" (Gray, 1995, 162). Outside of theological concerns, philosophers have not devoted much energy to the problems of good and evil as *natural* problems (Midgley, 1984). More scientifically inclined writers have tended to agree with the Nietzschean position. Norman Dixon in *Our Own Worst Enemy* (1987) sees the self-destructive side effects of human behavior, those characteristics propelling us towards extinction, as evolved by our ancestors over millions of years for survival in entirely different environments. As a result of cultural evolution we have created environments for which biology is inadequate to deal with. Thus: "man is a shoal of piranhas, directed by a computer which has been programmed by an archbishop" (Dixon, 1987, 49). Jared Diamond in *The Rise and Fall of the Third Chimpanzee* also has a sociobiological pessimistic view of human kind: "We are also unique in darker attributes, including genocide, delight in torture, addictions to toxic drugs, and extermination of other species by the thousand" (Diamond, 1991, 1). For the sociobiologist E. O. Wilson, the evolution of the human species is a tragedy for the Earth:

> Darwin's dice have rolled badly for Earth. It was a misfortune for the living world in particular, many scientists believe, that a carnivorous primate and not some more benign form of animal made the break-through. Our species retains hereditary traits that add greatly to our destructive impact. We are tribal and aggressively territorial, intent on private space beyond minimal requirements and oriented by selfish sexual and reproductive drives. Cooperation beyond the family and tribal levels comes hard. (Wilson, 1993, 25–6)

Lyall Watson in *Dark Nature: A Natural History of Evil* (1995) sees evil as "a force of nature, as a biological reality" (Watson, 1995, x) with rule number one among our genetic instructions being: "BE NASTY TO OUTSIDERS" (Watson, 1995, 48). For Howard Bloom, author of *The Lucifer Principle* (1995) "Evil is a by-product, a component, of creation. In a world evolving into ever-higher forms, hatred, violence, aggression, and war are part of the evolutionary plan" (Bloom, 1995, 2). Evil then is part of our biological nature (Wrangham and Peterson, 1996)[5]. Roy Baumeister in *Evil: Inside Human Cruelty and Violence* (1997) rejects pure culture and pure gene theories of the origin of human evil but recognizes the importance of biological factors:

> Human nature has not generally proved as pliable as the tabula rasa theorists have hoped. Hundreds of experimental utopian communes have broken down amid undone chores and minor bickering or, in some cases, have led to large-scale mass murder. America's ideological shift from the melting pot to multicultural diversity has not eliminated rancor between groups. Shifting control over upbringing from fathers to mothers has not resulted in a more sensitive and pacifist generation of young males; if anything, the statistics say they are worse than ever. (Baumeister, 1997, 382)

Culture itself can modify our basic, if somewhat base, human nature:

> A satisfactory understanding of human aggression is likely to invoke both culture and nature. It is unlikely that researchers will ever be able to trace specific violent actions directly to specific genes or other inherited physiological properties, but it is clear that nature has programmed people with some tendencies that can lead toward aggressive

responses. Rage appears very early in life and is expressed in lashing out at the source of frustration. The tendency to align with one's fellows and feel hostile toward potential opponents and rivals seems almost ineradicable. Yet culture can exert a great deal of influence in teaching people how to express and control their aggressive impulses. Culture also shapes the situations that form the context for those impulses, including the opportunities for response, the importance of proper response, and the norms of what is proper. And culture articulates the beliefs and myths about evil. (Baumeister, 1997, 382)

Dixon, Diamond, Wilson, Watson and Baumeister differ in their views of the causes of the dark nature of human beings, but their works *in toto* support the Nietzschean point that "evil features are not simply ineliminable but actually necessary if any good features are to be possessed at all" (Nehamas, 1985, 210). This in itself is another basic challenge to the received views of contemporary morality. Moral laws, however they are justified, are often seen to be almost like the laws of nature, universally valid and constraining. Sociobiological considerations, and we shall have more to say about this after our summary, challenge this.

In this section we have been discussing the "end of morality", radical philosophical challenges to orthodox ethics. The universalism and cosmopolitanism of orthodox ethics and moral theory is challenged by what we shall call, for want of a better description, various "postmodern" arguments, seen first most clearly by Nietzsche. These arguments are really part of a more general challenge to the theoretical progressiveness and rationality of philosophy as a cognitive enterprise (Smith, 1988a, b) that have led many (former) philosophers to propose that not only is the Enlightenment ideal of philosophy – as an enterprise supplying some sort of ultimate handguide to the universe by providing a *foundation* for the sciences and other forms of knowledge – a bankrupt enterprise, but Western (and possibly many forms of Eastern) philosophy is dead, because it has become irrelevant to the rest of culture (Rorty, 1982, 169). Philosophy has choked to death on richness, diversity, and plurality. We briefly examined two important attempts to save philosophy from its pluralistic grave – by N. Rescher and R. Sylvan – but concluded that their attempts failed. Elsewhere one of us (Smith,1988b) defended philosophy as a discipline against such charges in a minimalist sense: that at least philosophical progress occurs in that errors are exposed by analysis and unsound arguments exposed. We still hold to that position, but recognize now that this sort of hyper-rationality has cancer-like properties that threatens to undermine *all* arguments and positions. We will argue this in the next chapter through a consideration of some foundational issues in modern logic and meta-mathematics. We thus conclude that the "end of philosophy" argument means, logically, an end to ethics and morality as conceived as *rationally justified* conceptual systems. Western philosophy's code of honor – that one should not accept arguments "dogmatically" or "uncritically" – ultimately leads to acceptance of the view that dogmatism is inescapably part of the human condition just as evil is. We are all "racists" about our fundamental worldview.

In this section we have also introduced the thesis that sociobiological considerations offer a major challenge as well to conventional moral theory. We will now pick up the trail of the discussion and explore this issue in more detail. This will be done through a discussion of an excellent book which connects the themes of universalism, morality and biology: Mary Maxwell's *Morality Among Nations: An Evolutionary View* (1990).

UNIVERSALISM, MORALITY, BIOLOGY, AND RACE

Mary Maxwell opens her discussion in *Morality Among Nations* (1990) with the observation that there is a confusion about international morality. The blacks in South Africa under Apartheid gained the sympathies of the outside world, but this was "oddly selective". Events in other countries, including genocide are often "acceptable" (Maxwell, 1990, 2): such is the hypocrisy or double-standard of cosmopolitan media and intellectual opinion.[6] Maxwell does not find orthodox Western ethical philosophy particularly illuminating in understanding international morality. Twentieth century ethics, as MacIntyre and Gray have also observed, have intentionally or unintentionally undermined the basis of objective moral truth; Maxwell agrees that these philosophers were on the right track in doing this (Maxwell, 1990, 5). She believes that more fruitful insights are generated by sociobiology. The sociobiological view of international relations

> consists of the hypothesis that humans evolved in small groups and that intergroup hostility was a factor in the evolution of such behaviors as group loyalty and violence towards enemies. A behavioral characteristic of almost any group is to treat its members one way and nonmembers another way. The rightness of this is loudly proclaimed by the group in question and furnishes a "group morality". Correspondingly, it supports intergroup immorality or amorality, in a way that often contradicts the standard morality of its members – for example, it contradicts the "absolute" prohibition against killing. (Maxwell, 1990, 5)

Sociobiology's group morality supports the view that there cannot be a moral relationship between states maintaining that the welfare of the group has priority over all other objects of possible concern and evaluation (Maxwell, 1990, 6). Sociobiology thus lends support to the romantic anti-cosmopolitanism of "blood and soil" of Johann Gottfried von Herder (1744–1803), Wordsworth, Thoreau, Chopin and Wagner. There is a fundamental contradiction between the two theories of morality, Maxwell observes, that is responsible for the lack of development of the ethics of international relations (Maxwell, 1990, 124). Having said all this, Maxwell goes on to endorse the standard position that there is a moral relationship between states, not because of any objective ethical truths as such, which she claims do not exist (Maxwell, 1990, 130, 1995), but because of the "combination of our moral nature and our cultural history of ethical invention" (Maxwell, 1990, 130). But it is precisely the nature of our moral nature which is being called into question in this debate, and to adopt a position as Maxwell does is question begging insofar as we are playing the game of philosophical rationality. She admits on the one hand that the challenge of sociobiological group morality has not been dealt with by standard morality, but then claims without sustained argument a resolution in favor of standard morality. Her claim is undermined by her own excellent arguments for the group morality position.

The sociobiological group morality view – which we will call *biological particularism* – has been rejected by biologists and Marxists such as Stephen Jay Gould because of "possible socially undesirable results" (Williamson, 1996, 28) as it has been felt that the ethnocentrism of biological particularism conflicts with progressive liberal-left values. There are many points that can be made in reply to such a position. The great Australian playwright David Williamson remarks that what cultural determinists such as Stephen Jay Gould "have never acknowledged is that without a biological moral code, culture is as free to construct us to be psychopaths as saints" (Williamson, 1996, 28–9; Gardner et al. eds, 1994). Gould, the biologist, ignores the question of the philosophical and biological grounding of his own ideology and world view. The cultural determinism of Gould, an axiom of main-stream sociology, is under challenge. Sociology is in a state of epistemological crisis, which according to Irving Louis Horowitz, has proceeded now to a decline and breakdown; using the metaphor of sociology as a living body, Horowitz claims that sociology is *decomposing* (Horowitz, 1993). This is hardly an adequate perspective from which to criticize biological particularism. But in any case, even writers with a sociological perspective have not lightly dismissed particularism. Henry Pratt Fairchild in *Race and Nationality as Factors in American Life* (1947) was not afraid to say this:

> From time immemorial it has been inherent in the very nature of human group identification that the members of any particular group should

feel more warmly attracted and attached to other members of their own group than to outsiders. It is the very essence of human association that persons who live together continuously in more or less intimate bonds of society should be characterized by many similarities of thought, feeling, and action, and moreover that they should regard their own ways as right and good and preferable to those of strangers. Moreover, if the members of a particular group also possess distinctive observable physical traits of skin, hair, eyes, or other features, it is also in the established order of things that these particular endowments should be regarded as correct, admirable, and beautiful. (Fairchild, 1947, 4)

The sociologist William Graham Sumner, of Yale University, "used to say with emphasis that the United States is not a nation because of the presence of a large Negro element" (Fairchild, 1947, 47), meaning that nationality involves a "consciousness of racial kinship . . . embodied in a uniform racial group" (Fairchild, 1947, 47). A "consciousness of kind" played a fundamental role in the sociology of Franklin H. Giddings (1906)[7] and he proposed that "Discrimination . . . is the beginning of knowledge" (Giddings, 1898, 1). He rightly observed that "if the nerves of the skin detected no inequalities of pressure, the external world would remain, for our minds, a blank" (Giddings, 1898, 1). As another example, Sun Yat-Sen in his *San Min Chu I: The Three Principles of the People* (1932) sees the conservation of race as the key task of nation-building, but as well race could be used as a principle for uniting China: "The greatest force is common blood. Chinese belong to the yellow race because they come from the blood stock of the yellow race. The blood of ancestors is transmitted by heredity down through the race, making blood kinship a powerful force" (Sun Yat-Sen, 1932, 9). This sentiment is far from alien to the Chinese. For example, Singapore's ex-Prime Minister, Mr. Lee Kuan Yew, told a World Chinese Entrepreneurs' Convention in Hong Kong in 1993 that "the potential for economic networking is considerable . . . people feel a natural empathy for those who share their physical attributes. This sense of closeness is reinforced when they also share basic culture and language. It makes for easy business rapport and trust" (McCormack, 1996, 146). Harold Isaacs in *Idols of the Tribe* (1989) points out that "belief in the superiority of the race of Han and the view of all non-Chinese as "barbarians" are well-known features of the standard Chinese self-image" (Isaacs, 1989, 59). Isaacs found in his ethnic studies, among most races that, "Skin color and other physical characteristics figure critically in the shaping of every basic group identity and, with high visibility and powerful glandular effects, in relations between groups" (Isaacs, 1989, 53). More recently the philosopher Paul Feyerabend, a defender of radical pluralism and multiculturalism has said: " . . . if we disregard the racial features of a face, if we don't care for the rhythm of the sounds that emerge from its mouth, if we subtract the special and culturally determined gestures that accompany speaking then we have no longer a living human being, we have a monster and such a monster is dead, not free" (Feyerabend, 1991, 166–7). As a final example of an authority recognizing the social relevance and legitimacy of racial categories, we cite the American Jewish social theorist Nathan Glazer who said in an article in *The Australian* in 1994, that "discriminatory" immigration policies (as in Germany and Israel with its "law of return") are not "racist": "there is a difference between recognizing those who are in some sense one's own, with links to a people and a culture, and a policy based on dislike, hostility, racial antagonism" (Glazer, 1994, 9).

Those embracing biological particularism have usually seen a conflict or at least the potential for conflict between people, races, and ethnic groups; either in general or between such groups in the same region (Cattell, 1972; Alexander, 1987; Reynolds et al. eds, 1987; Allen, 1991; Nelson, 1994; Stove, 1995; Levin, 1997). This is also the view of the present authors, expressed in this work. However a conflict view of races is not the only position that could be argued for from the particularist perspective. L. Outlaw, in an article entitled "Against the Grain of Modernity: The Politics of Difference and the Conservation of 'Race'" (Outlaw, 1992), argues for the conservation of "races" and "ethnic groups" ("ethnies") from a distinctly "left" and progressive position, a politically correct racialism. Outlaw regards with concern racial and ethnic demographic developments in the United States, which are resulting in white European Americans fast becoming a minority group: "To say the least, such a development has the potential for decisive developments in the social, political, economic, and cultural dimensions of life in America, a nation that has been plagued for centuries by problems involving race and ethnicity" (Outlaw, 1992, 448).

The politics of race and ethnicity are part of the politics of difference, Outlaw says, and difference today has become a basis by which many groups participate in civil society (Outlaw, 1992, 448). Doubt has been cast on those universal principles of morality and sociality that were to enable the integration and assimilation of diverse races of people into the liberal American dream: "The celebration of universal principles has often turned out to be the rhetoric – rather than the realization – of liberal-democratic, socialist or communist principles of universality and equality in the midst of the domination of political, economic and cultural life by a particular race and/or ethnies" (Outlaw, 1992, 449). The politics of difference cuts against the grain of modernity in challenging liberalism, which is as John Gray has observed "the political theory of modernity" (Gray, 1986, 82). Liberalism requires that "morally irrelevant factors" such as race, ethnicity and gender be looked beyond, in favor of a human essence constituting personhood, and that essential quality is usually taken to be *reason* (Outlaw, 1992, 457). This Enlightenment conception of human nature, in Outlaw's opinion, is a false and fraudulent universalism: "it cannot encompass the concrete being of the person who is intimately and inextricably related to others by substantive factors, among them race and/or ethnicity, that are themselves *essential* (not "accidental") aspects of who we are" (Outlaw, 1992, 458). Michael Novak has also made a related point, about one of the philosophical problems of liberalism:

> The liberal personality tends to be atomic, rootless, mobile, and to image itself as 'enlightened' in some superior and especially valid way. Ironically, its exaggerated individualism leads instantly to an exaggerated sense of universal community. The middle term between these two extremes, the term pointing to the finite human communities in which individuals live and have their being, is precisely the term that the liberal personality disvalues. (Novak, quoted from Hardin, 1982, 177)

Outlaw's project for the conservation of race begins with W.E.B Du Bois' 1897 essay "The Conservation of Races" (Du Bois, 1992). Du Bois was aware that the idea of a racial "essence" had been discredited by late nineteenth century science, so that there was no set of fixed characteristics that rigidly divided human groups. But he still maintained the following:

> Although the wonderful developments of human history teach that the grosser physical differences of color, hair and bone go but a short way toward explaining the different roles which groups of men have played in Human Progress, yet there are differences – subtle, delicate and elusive, though they may be – which have silently but definitely separated men into groups. While these subtle forces have generally followed the natural cleavage of common blood, descent and physical peculiarities, they have at other times swept across and ignored these. At all times, however, they have divided human beings into races, which, while they perhaps transcend scientific definition, nevertheless, are clearly defined to the eye of the Historian and Sociologist.
>
> If this be true, then the history of the world is the history, not of individuals, but of groups, not of nations, but of races, and he who ignores or seeks to override the race idea in human history ignores and overrides the central thought of all history. What, then, is a race? It is a vast family of human beings, generally of common blood and language, always of common history, traditions and impulses, who are both voluntarily and involuntarily striving together for the accomplishment of

certain more or less vividly conceived ideals of life. (Du Bois, 1992, 485; Outlaw, 1992, 461)

Against this view Outlaw considers the opinion of Anthony Appiah (1986) who believes that races do not exist, but only cultures: "The truth is that there are no races: there is nothing in the world that can do all we ask 'race' to do for us" (Appiah, 1986, 36). And he continues: "Talk of 'race' is particularly distressing for those of us who take culture seriously . . . What exists "out there" in the world – communities of meaning, shading variously into each other in the rich structure of the social world – is the province not of biology but of hermeneutic understanding" (Appiah, 1986, 36). Outlaw does not directly refute Appiah's racial nihilism, so it is worthwhile to do this, albeit briefly, now. The idea that races do not exist because a concept does not do all that is asked of it, is an absurd argument. It would show that love, sexuality and a whole range of common world phenomena do not exist. Racial concepts are vague, but so are all concepts – we shall have more to say about vagueness in the next chapter. If vagueness is a ground for non-existence, then as we shall see in the next chapter, all common world objects and probably most scientific, logical and abstract objects do not exist either. If it is said that racial concepts have no part to play in a fully developed biological theory, then rather than directly challenging this view scientifically, we can force proponents of this view to ultimately become eliminative materialists, eliminating first common sense objects, then biological objects and accepting as scientifically legitimate only sub-atomic particles (Smith et al., 1997). If we approach Appiah's racial nihilism with a physically reductionist frame of mind, we should first ask how does he know that "cultures" and "meanings" exist? Racial concepts at least are empirical but Appiah's culturological concepts are not: they involve abstract essences and entities that physicalist, materialist and nominalist philosophers regard as ontologically highly problematic (Smith, et al., 1997). So if races do not exist, then, *a fortiori*, neither do cultures and all of the other cherished theoretical entities of sociology.

Outlaw responds to Appiah's racial nihilism by pointing out that Du Bois is not a biological reductionist or biological determinist. Race differences are not only physical but social, metaphysical and "spiritual", based upon the physical but transcending them. Human beings are such as to give social, philosophical and even theological meaning to racial concepts in the same "hermeneutic" sense mentioned by Appiah to produce a shared sense of identity. In this sense, racial categories are as real as any other categories in social theory; from a hermeneutical perspective it doesn't really matter whether physical racial characteristics exist "out there" in the "world" at all. Races are as real as anything else in the postmodern socially constructed world of social theory.

In this section we have discussed some challenges to received moral theory and other Enlightenment values based upon sociological and biocultural insights. We have also attempted to show that concepts such as race are still of relevance to understanding in a post-Enlightenment culture, insofar as "understanding" is possible at all. We conclude our brief outline of particularism and biological particularism with mention of Garrett Hardin's ecological challenge to universalism and cosmopolitanism, especially open-borders internationalism and free migration (Hardin, 1974, 1976, 1977a, b, 1978 a, b, 1979, 1980a, b, 1982, 1985, 1986).

For Hardin, universalism and the ideal of "One World", "in which clod equals cliff; the "rights" of all are equal whether friend or foe, native or foreigner, relative or stranger" (Hardin, 1982, 181), leads to the tragedy of the commons, to ecological destruction plunging everyone into the depths of Malthusian misery (Smith et al., 1997). This is most readily seen in the case of open migration, which even some internationalists (inconsistently) recognize supports the immigration-restrictionist case, seeing such openness as bringing "ecological *ruin to all*" (Milbrath, 1989, 331). Not only is the world's worth and resources finite and limited but the Earth faces an environmental crisis caused by both population pressure and economic growth. *Laissez faire* in population matters, meaning no borders and hence free migration, will create a suicidal commons, equivalent to city shops giving away their goods. They, like us, will be soon out of business (Hardin, 1993, 294). The "global village" in this sense, leads to "global pillage" (Hardin, 1993, 224). Hardin elaborates:

> The wisdom is very old: Don't put all your eggs in one basket. Given many sovereign nations it is possible for humanity to carry out many experiments in population control. Each nation can observe the successes and failures of the others. Experiments that have a good outcome can be copied and perhaps improved upon; unsuccessful experiments can be noted and not repeated. Such learning by trial and error is perilous if the borderless world created by unrestricted migration converts the entire globe into a single huge experiment. As long as the intelligence of the human species is less than perfect – which is forever – segmented parochialism is superior to unified cosmopolitanism in disclosing and capitalizing on the diverse possibilities of human nature. The formula for survival and progress is simple:
> *Unity within each sovereignty; diversity among sovereignties.*
> (Hardin, 1993, 295)

For most Americans, such thoughts seem contrary to the spirit of the poem on the Statue of Liberty and thus in some way, un-American. After all, isn't America a "nation of immigrants"? But Emma Lazarus, author of the poem on the Statue of Liberty, "was a wealthy woman who proposed sharing the wealth, the jobs of *other people* – our poor – with an unlimited number of immigrants" (Hardin, 1995, 125). The poem was not part of the original Statue, nor was it added to the Statue by Congress; the poem was added 17 years after the Statue was dedicated, put there by some of Lazarus' wealthy friends. It was not Lazarus' kind – the moneyed – who stood and stand to lose their jobs to new immigrants; in fact the wealthy stood and still stand to gain by being able to hire servants more cheaply (Hardin, 1995, 125). Lazarus' universalism and promiscuous altruism, if practiced without hypocrisy and with consistency (so that the wealthy, intellectuals, media moguls and the *literati* all felt the sting from the whip of *laissez faire*, equally) would eliminate Lazarus' type in an act of self-consumption. Hardin quotes Pierre-Joseph Proudhon (1809–1865), the French socialist and syndicalist, who was still enlightened enough to observe that "If everyone is my brother, I have no brothers" (Gray, 1946, 159; Hardin, 1982, 184). Garrett Hardin puts it even better: "Brotherhood requires otherhood. Civilization has been built upon, and can only survive with, a changeable mixture of discriminating altruisms" (Hardin, 1982, 184).

For Hardin the concept of ethnocentrism – where moral judgement is tied to the values of a particular ethnic group – is a major intellectual and moral advance: "The concept of rights that are unique and universal makes for intolerance, whereas sensitivity to the idea of ethnocentrism makes for tolerance" (Hardin, 1993, 296). Statements of universal human *rights*, such as the 1948 U.N. "Universal Declaration of Human Rights" – including rights such as freedom of speech, conscience and religion, the right to work, the right to social security, education and the arts – have a characteristic European bias that could only be applied to many Third World countries with absurd consequences (Hardin, 1993, 295). For example, the U.N. view that family size must solely be decided by individuals asserts that a right exists without giving consideration to *responsibilities*. The cost of raising children must be *commonized*, while the psychological benefits of parenthood are individualized – a highly unstable social arrangement (Hardin, 1994, 193). We will have more to say about the morality of the United Nations later in this book.

So much then for our discussion and defense of biological particularism against universalism. In the next section of this chapter we shall begin our attack upon liberalism and multiculturalism, having armed ourselves with postmodern weapons, laying the groundwork for the slaughter of other sacred cows later in this work.

LIBERALISM, MULTICULTURALISM, AND UNIVERSALISM

In concluding this chapter, seasoned and strengthened by a journey through the wild world of postmodern ethnocentrism and biological particularism, we shall now begin our attack upon liberalism and multiculturalism. Liberalism, as J. Dunn observes, is "an array of shreds and tatters of past ideological improvisation and highly intermittent current political illumination" (Dunn, 1985, 10 quoted from Mendus, 1989, 70). Liberalism has also been taken to be the view that there is nothing on which to base rational choice between different lifestyles (Ackerman, 1980). Hence it is illegitimate to impose values on another group and no one can assert the rational superiority of their own values. On the other hand liberals have asserted that there are objective values, or to maintain consistency, metavalues such as freedom and tolerance, transcendentally necessary for the flourishing of diversity, plurality and lifestyles – in short, multicultural societies. But even stated in this vague, but not unreasonable form, liberalism is only a logical deduction away from inconsistency. Poole notes one such incoherence: "In assuming the existence of a social world which is devoid of values, liberalism has assigned the task of creating them to the vagaries of individual choice. It then discovers that it has no strong argument against the individual who chooses values which are antithetical to those of liberalism" (Poole, 1991, 91; Rodewald, 1985).

Modern liberalism has become an inconsistent mix of tolerance and authoritarianism; authoritarianism is asserted on all the treasured politically correct issues such as racial and sexual equality, immigration and multiculturalism, but the common good is trumped by individual freedom on issues such as drug use, sexual freedom and criminal punishment (Berryhill, 1994). Liberals generally advocate gun control, using arguments conservatives use in other areas. Pornography must not be censored, but in general, racist propaganda and "hate" literature must be. Global redistributive justice must occur, even if this means that mass immigration destroys the ethno-cultural heritage of nations (Milne, 1996) – which in turn produces extreme nationalist resistance that destroys the possibility of realizing the original ideal at all. Even liberalism's commitment to tolerance is not free from paradox, facing a "paradox of tolerance", involving us in explaining why it is right to tolerate that which we believe to be wrong:

> In cases where toleration involves more than mere dislike, and has moral force, a paradox arises, which involves explaining how the tolerator might think it good to tolerate that which is morally wrong. In other words, we need to show how we can consistently claim *both* that toleration is a virtue in individuals and a good in society, *and* that

(strong) toleration necessarily and conceptually involves reference to things believed to be morally disreputable, or evil. (Mendus, 1989, 20)

Let us consider another example. Peter Singer in *Rethinking Life and Death* (1994), sympathises with the view that newborn infants "are not yet full members of the moral community" (Singer, 1994, 130–1). He rejects the sanctity of life doctrine and believes that, with qualification, infanticide, abortion and euthanasia are justified (Kuhse and Singer, 1985). Singer though is best known for his work on the ethics of animal liberation (Singer, 1990), where he has defended lobsters and lab rats (Robertson, 1991, 119–66). Isn't this a little odd: (with qualification) infanticide and abortion are alright but eating lobsters is not? Why doesn't a comprehensive green philosophy or deep ecology attack abortion? What about the life of the unborn child? Surely, by Singer's utilitarian criteria of rightness, where beings become moral on the basis of the capacity to suffer, an unborn child is at least as good a candidate for moral rights as a lobster? One would think so. But in thinking such thoughts, one must be careful not to become" speciesist", being racist and discriminatory in favor of one's own species. Singer says:

Why isn't species a legitimate reason? For essentially the same reason as we now exclude race or sex. The racist, sexist and speciesist are all saying: the boundary of my group also marks a difference of value. If you are a member of my group, you are more valuable than if you are not – no matter what other characteristics you may lack. Each of these positions is a form of group protectiveness, or group selfishness". (Singer, 1994, 203–4)

At this point we can ask, what exactly is wrong with that? Suppose that it is immoral: so what? Why be moral? Singer himself did a Masters thesis on this topic at the University of Melbourne and concluded at the time that there was no satisfactory answer to this question (Singer, 1993, ix–x). His answer now is to point to people he knows who have lived moral lives that are rich and exciting (Singer, 1993, x), which is not a satisfactory answer in an analytic philosophy exam because most human beings do not have moral lives (often by sins of omission) but many of these people still have rich and exciting lives. In the second edition of his book *Animal Liberation* (Singer, 1990), Singer proposes that moral opposition to racism and speciesism should be based on a basic principle of equality – the equal consideration of interests – that everyone's interests should have equal consideration (Rawls, 1972). From this principle Singer advances his master argument:

If a being suffers there can be no moral justification for refusing to take that suffering into consideration. No matter what the nature of the being, the principle of equality requires that its suffering be counted equally with the like suffering – insofar as rough comparisons can be made – of any other being. If a being is not capable of suffering, or of experiencing enjoyment or happiness, there is nothing to be taken into account. So the limit of sentience (using the term as a convenient if not strictly accurate shorthand for the capacity to suffer and/or experience enjoyment) is the only defensible boundary of concern for the interests of others. To mark this boundary by some other characteristic like intelligence or rationality would be to mark it in an arbitrary manner. Why not choose some other characteristic, like skin color? (Singer, 1990, 8–9)

Why not indeed, the racist or sexist might reply. The above argument could be taken by them as a *reductio ad absurdum* of the principle of the equal consideration of interests. This principle after all has radical egalitarian consequences with respect to the distribution of resources (Smith, 1991a) and arguably would lead to a tragedy of the commons situation in a world of limited resources in a state of ecological crisis. No skepticism-proof reason can be given for taking sentience as the criteria of moral rights, and it is easy to give intuitive counterexamples to the proposal (i.e. painless killings, instant obliterations, beings that do not suffer such as thinking machines, angels, and ontologically mixed entities such as ecosystems etc.) Singer says that if you reject speciesism, then you cannot have a basis for rejecting racism and sexism. But Singer's mode of argumentation is based upon a fallacy. As Hinckfuss has noted, a discriminator may prefer A over B solely because As are As and Bs are non-As. Such a response need not be irrational:

Discrimination is what morality is all about. The whole idea is to provide a rationale for discrimination in favour of certain sorts of acts, people and things and against other sorts of acts, people and things. So even if a particular discrimination seems bizarre to the liberationist (or, perhaps, *particularly* if it seems bizarre) it is not unlikely that the discrimination will have a basis in moral belief. It is ill-conducive to the elimination of discriminations which one dislikes or detests to fool oneself about the rationality or moral fervour of the discriminators. One's chances of bringing about what one takes to be social reform are unlikely to be enhanced by false beliefs about what is going on in the minds of others. (Hinckfuss, 1987, 11)

Singer's universalism is inconsistent with the beliefs of most civilizations and cultures that have existed on Earth, excluding the modern Western nations.[8] Allan Bloom in *The Closing of the American Mind* (1987) observes that ethnocentrism, identifying the good with one's own light, is as ubiquitous as the incest taboo. Bloom wishes to defend Western universalism against multicultural relativism and at one point in his book he attempts a *reductio ad absurdum* of multiculturalism. To do this, Bloom argues – rightly in our opinion – that there are very good reasons for non-Western closedness or ethnocentrism:

> Men must love and be loyal to their families and their peoples in order to preserve them. Only if they think their own things are good can they rest content with them. A father must prefer his child to other children, a citizen his country to others. That is why there are myths – to justify these attachments. And a man needs a place and opinions by which to orient himself. This is strongly asserted by those who talk about the importance of roots. The problem of getting along with outsiders is secondary to, and sometimes in conflict with, having an inside, a people, a culture, a way of life. A very great narrowness is not incompatible with the health of an individual or a people, whereas with great openness it is hard to avoid decomposition. The firm binding of the good with one's own, the refusal to see a distinction between the two, a vision of the cosmos that has a special place for one's people, seem to be conditions of culture. This is what really follows from the study of non-Western cultures proposed for undergraduates. It points them back to passionate attachment to their own and away from the science which liberates them from it. Science now appears as a threat to culture. . . . (Bloom, 1987, 37)

Bloom believes that people cannot be "fully human" if they remain in the cave of their culture, which he claims is what Plato meant by the image of the cave in the *Republic* (Bloom, 1987, 38). This interpretation of Plato is an arguable one, but is not the only one possible. The metaphor of the cave could be taken to be a snapshot of the Platonic epistemology and ontology; much of what Bloom takes to be science, because of its empirical basis and changeability would not be taken to be genuine knowledge by Plato; such genuine knowledge must be of the Forms. Beyond this thought, and against Bloom, we maintain that it is naive to suppose that people become "fully human" through science. Bloom does not examine the impact of reductionist doctrines such as physicalism and eliminative materialism (a program which attempts to eliminate mental phenomena and "folk" psychology, in favor of a de-humanized, de-personalized neurophysiology). Further, advanced science, as we shall show in the next chapter, has given us a metaphysical worldview which is literally absurd, surreal, contradictory and incoherent. For these reasons we believe that Bloom's *reductio ad absurdum* fails and his quoted argument can be taken as a defense rather than a refutation of ethnocentrism. The study of non-Western cultures does indicate, as Bloom observes, that it is natural to prefer one's own culture to others and to believe, even if it is false, that one's own race or people are superior to all others. Bloom is also right to assert that professors of openness should respect the closedness and ethnocentrism which is everywhere to be found (Bloom, 1987, 36–7). But "multicultural" consistency requires that Western people, and particularly people of Anglo Saxon-Germanic stock, should also recognize that they have a "multicultural" right to survive, rather than being used as the universal protoplasm of multicultural, multiracial societies in the West.

Summing up then, and returning to our example of Peter Singer's ethics, we can see that even broadly based liberal ethical principles, when pushed to a certain point, begin to disintegrate, indicating as philosophers such as John Gray and Alasdair MacIntyre have noted, that liberalism is itself an incoherent political philosophy.[9] In particular, liberalism, although purporting to be a philosophy of pluralism, and the basic justification for the existence of multicultural and multiracial societies in the West, is incapable of dealing with pluralism. This is dramatically illustrated by the Salman Rushdie *fatwa*, or death penalty, imposed upon Salman Rushdie by the Imam Ayatollah Khomeini in 1989 for blasphemy against Islam in his novel *The Satanic Verses* (Asad, 1990; Lewis, 1990; Ruthven, 1990; Sprigge, 1990). The Rushdie affair illustrates well the "clash of civilizations" and the cultural divide between the West and Muslim countries, and between secular and religious cultures. Salman Rushdie has argued that he has not committed blasphemy because he is not a believer (Rushdie, 1990). But the publishers of Holocaust-denial material are subjected to prosecution in Germany, where it is a crime to deny the Holocaust, whether they personally believe the contents of the books which they publish or not. An American neo-Nazi publisher has been imprisoned while on a trip to Germany, for publishing neo-Nazi material in the United States. In this case it seems that the neo-Nazi does believe what is published, but the criminal charge does not relate to the act of belief, but to the act of publication. Most "race hate" laws in the West relate to socially expressed views (such as acts of publication) rather than privately held beliefs. Hence Rushdie's defense based on "lack of belief" is not satisfactory. He has also argued on the eighth anniversary of the fatwa in favor of humanism over religion: "Gods may come and gods may go, but we, with any luck, go on for ever" (Rushdie, 1997, 15). He finds the liberalism of Europe one of its most attractive aspects (Rushdie, 1997, 15). But he condemns Europe for not taking a strong stand against Iran, being concerned with trade relations with Iran, rather than his freedom of speech. When Enlightenment ideals "come up against the powerful banalities of what is called 'reality' – trade, money, guns, power – then it's freedom that takes a dive" (Rushdie, 1997, 15). This remark indicates that Rushdie has correctly perceived that there is a fundamental contradiction between Enlightenment ideals and the money-powered world of *realpolitik*. However he has not recognized that it is liberalism that first legitimated, and continues to legitimate, the *realpolitik* of capitalism.

The Rushdie affair is an example of what John Harris has called "A Paradox of Multicultural Societies":

> The problem arises in connection with any culture which does not equally respect its own members. It looks as though a society committed to equality and containing such cultures or sub-cultures within it, is caught in a genuine and uncomfortable dilemma. If the society wishes to show to each individual the same concern and respect that it accords to any, then it may be required to outlaw, frustrate or at the very least condemn, important features of a constituent and discriminatory culture. While if it respects all cultures equally, a society may find itself endorsing culturally enshrined inequalities.
>
> For example, a culture which discriminates against women, which denies them equal opportunities, equal freedom, or equal standing with men in their community, may itself require that, as a culture, it be accorded the same concern and respect as that commanded by any other culture within the society. (Harris, 1982, 224)

He observes that multiculturalism in education is about eliminating "institutional racism" rather than the education of children about other cultures, but "the very same principles that mandate the achievement of these goals also and for the same reasons require the abolition of the institutionalised sexism of certain cultures" (Harris, 1982, 232). Charles Taylor is well aware of this problem. Western liberalism is an "organic outgrowth of Christianity" with a separation between Church and State: the "very term *secular* was originally part of the Christian vocabulary" (Taylor, 1992, 62). Fundamentalist or mainstream Islam does not recognize as valid the Western liberal distinction between Church and State. Thus: "Liberalism is not a possible meeting ground for all cultures, but is the political expression of one range of cultures, and quite incompatible with other ranges" (Taylor, 1992, 62; Tully ed., 1994). Taylor recognizes the dilemma which this presents for Western liberal societies, but elsewhere merely concludes "We're in for a rough ride on our shrunken planet." (Taylor, 1989b, 121).

Max Charlesworth, an Australian supporter of mass immigration and multiculturalism, in his book *Bioethics in a Liberal Society* (1993), agrees that the Salman Rushdie affair is "a dramatic example of the severe and apparently intractable religious-ethical problems that can arise in a multicultural society" (Charlesworth, 1993, 164). He then goes on to consider the question of whether the idea of multiculturalism is a secular idea. He concludes that religious pluralism and tolerance are possible only in a society founded on the secular separation of Church and State. No religion can claim to be absolutely true and divinely ordained so that there is a contradiction between multiculturalism and exclusivist absolutist religions: " . . . if any of the constituent subcultures were to say in effect: we can only live in social relationships with other groups if the values of *our* particular subculture are adopted as the basis of a unitary cultural consensus – then, by definition, a multicultural society is not possible" (Charlesworth, 1993, 165). And this is the point: a genuine multicultural society is not possible. Consider the case of the Party of Liberation, an international movement for the creation of a global Islamic State under Islamic law (*Khilafah*), the British chapter of which has proposed that "the only place to meet Jews is on the battlefield" (Vulliamy, 1996, 23). The group's exponent, Farid Kassim, a second generation British-Iraqi has said: "When I look at what is around me, it does not belong to the Anglo-Saxon . . . but to God. I am not obliged to obey British law" (Vulliamy, 1996, 23; Mortimer, 1990). There is little point now in raging against the "terrors of Islam" (Flew, 1994) – the Islam problem is itself generated by the promiscuous altruism and openness of liberalism, and consequently cannot be solved by merely reaffirming those values any more than a person suffering from poisoning can be saved by further administration of the same poison. Clearly, different values are required.

A failure to understand the *realpolitik* of the world characterizes many intellectual musings about multiculturalism, illustrated by the inadequacies of the works considered above. As another example consider the foreword of the book *Multiculturalism, Difference and Postmodernism* edited by G.L. Clark, D. Forbes and R. Francis, about Australian multiculturalism. Multiculturalism is seen as giving an audience to "voices excluded" by contemporary public discourse which they see as giving "privilege" to "Anglo-Celtic readings of the landscape" of Australia (Clark et al. eds, 1993, x). Postmodernism aims to give voices to those suppressed by the "dominant discourse." Of course: "Australia's New World history is so much about the dispossessed and oppressed seeking refuge and new opportunity. Many new arrivals are perplexed by the oppression and exclusion the white Australian state visits upon its indigenous people" (Clark et al. eds, 1993, xi). This is all asserted without any empirical evidence that Italian, Greek or Asian migrants were, and are, particularly concerned about the plight of the Australian Aborigines; indeed as they are, according to this view, by definition, "oppressed" groups, surely their concern would be with their own oppression. Regardless of this, the editors assert that there is a need to attack Anglo Saxon culture, particularly its idea of mateship, as multiculturalism "aims to fracture the coherence of inclusive symbolism and expose the plurality of Australian experience" (Clark et al. eds, 1993, xi). For them, multiculturalism is about power politics, "the assertion of the legitimacy of difference counter-posed to the power and influence of dominant cultural groups of society" (Clark et al. eds, 1993, xi). They see "Anglo-Celts" as a dominant cultural group in Australian society, absurdly proposing that they (the category itself mixes together the English on the one hand, and the Scots, Irish and Cornish on the other – hardly a unified cultural group) act as a united front. They ignore the role of ethnic elites (who are organized as a united front), business leaders and "new class" intellectual elites and their role in domination and oppression. No doubt it sounds good to be proclaiming the moral superiority of the "oppressed". Finally, these editors express their amazement that multiculturalism is "politically disputed" in Australia: "It is regrettable that many people would like to reimpose an institutional commitment to a simple, homogeneous world. The remarkable diversity of Australia, the political strife in Germany which is reeling from reaction to refugee and guest-workers' settlement, the scars stemming from the Los Angeles riots and the long-standing separatist stance of Quebeckers are permanent testimony to the complexities of multicultural societies" (Clark et al. eds, 1993, xii). Commonsense alone would surely have led these theorists to begin to doubt whether their commitment to multiculturalism was, from a rational point of view, sound. And if they had abandoned Enlightenment rationality in favor of the simple pleasures of postmodern relativism, why should they suppose that their fairy-tale is any more believable than the Anglo Saxon one they caricaturize and despise?

THE STATE OF THE ARGUMENT

Although recognizing the worth of cultural, ethnic and racial pluralism, we have been concerned to oppose in this chapter both orthodox multiculturalism, which seeks to increase cultural pluralism by mass migration at the expense of a dominant cultural group (a group which is in turn vilified and attacked by intellectuals), and globalism/universalism/cosmopolitanism/internationalism which also aim to steamroll cultures into the flat homogeneity of the global free market. Multiculturalism can be defended on postmodernist grounds, but it is typically defended by recourse to liberalism, so the two broad positions which we wish to oppose here have a common philosophical heart. By use of postmodern skeptical arguments, we have attempted to destroy this common heart and defend, or at least illustrate, the plausibility of various forms of particularism against the dominant universalism of our age. We have been critical of Enlightenment values and much which conservatives cherish as being characteristic to the West, but we believe that it is more important that *all* cultures, races and ethnic groups survive – than some abstract, fleshless ideal. W.F. Smyth has put this point well:

> The reader should not imagine that I am opposed to people who wish to preserve their culture and identity. On the contrary, it is precisely be-cause I very much wish to preserve my own way of life, that I am able to understand those who feel the same way about theirs. The point is, however, that I do not wish *them* to preserve *their* culture at the ex-pense of mine. If my culture corresponds to one political jurisdiction and somebody else's corresponds to another, then with a little good will major problems can likely be avoided: each jurisdiction can manage its own culture in its own way. But if two or more cultures compete within a single political jurisdiction, then polarisation is sure to arise. It is the policy that encourages and exacerbates this polarization – that per-versely ignores facts of nature – which I oppose. Indeed, the herd in-stinct is strong in human beings and is not to be despised: it is certainly related to those instincts which allow us to cooperate and to build to-gether. . . . [It] is a kind of loyalty to what we are and to what we have been formed by. We should respect it rather than call it names. (Smyth, 1991, 434)

In the next chapter we will further develop our critique of universalism and cosmopolitanism by attacking universalism in the hard sciences as well – producing then, the "balkanization of everything".

3 Shipwrecked by the Laughter of the Gods: The Epistemological Limits of Universalism

> Whoever undertakes to set himself up as a judge in the field of Truth and Knowledge is shipwrecked by the laughter of the gods.
> — Albert Einstein (1982, 28)

In a review of John Horgan's *The End of Science* (1996), John Caiazza (1997) views with alarm Horgan's central thesis that modern science is at an end because of theoretical impasses in almost every field. Caiazza takes Horgan to task for failing to consider the cultural implications of this thesis. He says: "With the 'end of science', the entire Enlightenment project – which includes capitalism, individual rights, mass education, rationalism, and representative government – is brought into question" (Caiazza, 1997, 28). The "end of science" "is the final nail in the coffin of Western culture, leaving us stranded without hope of apprehending truth, exercising reason, or justifying standards of morality" (Caiazza, 1997, 29). In this chapter we will also argue for the "end of science" thesis, based upon an analysis of scientific theories rather than the testimony of scientists as Horgan does. Caiazza is right to regard the entire Enlightenment project as being brought into question, but he is wrong to suppose that such a critique is an "argument" for or advocacy of irrationalism. Rather, recognizing the limits of science, logic and reason, recognizing that faith, commitment, dogma and prejudice are part and parcel of human epistemic affairs, should be a liberating event rather than a depressing one. There is more to Heaven and Earth than dreamed of in the theories of philosophers and scientists; man is more than a rational animal. The limits of science must make us cautious about "One World" dreams of creating a global culture. Such dreams are likely to be shipwrecked by the laughter of the gods.

THE CRUEL LOGIC OF PARADOX: THE LIMITS OF LOGIC AND MATHEMATICS

The failure of the Enlightenment project can be first illustrated by a consideration of the epistemological foundations of mathematics, a discipline once thought to supply secure knowledge and necessary truths. Morris Kline in his excellent survey of the development of mathematics, *Mathematics: The Loss of Certainty* (Kline, 1980) opens his book with these words:

> There are tragedies caused by war, famine, and pestilence. But there are also intellectual tragedies caused by limitations of the human mind. This book relates the calamities that have befallen man's most effective and unparalled accomplishment, his most persistent and profound effort to utilize human reason – mathematics. (Kline, 1980, 3).

Kline is concerned with "the rise and decline of the majesty of mathematics" (Kline, 1980, 3). The methodology of mathematics has been, and still is, deductive proof from self-evident or merely given principles or axioms. Deductive logic guarantees the truth of conclusions deduced from the axioms. Kline observes that by "utilizing this seemingly clear, infallable, and impeccable logic, mathematicians produced apparently indubitable and irrefutable conclusions" (Kline, 1980, 4). This deductivist foundation to mathematics was rocked by nonstandard geometries and algebras in the nineteenth century and by the set-theoretic and logical-semantical paradoxes, as well as Gödel's incompleteness theorem, in the twentieth century. Kline concludes:

> Mathematicians have been worshipping a golden calf – rigorous, universally acceptable proof, true in all possible worlds – in the belief that it was God. They now realize it was a false god. But the true god refuses to reveal himself, and now they must question whether god exists. The Moses who might relay the word has yet to appear. There is reason to question reason. (Kline, 1980, 316)

Kline's "postmodern" survey contrasts with survey books on mathematics published earlier in this century, such as E.T. Bell's *Mathematics: Queen and Servant of Science* (Bell, 1987 [reprint]). Bell's book is highly optimistic, being primarily concerned with applications rather than foundations. However he does conclude on a "note of doubt" (Bell, 1987, 416) in the light of Gödel's theorem. Kline's book though is consistent in skeptical flavor with more recently published survey books such as P.J. Davis and R. Hersh's *Descartes' Dream* (Davis and Hersh, 1986). Unlike Kline they discuss the social consequences of mathematization and conclude, *"We'd better watch it, because too much of it may not be good for us"* (Davis and Hersch, 1986, xv). These writers also speculate (albeit briefly and without the necessary depth of argument), that the Jewish Holocaust was a product of "advanced mathematization, through abstraction and subsequent loss of meaning" (Davis and Hersh, 1986, 291; see also Barrett, 1978; Winner, 1986).

Keith Devlin, author of *Logic and Information* (Devlin, 1991) argues that the attempt to produce a formal language of the mind, is a failure. The inside flap of the book's dust jacket explains:

> . . . if our thought and language are so logical . . . why have all efforts to re-create them fallen short? The most advanced artificial intelligence and natural language programs do not begin to approximate actual human abilities. Computing machines, of any kind, cannot and probably never will think like us. It is time . . . to come to terms with the fact that logic simply can't capture the real processes of human thought. . . . many ways of thinking that are perfectly rational are at the same time entirely illogical, and that the exquisite verbal tango of human communication has little to do with logical processing. (Devlin, 1997, dust jacket)

Devlin goes on to argue in detail in his book that computers face intrinsic limits to understanding because of the problem of logical ambiguity. Humans have the capacity to make logical jumps and to operate "illogically" with vagueness, ambiguity and contradictions on an intuitive but socially learned basis. Computers, being superb logical operators, even when operating on the basis of fuzzy logic, still require precise instructions. If computers operate "irrationally", disaster usually follows. Human irrationality and illogicality is usually manageable in defined social contexts, which is what artificial intelligence (AI) lacks. Socially defined norms may not be captured by formal logical rules. The physicist Roger Penrose, although not as radical as Devlin in his rejection of formalism, also argues that there are some facts about human thinking that will never be duplicated by a machine. As a mathematical realist/Platonist, believing that mathematical truth has its own "independence", he argues that apart from Gödel's theorem, mathematical truth goes beyond mere formalism. In setting up a formal system, axioms and rules of procedure used are decided by an intuitive understanding of that which is self-evidently true (Penrose, 1989, 1994, et al., 1997). A mechanistic philosophy of mind, by contrast, works on the assumption that "the human mind is a system of *computational* or *recursive* rules that are embodied in the nervous system; that the material presence of these rules accounts for perception, conception, speech, belief, desire, intentional acts, and other forms of intelligence" (Nelson, 1982, xiii). This mechanist theory or approach to mind, in both its reductive (intentional states are identical brain states) or eliminative (there are really no such intentional states) forms typically proposes that the commonsense framework of daily life is a "false and radically misleading conception of the causes of human behavior and the nature of cognitive activity" (Churchland, 1984, 43; see also Heffernan, 1978; Horgan and Woodward, 1985; Baker, 1987; Maloney, 1987; Hunter, 1988; Cling, 1990; Fetzer, 1990; Robinson, 1992; Bechtel, 1993; Bickle, 1993; Christie, 1993; Dennett, 1993; McLaughlin, 1993; Sprigge, 1993; McClintock, 1995). In the AI/mind debate it is typically assumed by both sides of the debate (mentalists and mechanists) that modern deductive formal logic is essentially correct and is the appropriate logic for science, computing, artificial intelligence and mathematics (Dreyfus, 1979; Hofstadter, 1980, 1986; Hofstadter and Dennett, eds, 1981; Dennett, 1981; Manning, 1987; Pylyshyn, ed., 1987; Weizenbaum, 1987; Graubard, ed., 1988; Sylvan, Goddard and da Costa, 1989; Lormand, 1990; Hooker and Penfold, 1995; Preston, 1995).

It will be argued here that modern mathematical or formal logic is tending towards self-destruction and ultimately self-elimination: advances in formal logic have generated methods of such power that it is possible to devise paradoxes that are seemingly unsolvable and to counter-model propositions of standard logic that were once thought to be secure logical truths. Later in this section, after developing our thesis about the possible incoherence of the world, we will examine the epistemological situation in theoretical physics which also, we will argue, supports our thesis about the bankruptcy of the Enlightenment project. But first we will now give an outline of formal deductive logic.[1]

What is formal deductive logic? Bertrand Russell in his *Introduction to Mathematical Philosophy* (Russell, 1919) states that "logic (or mathematics) is concerned with *forms*, and is concerned with them only in the way of stating that they are always or sometimes true – with all the permutations of 'always' and 'sometimes' that may occur" (Russell, 1919, 199–200). Formal logic is thus concerned with the *form* of an argument rather than its content or subject matter and an assessment of whether the argument is an instance of correct or incorrect reasoning can be made on the basis of a consideration of form.

Formal deductive logic is concerned primarily with the study of arguments within logistic systems or languages. Such systems or languages, much like natural languages have a *syntax* (grammar) and a *semantics* (meaning/interpretation). The syntax is a sort of "logical skeleton", outlining the formal relations between signs or expressions in the language. The syntax of the system constitutes the vocabulary, rules of formation, axioms, and rules of inference of the system. (So called "natural deduction systems" have no axioms, but only rules of inference.) The *semantics* of a logistic system outlines relationships between syntactical expressions and non-linguistic objects, supplying an *interpretation* of a system. This formal structure constitutes the *object language* of the logistic system L. There is also an unformalized language (but it can be formalized as well) M known as the *metalanguage* of L (if the metalanguage is formalized then there is another unformalized language, the meta-metalanguage MM and so on) where one describes L. It is usually a natural language such as English or a suitably regimented part of English.

Proof theory is a syntactical study of logistic systems with respect to the structure of proofs in the system. A proof is a sequence of well formed formulae (wff), such that each member of the sequence is either an axiom of the system or can be derived by means of the rules of inference of the system. Various proof-theoretic concepts may be defined such as *consistency*: a logistic system L is syntactically consistent if and only if there is no wff such that both W and its negation ("not-W") ~ W is provable in L.

Model theory is concerned with the relationship between the syntax of logistic systems and their models or interpretations (usually represented in set-theoretical form). The key concepts of model theory are *validity*, *consequence* and *independence*. If A and B are wff of L, then B is a *logical consequence* of A in L if and only if B is true in all models of L in which A is true. A is *valid* in L if and only if A is true in all models of L. B is *independent* of the axioms of L if and only if there exists a model of L in which B is true and a model in which B is false. *Truth* in these interpreted formal systems is usually defined in a way first suggested by the logician Alfred Tarski, by assigning objects to names and outlining *satisfaction conditions* for the predicates of the language so that by a recursive procedure the values of all the sentences of the language can be determined. True sentences are just those sentences satisfied by all sequences of objects in the domain of L and false sentences by no sequence of objects.

The syntactical and semantical natures of L are "held together", so to speak, by two results. According to *Gödel's completeness theorem* if S is any sentence in a *first order language* (typically meaning the classical first order predicate calculus) and K is an arbitrary set of sentences of L

(GCT)   If K $\models$ S, then K $\vdash$ S

Where " $\models$ " is model-theoretic consequence and " $\vdash$ " is proof-theoretic consequence. The *soundness theorem* is

(ST)   If K $\vdash$ S, then K $\models$ S

Logicians, as we shall see, can live with incompleteness, but they cannot tolerate *unsoundness*. Soundness requires the truth of the premises as well as the validity of the argument form. It is a fundamental presupposition of formal deductive logic that if the form of an argument is valid, and its premises are true, then its conclusion *must* be true. In a valid *deductive* argument it is impossible to assert the premises and deny the conclusion without contradiction, which is not so for inductive or statistical arguments.

In *classical deductive logic* it is a necessary and a sufficient condition of the validity of an argument that it should be impossible for the premises to be true and the conclusion false. On this account of validity all arguments with a necessarily true conclusion, and all with inconsistent premises are valid. By way of example:

p & ~p
q

where q is an arbitrary proposition is classically valid. This can be proved by the following argument known as the "Lewis argument" (Read, 1988, 31):

(1)	p & ~p		Assumption
(2)	p	(1)	Simplification
(3)	~p	(1)	Simplification
(4)	p v q	(2)	Addition
(5)	q	(4),(3)	Disjunctive Syllogism

Relevant or relevance logics reject the validity of p & ~p → q and (p v q) & ~p → q on the grounds that A → B should express the idea that there is a logical connection between the premises and conclusion of an argument, that the logical content of B should be contained in A (Routley et al., 1982).[2] The difficulty is to state formally what this idea of "relevance" actually is, rather than merely construct logistic systems which are said to be "relevant." Various proposals can be found in the literature offering an explication of the concept of relevance but all of these accounts are open to logical and philosophical objections (Iseminger, 1980). For example the idea of the relevant meaning connection between A and B has been explicated by means of variable-sharing: for propositional formulae A and B, if A entails B then A and B share a variable (Read, 1988, 126). This proposal would allow us to reject p & ~p → q but not the disjunctive syllogism, which by the Lewis argument allows us to prove p & ~p → q in any case. For this reason contradictory situations have played an important role in the formal semantics of relevant logics. Nontrival contradictory situations have been used as countermodels or counterexamples to theses such as p & ~p → q. Consider a nontrival model C. Then for some A and B, A and ~A both hold in C but B does not hold. Hence A and ~A does not entail B. Classical logic rejects the idea that there could be propositions for which both A and ~A could both be true, that is, for which there could be *true contradictions*. A major foundational debate exists in formal logic about this point and we shall have more to say about it below.

There have been, of course, many other attempts and programs implicated to solve the problem of *relevance* (Sylvan, 1989b). Most, if not all of these attempts face philosophical difficulties of their own. For example S. McCall's connexive implication systems begin with the correct intuition (we believe) that classical quantification theory is mistaken in rejecting the validity of the inference from "All A is B" to "Some A is B" in the situation where there are no A's (McCall, 1966, 1967). This arises because of the existential loading of the "some" quantifier "($\exists x$)" which reads "there *exists* an x". Thus we cannot validly infer the false proposition "Some unicorns have golden horns" from the true proposition (classically true in the absence of unicorns), "All unicorns have golden horns" (McCall, 1967, 347). To solve the problem of granting the universal validity of inferring "Some A is C" from "All A is C" as well as the paradoxes of strict implication, McCall devised a system of *connexive implication* where the thesis:

(McC) $(a \rightarrow c) \rightarrow \sim (a \rightarrow \sim c)$

holds. But the price now paid is the failure of conjunctive simplification (p & q) $\rightarrow$ p, which cannot be accepted without a contradiction arising in the system (Smith, 1986a, 179). Thus, it is not a logical truth in connexive logic that green apples are apples, even though this is clearly intuitively correct.

The attack on the foundations of classical logic has also come from another direction. In 1990 the standard account of the concept of logical consequence came under attack by John Etchemendy in a book entitled *The Concept of Logical Consequence* (Etchemendy, 1990). Etchemendy attacked the orthodox Tarskian model-theoretic definitions of logical truth and logical validity, namely, that a sentence ø of a language L is logically true if and only if it is true in all models and an argument is logically valid if and only if its conclusion is true in every model in which the premises are true (Tarski, 1956). Etchemendy argued that the standard model-theoretic account of logical consequence is mistaken, since it "will declare certain arguments invalid that are actually valid, and declare others valid that in fact are not" (Etchemendy, 1990, 8). For example the infinitary inference called the *Omega rule*:

(OR) 0 is P, 1 is P, 2 is P, . . . Therefore all numbers are P

is an intuitively valid inference, as Tarski himself recognized (Etchemendy, 1990, 83). Indeed Tarski himself used the phenomenon of *ω-incompleteness* to argue for the inadequacy of the syntactical definition of logical consequence. An ω-incomplete theory allows us to derive the following sentences from the axioms of the theory:

(A$_0$)   0 possesses the property P.
(A$_1$)   1 possesses the property P.

...

In general we can deduce all sentences such that

(A$_n$) n possesses the property P, for a natural number n.

An ω-incomplete theory does not allow us to derive by the standard rules of inference the universal generalization:

(A)   Every natural number possesses the property P.

Tarski thought that this was a problematic state of affairs:

> This fact seems to me to speak for itself: it shows that the formalized concept of consequence, as it is generally used by mathematical logicians, by no means coincides with the ordinary concept. For intuitively it seems certain that the universal sentence A follows in the ordinary sense from the totality of particular sentences A$_0$, A$_1$, ... A$_n$, ... provided all these sentences are true, the sentence A must also be true. (quoted from Etchemendy, 1990, 83)

The Omega rule, Etchemendy argues, also poses a problem for Tarski's theory because if we do not take numerals and "number" to be logical constants then the inference is invalid by orthodox model theory. The suggestion that these symbols be taken to be logical constants is refuted by Graham Priest on the grounds that the sentence "there are two distinct numbers" would contain only logical constants and be vacuously satisfied (Priest, 1995a, 289). It is counterintuitive to suppose that this sentence is a logical truth. Priest then argues that the problem could be solved by supposing that the Omega rule is invalid. What is valid is the argument with the suppressed premise: if C then all numbers are P, where C is the conjunction of (A$_0$), (A$_1$), etc. But this is also counterintuitive. The Omega rule is used in mathematical reasoning in the form in which it is stated. Before doubting standard mathematical practice we should be given good reason for doing so. Etchemendy in our opinion has made his point with the argument about the Omega rule, although a number of his other alleged counterexamples are problematic (Priest, 1995a, 289–90).

Stephen Read in his book *Thinking About Logic* (1995), argues that the classical account of logical consequence *undergenerates*, in failing to count as valid arguments which have intuitively valid logical consequences. Classical logical consequence is *compact*: "any consequence of an infinite set of propositions is a consequence of some finite subset of them" (Read, 1995, 43). Compact classical consequence undergenerates: "there are intuitively valid consequences which it marks as invalid" (Read, 1995, 44). Read also takes as an example the ω-rule, which is not classically valid because of the compactness condition, and more technically because of arguments concerning *non-standard models*: "whatever proposition instantiates A(n), . . . can hold of all the standard numbers 0,1,2, and so on, and still fail to be true of every number in the model – so that although all premises of the ω-rule, A(0), A(1), and so on are true in this model, the conclusion, 'for every n, A(n)' is false" (Read, 1995, 47). However, Read responds, effectively, to the "non-standard model" objection as follows: "The non-standard models of first-order logic are just that, non-standard. They contain objects which are not numbers" (Read, 1995, 48).

The logician Vann McGee of Rutgers University Philosophy Department, also argued that Tarski's concept of the concept of logical validity "is an utter failure" (McGee, 1992; see also Johnson, 1992, 83–121).[3] The idea that a sentence of a formalized language is valid if and only if it is true in every model, has two major problems. First is the *contingency problem*: what sentences are valid ought not be a matter of contingent fact, but this is so by Tarki's theory. For a sentence to be valid we need to know that there couldn't possibly be a model in which the sentence is false. McGee believes that this problem could be overcome with "sufficiently heavy-handed metaphysical assumptions" (McGee, 1992, 292). The second problem is the *reliability problem*: what good reasons have we for believing that being true in every model is any guarantee that a sentence is true? There is, we believe, an even more basic difficulty than this, an epistemological problem which has been stated precisely by Graham Priest:

> If the validity of an inference is to be identified with the truth of a universal generalization, then we cannot know that an inference is valid unless we know this generalization to be true. But we cannot know that this generalization is true unless we know that its instances are true; and we cannot know this unless we know that every instance of an argument form is materially truth preserving. Hence, we could never use the fact that an argument form is valid to demonstrate that an argument *is* materially truth preserving. Thus the prime function of having a valid argument would be undercut. (Priest, 1995a, 287)

Priest believes that this argument fails because the "epistemic order" need not coincide with the "definitional order". He says that we may be able to tell that an argument is valid without consulting the definition. He then recognizes that this in turn raises the question of how we can tell that an inference is valid – and that is precisely the epistemological problem which the formal logician faces. We are not denying that some arguments are valid. Recognizing the limits of formal universalistic modes of reasoning does not commit one to *logical nihilism*, the view that no arguments are valid at all. The thesis that no arguments are valid cannot be coherently *argued* for, because if an argument were given for the thesis it would be invalid. The formal deductive logician does face a problem of deduction in many ways analogous to the notorious problem of justifying induction (Haack, 1976, 1982).

Stephen Read expresses other criticisms of the classical account of logical consequence in his book *Thinking About Logic* (Read, 1995). Classical logical consequence makes argument validity a matter of *form*: "An argument is valid if it instantiates a valid form; and a form is valid if there is no (permissible) interpretation of the schematic letters (over some domain) under which the premises are true and the conclusion false" (Read, 1995, 50). This account is advanced in an attempt to avoid a modal metaphysics of *necessity*. The model-theoretic accounts dismisses a range of valid consequences as not valid by virtue of their form. Read's example is of a necessary truth "Nothing is both round and square at the same time", where neither "round" nor "square" are logical expressions and the formalized statement is not a logical truth, true by virtue of its logical form alone. Read goes the modal metaphyics way, rejecting the classical model-theoretic account as inadequate: "Logical consequence is really a matter of what would be the case if the premises were true. One proposition is a logical consequence of others if it would be true if those others were true, that is, if it is impossible for the one lot to be true and the other false" (Read, 1995, 53). The logical consequence relation, thus, should be materially valid, having an analytic connection between the premises and the conclusion of an argument, "valid in virtue of matter, not of form" (Read, 1995, 53). However the modal account of logical consequence is not free of philosophical problems. How, for example, do we know the truth of modal propositions? How can the truth-value of propositions in "other worlds/universes" be discovered from the position of this universe when by definition we cannot empirically access these worlds? What is a "possible world"? If a characterization of a "possible world" depends upon formal consistency, then the modal view collapses back into the classical model-theoretic view. Read believes that because of these epistemological problems, *necessity* must be identified with the *a priori* (Read, 1995, 111). Read acknowledges that the alleged cogency of the concept *a priori* has been under attack by empiricists (Read, 1995, 111–17) and he also admits that the necessary and the *a priori* are not coextensive (Read, 1995, 117). This in itself means that the problem of necessity is outstanding.

The problem of the justification of basic logical principles has become acute given the power of modern logic to construct exotic models to countermodel and refute more and more propositions, as Chris Mortensen has observed:

One of the directions of recent logical research has been into the semantical conditions under which various propositions hold and fail. One of the upshots has been a growing body of information about how to construct models to refute more and more propositions. It is, for example, no news that countermodels can be constructed to large numbers of the theorems of the very natural modal logic S5, on which David Lewis' modal realism is based. It is also a straightforward matter to construct countermodels to the laws of excluded middle and noncontradiction. Recent work by Errol Martin has even shown how to construct countermodels to every instance of A → A. In the light of these kinds of results, it seems to me that it would be a bold claim that there is *any* proposition that cannot be made to come out false in *some* structure. (Mortensen, 1981, 157; see also Martin and Meyer, 1982; Meyer and Abraham, 1984; Mortensen, 1989; Priest, 1995b)

The minimum skeptical conclusion which follows from these considerations is that formal logic is a myth, as D.C. Stove recognized in his book *The Rationality of Induction*:

There are no logical forms, above a low level of generality, of which every instance is invalid: every such supposed form has valid cases. There are few or no logical forms, above a low level of generality, of which every instance is valid: nearly every such supposed form has invalid cases or paradoxical cases. The natural conclusion to draw is that formal logic is a myth, and that over validity, as well as over invalidity, forms do *not* rule: cases do. (Stove, 1986, 127)

Graham Priest in his paper "What is a Non-Normal World?" (Priest, 1992), has observed that "the idea that there are situations in which an arbitrary formula may fail is part of the folklore of relevant logic" (Priest, 1992, 291). Routley and Meyer in their semantics for relevant logic have constructed "worlds" where any formula of the form α → β may fail (Routley et al., 1982) and non-normal worlds where theorems and logical truths may fail. Priest says:

the prime notion of logic is inference; and valid (deductive) inferences are expressed by statements of entailment, α → β, (that α entails that β). Hence, in a logically impossible world we should expect statements of this form to take values other than the correct ones. Is there a limit to the value that such a conditional might take? I do not see why. Just as we can image a world where the laws of physics are arbitrarily different, indeed, an anomalous world where there are no such laws; so we can imagine worlds where the laws of logic are arbitrarily different, indeed an anomalous world where there are no such laws. (Priest, 1992, 292–3)

Richard Routley/Sylvan has taken this idea to its "logical" conclusion, in his theory of items (Routley, 1980). Items include everything that can be talked about, and things which cannot – paradoxical items, ineffable things, contradictory objects, nondescript items – anything goes! Whatever is not an item, such as Bugboo = that object not an item, is an item. Items may be as odd, vague, paradoxical as one likes and more so (Sylvan, n.d.). Sylvan adopts item theory because of the failure of the semantical theory of classical logic, which attempts to either reduce or eliminate problematic logical items such as vague, indefinite, non-existent and paradoxical objects. Sylvan thus is free to speculate about the mathematical properties of a prime number m between 11 and 13 (although Peano arithmetic has no such m): "there is no impressive reason why a pluralistic noneist framework should not recognize *all* these sorts of arithmetic (and others): standard arithmetic as neutralised, Peano arithmetic as neutralised, assumption-enriched and qualified arithmetic, dialethic arithmetic, and so on. Let's have them all, let's hear it for them all!" (Sylvan, n.d., 3–4). At this point we can see very clearly how modern formal logic has swallowed its own head; there can be no *general* laws of form or *universally* valid rules of inference. Logical truth and validity are relative to a logistic system and as we have seen, there anything goes.

This conclusion can be supported, albeit briefly, by a consideration of the paradoxes. A paradox is an argument with seemingly true premises, obtained by valid reasoning which has a conclusion which is false, contradictory or in general, not true. Formal deductively valid arguments with true premises and a valid "law of form" *must* transmit truth from the premises to the conclusion. Only truth should be obtained from truth. The existence of logical and semantical parodoxes challenges this fundamental dogma of logic. It does seem possible to be able to derive absurdity from truth by logic. This is so for both semantics and set theory. We shall give examples.

In semantics, the best known paradox is the Liar paradox which arises from considering an arbitrary sentence S which is asserted not to be true. Using Tarski's scheme we have

(1)   "S is not true" is true, if and only if, S is not true.

Suppose then that

(2)   S = "S is not true".

Substitute S for "S is not true" in (1) to obtain:

(3)   S is true, if and only if, S is not true.

But this is a contradiction (Post, 1970, 1978–9; Bartlett and Suber eds, 1987).

The Liar paradox can also be stated as a syllogism, a Liar syllogism (Read, 1979; Drange, 1990). Let (B) be the argument:

(B)   This argument is valid
       Therefore, this argument is invalid.

Assume that (B) is valid, then it has a true premise and a false conclusion, and is therefore invalid. So if (B) is valid, then it is invalid, so by *reductio ad absurdum* it is invalid. But the invalidity of (B) has been deduced from the premise that (B) is valid which is what (B) asserts. Therefore (B) is valid. Therefore (B) is both valid and invalid (Read, 1979, 267).

Another argument producing a paradox which uses no semantic or set-theoretic notions, and hence cannot be "solved" in the familiar ways, has been given by G. Littman (1992). Laura Goodship (1996) states this argument as follows: "Consider the proposition: it is irrational to believe this proposition. Call this A. Suppose that someone believes A. Then they believe A and at the same time, believe that it is irrational to believe it. This is irrational. Hence, it is irrational to believe A. But this is just A. Hence, we have demonstrated A, and so it *is* rational to believe it" (Goodship, 1996, 154). There seem to be propositions which are *both* rationally acceptable and rejectable. If this is correct, it would seem to constitute a major defect in the standard view of rationality, which is based on classical logic (Priest, 1995b).

Other interesting semantical paradoxes exist, establishing that all sentences are true (*Löb's paradox*) and also that all sentences are false (*Windt's paradox*). M.H. Löb argued as follows. Let (L) be any sentence and let (M) be the sentence:

(M)   If this sentence is true, then so is (L)

Now if (M) is true, then so is (L), that is , (M) is true. Hence (L) is true. Therefore every sentence is true (Löb, 1955; Van Benthem, 1978). Peter Windt has asked us to consider two propositions:

(I)   *P*
(II)   There is no sound deduction of (I) from (I) and (II).

Here is an argument schema which purports to disprove (I), whatever "*P*" is:

(1)   There is a *valid* deduction of (I) from (I) and (II).

(2)   There is a *sound* deduction of (I) from (I) and (II) iff (I) and (II) are true. (From (1) and the definition of "sound".)

(3)   Suppose (I) is true. (Assumption for a *reductio.*)

(4)   If (II) is true, there is a sound deduction of (I) from (I) and (II). (From (2) and (3).)

(5)   If (II) is true, there is no sound deduction of (I) from (I) and (II). (Consider what (II) says.)

(6)   (II) is not true. ((4), (5))

(7)   There is no sound deduction of (I) from (I) and (II). ((2), (6))

(8)   (II) is true. ((7), and consider what (II) says.)

(9)   (II) is and is not true. ((8), (6))

(10)   (I) is not true. ((3)–(9), *reductio ad absurdum.*) (Windt, 1973, 65)

Curry's paradox, first stated in 1942 by Haskell Curry (Curry, 1942) has both a semantic and set theoretical version, in both cases establishing triviality (Irvine, 1992). Consider a sentence scheme:

(CS)   This sentence entails that S

for an arbitrary contingent sentence S. Is (CS) true? (CS) is true if it is impossible for (CS) to be true and S to be false. Now given that entailment is truth-preserving if (CS) were true, then S would be entailed by it, so that whenever (CS) is true, S will be true. So it is not possible for both (CS) to be true and S to be false. Hence (CS) is true. But since S is entailed by (CS) and (CS) is true, S must be true. But S is an arbitrary contingent sentence (Irvine, 1992, 273–4). Meyer, Routley and Dunn have also shown that a set-theoretical version of Curry's paradox follows on minimal logical assumptions (Meyer, Routley and Dunn, 1979; Geach, 1954; Laraudogoitia, 1989; Hazen, 1990).

It is well known that there are many programs that have been implemented to solve the paradoxes. The set theoretical paradoxes such as Russell's paradox have not been solved, so much as avoided by axiomatic set theories (Safir, 1976; Slater, 1984). The semantic paradoxes have been more difficult to deal with, and there is no generally accepted way of avoiding every paradox, let alone solving them. Graham Priest has observed:

There is certainly no generally accepted solution. The strategies or "heuristics" for solving the problem are but few. There is the "meaningless" strategy, the "neither true nor false strategy" and so on. Yet within this framework, purported solutions have multiplied in a way that makes the breeding habits of rabbits look like family planning. Show that one distinction does not work and a dozen appear in its place; show that a theory runs into trouble with a well-supported philosophical theory and a dozen patched-up versions appear to replace it. This is not the place to chart the historical details of this process, which are, in any case, widely known. However, one can see in this process what Lakatos has called a "degenerating research programme". Characteristic of this is that no essential progress is made towards solving the central problem. Rather, enormous time is spent trying to solve problems of equal or greater acuity created by the programme itself. An extreme form of this is where the proposed problem solution does not really solve the problem at all but merely one of its manifestations. The original problem is then transferred, and appears in a different place. It may sometimes appear in a slightly different guise, whence to a cursory glance the proposed solution may appear more successful than it actually is. (Priest, 1987a, 145–6)

Indeed, it is possible to construct "obstinate paradoxes" that seemingly escape all proposed solutions. J.L. Mackie in *Truth , Probability and Paradox* gives examples of such sentences (Mackie 1973, Lehrer, 1990 20–4). One which we can construct here which seems particularly difficult to solve is this:

> (JWS)   If this very sentence has a truth value or doesn't have a truth value or is said to be ø, then it entails an arbitrary sentence S

where "ø" is any proposed solution to the semantic paradoxes such that the sentence (JWS) is systematically unstable in its semantic valuation (Herzberger, 1982).

Patrick Grim has also produced a challenging set of paradoxes in his book *The Incomplete Universe* (Grim, 1991). Grim attempts to show that there is no set of all truths, that there is no proposition that is genuinely about all propositions, that all propositions cannot be put in a one-to-one correspondence with themselves and so on. A number of reviews have demonstrated that Grim has failed to solve these paradoxes, and they remain outstanding as well (Sylvan, 1992; Kvanvig, 1994).

Metaphysical paradoxes sometimes present a challenge to logical theory. The *Sorites paradox* is one such paradox (Sanford, 1975a, b; Unger, 1979a, b; Peacocke, 1981; Travis, 1985; Sorensen, 1986, 1988; Clark, 1987; Goldstein, 1988; Heller, 1988; Deas, 1989; Burns, 1991; Sainsbury, 1991; Williamson, 1992, 1994; Wright, 1992; Heck, 1993; Hyde, 1994; Kosko, 1994; Koons, 1994; Tye, 1994; O'Leary-Hawthorne and Cortens,

1995). The Sorites paradox is part of a general philosophical problem about vagueness which, Napoli observes, "has become a philosopher's nightmare" (Napoli, 1985, 115). Bertrand Russell recognized that the law of excluded middle (A or not-A) is true when precise symbols are used, but not when the symbols are vague, Russell adds "as, in fact, all symbols are" (Russell, 1923, 86). This vagueness is present to a lesser degree "in the quantitative words which science has tried hardest to make precise, such as metre or a second" (Russell, 1923, 86). Russell then goes on to argue that vagueness affects the words of pure logic such as "or" and "not" because their explication in turn involves the concepts of "true" and "false" and these terms can only have a precise meaning when the symbols employed are precise. Thus: "It follows that every proposition that can be framed in practice has a certain degree of vagueness; that is to say, there is not one definite fact necessary and sufficient for its truth, but a certain region of possible facts, any one of which would make it true" (Russell, 1923, 88). Vagueness also raises a severe difficulty for metaphysical realism:

> The problem is that the realist can find no fit between vague language and the world. Language may contain vague terms but the world, according to realists, cannot contain vague things and properties. Realists suffer acute embarrassment as a result of vagueness because they adhere to the correspondence theory of truth and reference. How are vague terms to correspond to precisely bounded objects? This problem can be put quite sharply for the realist. It is a tenet of realism that for each thing and each property the thing either has the property or it fails to have the property. ... Apparently, then, such ordinary predicates as 'is red'; 'is a table', and 'is a person' cannot express properties. Since the predicates are vague, they allow of borderline cases – cases of which they neither determinately hold nor fail to hold. Indeed, given this it is hard to see how any ordinary thing- or perception-predicate could express a property, since the predicates are all vague. (Schwartz and Throop, 1991, 347)

The Sorites paradox can be stated as follows: "One thousand stones, suitably arranged, might form a heap. If we remove a single stone from a heap of stones we still have a heap; at no point will the removal of just one stone make sufficient difference to transform a heap into something which is not a heap. But, if this is so, we still have a heap, even when we have removed the last stone composing our original structure" (Burgess, 1990, 417). Paradoxes of this form can be advanced by use of suitable premises and the principle of mathematical induction or by finitely many applications of *modus ponens* to the conditional premises, or in non-standard versions of the sorites paradox, by use of the substitutivity of identicals

(Priest, 1991). We cannot explore here the present state of this paradox cataloguing the failure of solutions. Richard DeWitt in his survey article concludes that "all the proposals offered to date as ways of blocking the paradox are seriously deficient" (DeWitt, 1992, 93–4) and Graham Priest concludes his own paper stating that "no extant solution to the Sorites paradox works" (Priest, 1991, 296).

There are other areas in mathematics and logic where paradoxes arise, and one in particular relates to Gödel's first incompleteness theorem, the most famous result in modern logic. Although there have been some logical and philosophical criticisms of this result (Butrick, 1965; Barbó, 1968; Johnstone, 1981) the result is generally taken to be as secure as any other accepted result in mathematics and metamathematics (Chaitin, 1987a, b).

Gödel's second incompleteness theorem, asserts that the consistency of $\overline{N}$, the (classical) formal theory of arithmetic is not provable within $\overline{N}$ so that the consistency of a reasonably strong theory of arithmetic is not finitary provable. The proof however assumes classical logic. The system R# of relevant arithmetic based on the relevant logic R is strong enough to represent all recursive functions but the system has a simple finitary consistency proof, which can be represented within the system itself. R. Meyer has given an absolute finitary consistency proof of ultramodal arithmetic DKA such that neither $0{\neq}0$ or $1{=}0$ is a theorem. Routley says in commentary on this non-classical result: " . . . the proof is enough to undermine all the philosophical applications that have been made of Gödel's second theorem, and to imperil the scope of the theorem as well" (Routley, 1980, 931).

Gödel's first incompleteness theorem (hereafter "Gödels theorem") has been taken to show that there is an unprovable sentence of arithmetic which is true. This idea has been decisively refuted by Hugly and Sayward: Gödel's result is *syntactical* and does not make use of the concept of *truth* in its proof (Hugly and Sayward, 1989). Nor has Gödel shown that there is some sentence saying "I am unprovable". Shen Yuting (1955) has proved that the sentence, "What I am saying is unprovable" is paradoxical. Further, as John Myhill has noted, there is an absolute or informal sense of *probability* in which Gödel's undecidable sentences are *provable* (Myhill, 1960). This claim is not in itself contradictory because Gödel's result is a systems-internal result, concerned only with provability in a particular formal theory. It cannot show in itself that the identification of mathematical truth with (informal or absolute) provability is incorrect. One could argue for this position of course, but it would have to be done on an independent basis involving further philosophical considerations.

Graham Priest, in chapter 3 of his book *In Contradiction* (Priest, 1987b), advances a Gödel-based argument to show that naive proof theory is inconsistent. He notes that naive proof theory is that which formal logic formalizes. Since informal mathematics could be formalized, it makes sense to call it a formal theory. Naive proof theory can represent all recursive functions. Priest argues that naive proof theory is also recursive, because it is part of our very concept of a proof that a proof should be effectively recognizable, so by Church's thesis it must be recursive. There are arguments against this which Priest adequately counters. Hence naive proof theory satisfies the conditions of Gödel's theorem. Let T be a formalization of naive proof theory. If T is consistent then there is a sentence ø which is not provable in T but can be established as true by a naive proof. Therefore it is provable in T: contradiction. This shows, Priest believes, the inconsistency of naive proof theory, which is what Priest wants to prove to support the position of dialetheism, that there are true contradictions. In our opinion Priest has not adequately followed through his own argument.

If we probe more deeply we should note that Gödel's theorem assumes a non-paraconsistent logic as its basis. It must at least assume that the system to which it is applied is *consistent*. If T can be shown to be inconsistent, then Gödel's theorem is not applicable. But Gödel's theorem was used to show that T is inconsistent. Hence Gödel's theorem is both applicable and not applicable to T. As well, Gödel's theorem is based on a logistic system that formalizes naive proof theory itself. So given Priest's argument, Gödel's theorem itself is contradictory. Gödel's theorem, applied to Gödel's system itself, generates, so to speak, a self-referential inconsistency. In a logistic system, we make reference to naive or informal proof theory in the meta-language or meta-meta-language, or somewhere in the Tarskian hierarchy of languages. Informal proof theory must then be presupposed at some stage in this hierarchy of languages under pain of vicious infinite regression, so Priest's problem cannot be avoided by the formalist (Priest, 1979, 1984, 1995b; Chihara, 1984).

Priest argues that the argument from Gödel's theorem shows (along with other arguments) that no consistent approach to the paradoxes can be satisfactory, that we are stuck with "true contradictions". Smith (1988a) has argued that the paraconsistent logical view that the paradoxes represent "true contradictions" is essentially an arbitrary assumption, assumed to save formal deductive logic from unsoundness. The paradoxes show that our formal deductive systems do break down and fail us. The paraconsistency tradition has failed to show how "true" or "good" contradictions can be distinguished from "false" or "bad" contradictions (Smith, 1988a). Without this distinction logical anarchy results. Thus, we are faced with the prospect of accepting that the paradoxes are unsolvable and that formal deductive logic is, as David Stove has noted, a *myth*.

Perhaps even more interesting speculations relate to the consistency of standard mathematics. Bertrand Russell, during his idealist phase, maintained that geometry was inevitably contradictory (Russell, 1897, 188–99; Hylton, 1990, 84–101), but his arguments were based upon Hegelian dialectical considerations which he later rejected. More recently Graham Priest has argued that arithmetic is inconsistent (Priest, 1994a). Based on an argument which he attributes to Uwe Petersen, he says "we can *prove* that there is a number x such that $x = x+1$" (Priest, 1994a, 341). Here is Priest's informal proof:

> Let π be an abbreviation for the following description:
> the least number such that this description refers to it (or 0 if it fails to refer) + 1.
> Note that "π" does refer to a number. For if "π" failed to refer, it would refer to 1. Hence we have:
> $$\pi = \text{(the least } x \text{ such that "}\pi\text{" refers to } x) + 1 \qquad (*)$$
> Now, clearly, "π" refers to π, and since reference is unique π is the least thing that "π" refers to. Hence by (*),$\pi = \pi+1$, and so:
> $$\exists x\, x = x+1 \qquad\qquad (**) \qquad \text{(Priest, 1994a, 341)}$$

Priest then adds: "The argument does not tell us *what* the x in question is, in any particularly illuminating way. *A fortiori*, it does not tell us that it is so large as to have no psychological or physical significance in the appropriate sense" (Priest, 1994a, 341–2). In his paper "What Could the Least Inconsistent Number Be?" (Priest, 1994b) Priest states that he has no answer to the question "what is n?," what the least inconsistent number actually is, and nor does he believe that an answer is likely to be forthcoming (Priest, 1994b, 3). Nicholas Denyer (1995) has given a parallel argument to Priest's, that the least inconsistent number is less than or equal to 10, and hence that standard arithmetic is trivial, generating $1=0$:

> Let μ be an abbreviation for the following description:
> the least number ≤ 10 such that this description refers to it (or 0 if it fails to refer to such a number) + 1.
> Note that "μ" does refer to a number ≤ 10. For if "μ" failed to refer to such a number, it would refer to 1, and $1 \leq 10$. Hence we have:
> $$\mu = \text{(the least } x \leq 10 \text{ such that "}\mu\text{" refers to } x) + 1. \qquad (*)$$
> Now "μ" clearly refers to μ, and since reference is unique μ is the least thing ≤ 10 that "μ" refers to. Hence, by (*), $\mu = \mu + 1$. Thus the magic number is $\leq \mu$. But $\mu \leq 10$. Hence the magic number is ≤ 10. (Denyer, 1995, 573)

Later, Priest (1996, 651–2) rejected Denyer's version of Petersen's argument, as well as his own version of it (Priest, 1996, 652). J.W. Smith

(1991c) however has given an alternative argument, not based on self-reference or Gödel diagonalization for the inconsistency of real number theory. The number 0.999. . . can be shown by elementary algebra to be equal to 1 (Rucker, 1982, 79). The proof as it stands is correct. But it is also possible to show that 1 is not equal to 0.999. . . , Smith argued (see also Georgescu-Roegen, 1971, 384). The claim is controversial, but Smith's intuitive proof was accepted by some logicians such as (the late) Richard Sylvan. On a speculative note, it may be possible to produce contradictions in number theory by a paraconsistent reinterpretation of certain proofs producing a situation of "proof- overdetermination". For example 1^{∞} is standardly said to be undefined (Thomas, 1966, 819–20). Yet could we not accept this *and* argue as well that as $1^{\infty} = 1.1.1. . . . 1^{\infty}$ is not *only* undefined, but is also definable as 1? One could perhaps attempt to argue this out by use of the recursive definition of the power notation: if $n = 0$, $a^{n} = 1$; if $n > 0$ $a^{n} = a.a^{n-1}$. This point is a speculative one, and further thought may show that it is incorrect. However, paraconsistent logic and the inescapability of avoiding the logical, semantic and set-theoretic paradoxes, also commit us to rethinking the orthodox view of the consistency of elementary mathematics. An expression such as 0/0 is known as an indeterminate form, and is not a well-defined expression and, "if I is an indeterminate form, $x = I$ has (possibly) *infinitely many* finite solutions, at least in the sense that there are infinitely many well-defined expressions that are equivalent to I, yet each of which sets x to a different value" (Zangari, 1994, 193). Could, paraconsistently, 0/0 be regarded as an "inconsistent number"? If so, then it may be possible to support certain mathematical theories that have long been discarded. The great mathematician Euler, for example, argued against Bishop Berkeley's attack on the calculus, maintaining that 0/0 was not undefined but could have many values: "Euler's argument was that $n.0 = 0$ for *any* number n. Hence, if we divided by 0, we have $n = 0/0$. The usual process of finding the derivative determines the value of 0/0 for the particular function involved" (Kline, 1980, 147). Euler's argument is mathematically flawed but it may be possible to rehabilitate his approach to the calculus from the perspective of paraconsistent logic (Priest and Routley, 1984, 155–7). On the other hand, the possibility of satisfactory proofs of 1=0 emerging from the paraconsistency position clearly pushes us to the limits of cogent thought. It seems that at this point even our concept of number seems to slide away into an abyss of skepticism.

PHYSICS AND SKEPTICISM

We turn now away from mathematics and metamathematics, to physics. Recall that our central thesis is the failure of the Enlightenment project, the attempt to present a coherent and comprehensive account of reality, or a theory of everything. Recently a number of books have dealt with the question of the limits of physical explanation and whether theories of everything (Barrow, 1991; Peat, 1991) are possible or likely (Casti and Karlqvist eds, 1996; Horgan, 1996). These works have not addressed the central question in the field: is there at present or given foreseeable advances a *consistent* physical theory of reality? Alternatively: are our best physical theories consistent? This question essentially amounts to a consideration of whether quantum mechanics on the one hand and the special and general theories of relativity on the other, are mutually consistent. There are good reasons for supposing that they are not. Due to space limitations it is not possible to outline the basic theories of quantum-mechanics and the special and general theories of relativity. Nor is it necessary. Since about 1980 a popular science industry has emerged producing largely uncritical "pot boiler" books consisting of great smatterings of quantum mechanics, relativity and whatever other part of science is regarded as "flavor of the year". Chaos and complexity theory, artificial intelligence, Eastern philosophy and New Age musings are often tied together with Gödel's theorem and other results from mathematics and logic which seem suitably "deep". Despite the obvious limitations of this genre of books due to commercial exploitation, the cautious reader can still find a generally sound basic introduction to the problems and paradoxes of physics. What will not be found is any sort of critical evaluation of the underlying physical theories. For this, one must turn to the popular and technical writings of experts in the field, rather than science journalists and commentators.

First, from the quantum mechanics side. Ignoring all the quantum mechanical paradoxes (Bub, 1981; Ginsberg, 1984; Gibbins, 1987; Jauch, 1989; Mittelstaedt, 1991; Scully et al., 1991; Buchanan, 1997) the mathematical inconsistency of quantum theory can be readily seen from a consideration of the use made of the Dirac delta function (Davies, 1984), which has been long recognized to be self-contradictory (see Priest and Routley, 1984, 157–8; Mortensen, 1995, 67–72). The problem can be solved in Schwartz's theory of distributions in quantum mechanics, but at the cost of a great increase in complexity (Mortensen, 1995, 67). Second, the problem of the "infinities" in quantum electrodynamics (QED) (Noyes, 1975; Schlegel, 1980; Morris, 1990), allegedly solved by renormalization, is regarded by at least one of the founders of the theory of QED as unsolved. Richard Feynman has said: "Having to resort to such hocus-pocus has prevented us from proving that the theory of quantum electrodynamics is mathematically self-consistent. It's surprising that the theory still hasn't been proved self-consistent one way or other by now; I suspect that renormalization is not mathematically legitimate" (Feynman, 1985, 128).

The physicist Roger Penrose (1989) has said this on the question of the self-consistency of physics:

> we do not know the basic laws governing the mass-values of the sub-atomic particles of nature nor the strengths of their interactions. We do not know how to make quantum theory fully consistent with Einstein's special theory of relativity – let alone how to construct the 'quantum gravity' theory that would make quantum theory consistent with his *general* theory of relativity. (Penrose, 1989, 4)

Penrose argues for a fundamental change in the quantum-mechanical world view because of the paradoxes of quantum theory. He observes in his book *Shadows of the Mind* that those "who are most vehement about accepting [quantum theory] as being in no way in need of modification tend *not* to think that it represents the actual behaviour of a 'real' quantum-level world" (Penrose, 1994, 309). In his book *The Emperor's New Mind* Penrose notes that in the famous two-slit experiment "each individual photon behaves like a wave entirely on its own! In some sense, each particle travels through *both slits at once* and it interferes with itself!" (Penrose, 1989, 235). Quantum linear superpositions means that any two states can coexist in any complex linear superposition. Hence "any physical object, itself made out of individual particles, ought to be able to exist in such superpositions of spatially widely separated states, and so 'be in two places at once'!" (Penrose, 1989, 256). Penrose also discusses the most famous thought experiment illustrating the "large scale" paradoxical nature of quantum linear superpositions, the Schrödinger cat paradox. He gives a survey of responses to these paradoxes but concludes that variants of these paradoxes exist in all interpretations of quantum mechanics. He concludes that it is likely "that quantum mechanics is simply *wrong* when applied to macroscopic bodies. . . " (Penrose, 1989, 297). Penrose is also of the opinion that there is an "essential conflict" between special relativity and the non-local quantum mechanical view of physical reality, that has emerged from EPR-type experiments. The non-local "influences" in EPR-type experiments do not formally violate special relativity, because they do not constitute messages or signals in the ordinary sense (Penrose, 1989, 286), but the experiment does generate a metaphysical paradox in Penrose's opinion: "Two different observers form mutually inconsistent pictures of 'reality' in an EPR experiment in which two photons are emitted in opposite directions . . . The observer moving to the right judges that the left-hand part of the state jumps *before* it is measured, the jump being caused by the measurement on the right. The observer moving to the left has the opposite opinion!" (Penrose, 1989, 287)

The present inability to reconcile quantum theory with general relativity is recognized by Isham (1992) who states that "the apparently fundamental linear structure of quantum theory is only an approximation to something else, and it is precisely in the context of quantum gravity that this approximation will be seen to fail" (Isham, 1992, 93). On the other hand Von Borzeszkowski and Treder in their book *The Meaning of Quantum Gravity* (1988) argue that "there does not exist a physically meaningful rigorous quantization conception for Einstein's theory" (Von Borzeszkowski and Treder, 1988, vii). In their opinion Planck's units constitute a domain in which the gravitation conception loses its physical meaning. The consistency of the quantum theory with black hole physics may also require a form of nonlocality not present in ordinary field theory (Lowe, 1995).

The logical incompatibility between quantum theory and the special theory of relativity has been argued by Nicholas Maxwell. His argument proceeds by showing that the quantum theory is committed to the position of *probabilism* and that probabilism is inconsistent with the special theory of relativity:

Probabilism, as understood here, is the thesis that the universe is such that, at any instant, there is only one past but many alternative possible futures—the fundamental laws of the universe being probabilistic and not deterministic. According to probabilism, then, there is a physically real difference between past and future events—the future alone containing physically, ontologically real alternative possibilities. Because of this physically real difference between past and future, probabilism requires that, at any instant, there be a universal, absolute, unambiguous distinction between past and future—to divide off the *one* past from the *many* alternative possible futures. Probabilism, in short, is only true if there does exist such an absolute distinction between one past and many possible futures.

Special relativity, on the other hand, is only true if there is *no* universal, absolute, unambiguous distinction between past and future. According to special relativity, given any two physical events, E_1 and E_2, having space-like separation from each other (so that they lie outside each other's past and future light cones), then there is no absolute, frame-independent way in which E_1 is unambiguously either earlier than, simultaneous with, or later than E_2. Which relationship holds depends on the choice of inertial reference frame, all such choices being physically equivalent. Thus special relativity denies that there exists the kind of absolute, universal, frame-independent distinction between past and future, which must exist if probabilism is to be true. (Maxwell, 1985, 23–4)

Therefore probabilism, and hence the quantum theory is inconsistent with the special theory of relativity. Although we cannot develop this argument here, Maxwell's basic point can be substantiated by a consideration of the quantum measurement problem, especially as this problem is dealt with by some versions of quantum theory such as the many-worlds view. The splitting of the universe which this theory requires also seems to introduce an absolute distinction between past and future. Maxwell's aim was to show that given probabilism, the special theory of relativity must be rejected (Maxwell, 1988, 640). However, before Maxwell, Rietdijk (1966, 1976) argued that given the special theory of relativity, probabilism and hence the quantum theory must be rejected. One could, on the basis of Maxwell's argument, reject either the special theory of relativity or the quantum theory, given extra argument, evidence and independent reason. Maxwell has defended his position against criticisms by Dieks (1988) and Stein (1991) (Maxwell, 1993). In his 1993 paper in *Philosophy of Science*, Maxwell adds further comments on the problem of the consistency of physics:

> The general program is to (help) discover how to unify all of theoretical physics. This means, in particular, to discover how to unify ostensibly *probabilistic* **QT** and *deterministic* general relativity (**GR**). The structure of *orthodox* **QT** is, however, such as to obstruct the quantization of **GR**. Orthodox **QT** is such that, in assigning a quantum state to a physical system we are obliged to assume the existence of an external measuring instrument. This creates an insuperable difficulty the moment one seeks to assign a quantum state to curved spacetime, for how can one have a measuring instrument *external* to spacetime? (Maxwell, 1993, 346)

The physicist Mendel Sachs (1982) also gave a very comprehensive argument for the logical incompatibility of quantum theory and the special theory of relativity. One of the conflicts between the two theories relates to ontology. The special theory of relativity, even though it forced us to revise our Newtonian view of space and time, remains a broadly realistic theory committed to the idea of an objective reality. Quantum mechanics challenges our realist understanding of the world. A.H. Goldman, who attempts to defend realism in his book *Empirical Knowledge* (Goldman, 1988) acknowledges this point. The quantum-jump for example introduces a discontinuity in space-time trajectories which "already violates our concept of a physical particle and its possible world-lines" (Goldman, 1988, 245). Worse yet is wave-particle duality which "if ineliminable, itself blocks a coherent physical model of the entire domain of quantum mechanics. Particles and waves have incompatible properties" (Goldman, 1988, 248). Goldman concludes that the prospects are poor for a realist interpretation of quantum mechanics:

> Thus there seems to be no coherent realist mode, no single physical analogue, of the quantum theory as it was developed. Yet the enormous success of the theory requires re-emphasis if the realist is to confront the problem honestly. With the Pauli exclusion principle, the theory accounts for the assumptions of the Bohr model, which in turn account for chemical properties and reactions. Also predicted are such phenomena as alpha decay, the photoelectric effect, specific heats, and scattering and spectroscopic phenomena. If we are to be realists about atoms, we must also admit that quantum theory is at present the only theory of the atom. The problem created for scientific realism therefore looms large, although some physicists might question that concession. They might argue, as Bohr himself did, that the problem derives from the attempt to extend uncritically and without limit concepts from classical physics into the quantum domain. While such concepts provide visual metaphors there, we should not expect reality at that level to be exhaustively characterized in those terms. (Goldman, 1988, 251)

Faced with this metaphysical quagmire of quantum quandaries, the realist's hopes are inevitably pinned on a new physical theory, perhaps making use of explanatory principles below the level of space-time (Matthews, 1997). One of the few attempts to produce such a theory, in a mathematically rigorous way, the theory of indistinguishables by A.F. Parker-Rhodes, has unpalatable consequences for realism. Apart from using some unusual mathematics, which could be inconsistent, the fundamental entities of the theory, *indistinguishables* "cannot be observed and have no real properties" (Parker-Rhodes, 1981, 200), constituting "metaphysically impenetrable bedrock" (Parker-Rhodes, 1981, 200). Elsewhere Parker-Rhodes says:

> Idealist philosophy is criticized for not describing the real world, and is rightly discredited; but what if there was some field where it could be used literally? Applied to mathematical notations it is pedantic and unhelpful; but my hypothesis is that in the foundations of the world, a context antipodal to that of moral and aesthetic values where the notion was born, there are things of which the real and ideal coincide. Here one need made no apology for treating inscrutables as indistinguishables; the categories are clear-cut, their properties plain, and observation either impossible or infallible. (Parker-Rhodes, 1981, 11)

In short, there is no good reason for supposing that a replacement of quantum mechanics, involving explanatory principles below the level of space-time will support either realism or determinism. This hypothetical super-theory may well see space-time itself as an abstraction or a construct to be either reduced to some more fundamental phenomena, or eliminated in much the same way that eliminative materialists wish to eliminate mental phenomena.

We have to date been considering the question of the consistency of physics and the self-consistency of nature from the perspective of quantum mechanics. Let us now look at this issue from the perspective of Einstein's special and general theories of relativity. As we have already seen, Maxwell rejects the special theory of relativity on the basis of its incompatibility with the doctrine of probabilism. There is an extensive literature of very mixed quality criticizing primarily the special theory of relativity (critics and some replies include (Ideström, 1948; Heason, 1963; Larson, 1963, 1964, 1965; Aspden, 1969, 1972; Nordenson, 1969; Brillouin, 1970; Essen, 1971; Dingle, 1972; Kingsley, 1975; Brown, 1976; Grøn and Nicola, 1976; Chatham, 1976; Hazelett and Turner eds, 1979; Cullwick, 1981; Karlov, 1981; Santilli, 1984; Herbert, 1987; Cohen, 1989, 1992, 1995; White, 1991, 1993; Stiles, 1994; Walton, 1995). It is most unlikely in our opinion that there is some mathematical or logical flaw in the special theory of relativity, invariably because critics usually implicitly adopt assumptions of classical physics which relativity theorists would reject. As Paul Davies observes:

> Ultimately, all these clever attempts to find a loophole in special relativity are doomed to failure on logical grounds. If the basic principles of relativity are always adhered to, then it is automatic that one will obtain internal consistency from the theory. For example, Maxwell's theory of electrodynamics has special relativity built into it mathematically. If a thought experiment appears to give a result in contradiction to relativity, a logical or mathematical error must have been committed. (Davies, 1980, 465)

The general theory of relativity has been put to experimental test and is generally regarded to be "beyond a show of doubt" (Will, 1995; Price, 1996). In our opinion, the conflict between quantum mechanics and the special and general theories of relativity is most likely to be resolved, if it can be resolved at all, by keeping the special and general theories of relativity intact and modifying quantum mechanics. We have, however, no idea about how this could be satisfactorily achieved (Sachs, 1982). Apart from this question though it is interesting to observe that the general theory of relativity allows "time travel". Gödel showed that a solution to Einstein's field equations contains under certain conditions closed time-like curves (Gödel, 1949; Stein, 1970; Meiland, 1974; Horwich, 1975; Lewis, 1976; Weingard, 1979; Malament, 1985; Ray, 1991). Gödel's solution to Einstein's field equations involved a rotating universe which essentially tipped the line cones of a particle on its side, resulting in a particle's world-line forming a closed time-like curve (for an explanation cf Davies, 1995, 242). Hawking and Ellis in their book, *The Large-Scale Structure of Space-Time* (1973) regard the existence of such closed time-like curves as paradoxical

> for one could imagine that with a suitable rocketship one could travel round such a curve and, arriving back before one's departure, one could prevent oneself from setting out in the first place. Of course there is a contradiction only if one assumes a simple notion of free will; but this is not something which can be dropped lightly since the whole of our philosophy of science is based on the assumption that one is free to perform any experiment. (Hawking and Ellis, 1973, 189)

Hawking and Ellis advanced a *chronology condition* – that there are no closed timelike curves – to explicitly rule out such situations. Recently K.S. Thorne has shown that wormholes may permit "time travel" if held open by exotic materials. The wormholes themselves are a mathematical solution to Einstein's field equations (Thorne, 1995, 483–521). Thorne attempts to deal with causality paradoxes by appeal to quantum gravity considerations (Thorne, 1995, 515) but concludes "*the laws of quantum gravity are hiding from us the answer to whether wormholes can be converted successfully into time machines*" (Thorne, 1995, 521). A substantial debate exists about the theoretical possibility of time travel (Gonella, 1994; Antonsen and Bormann, 1995; Earman, 1995; Woodward, 1995). As Paul Davies has noted, if time travel occurred "even under the most peculiar and contrived circumstances, then it would threaten the very consistency of physics itself" (Davies, 1990, 21). A popular account of the problem of causality violation, published by D.H. Freedman in *Discover* in June 1989, puts the dilemma which theoretical physicists face in sharp focus:

> The whole issue may sound a little silly, but it is not to be taken lightly. If physicists cannot resolve the causality-violation paradox, they will be forced to choose among three unattractive conclusions: causality is not inviolable in our universe; general relativity is wrong, and thus the timeholes it describes are irrelevant; or, timeholes can't exist, even though no one yet knows a reason why they can't.
> The price of embracing causality violation would be high: physics as we know it might go out the window. "What physics does for you,"

explains John Friedman, an astrophysicist at the University of Wisconsin at Milwaukee who has been working with Morris on timeholes, "is let you specify a set of initial conditions, then use your equations to tell what things will look like at some later time. But things won't always work that way if there is causality violation." The problem, of course, is that after the initial conditions are specified, something might come back in time and change them.

Nevertheless, the ban on causality violation is not sacrosanct. "The statement that there can't be causality violation in the universe is very much a matter of opinion rather that fact," says Wald. "General relativity allows one to talk meaningfully about situations where there is causality violation." Einstein himself was vexed by this, notes Tipler: "He was aware of the possibility of causality violation right at the very beginning. He refused to rule it out a priori as nonsense, but hoped it would be ruled out on physical grounds." (Freedman, 1989, 63)

If Einstein's General Theory of Relativity is "correct" (as far as physical theories can be "correct") and exotic matter is at least theoretically possible, physicists must find a way to avoid causality violation: if not, physics itself collapses into inconsistency (Ayer, 1989). There are a number of hypotheses about how time travel can occur without causality violation. One hypothesis is that some mysterious force (possibly quantum mechanical) prevents causality violation (Redmount, 1990). Perhaps this is so, but without a specification of what this force is, we do not have a scientific explanation at all. Another hypothesis has it that causality violations would destroy the universe (as a "real" contradiction would exist, and contradictions (at least on one account) "annihilate" themselves). But by far the most popular escape hypothesis is to say that parallel universes exist and that only travel into the past of another universe is permitted. David Deutsch, in his book, *The Fabric of Reality* (1997), develops the idea of parallel universes in great depth. The idea of parallel universes is familiar to us from the many worlds version of quantum mechanics, which proposes that every time there is a collapse of the wave packet, the universe splits into different universes (Leslie, 1989). Deutsch goes further and conjectures that the "parallel-universe-multiplicity" is the real reason for the unpredictability of the weather, presumably because the universes interact. Time travel as well involves visiting a different universe, so the consistency of physics is allegedly saved (Chown, 1992). Phil Bagnall in a commonsense article published in *New Scientist* in 1996 disputed the parallel universe solution to the paradoxes of time travel (Bagnall, 1996). He notes the obvious: "surely that is not real time travel? It is simply space travel. If I fly off to the US I shall end up in a different time zone, sure, but I have not, by any stretch of the imagination, travelled through time" (Bagnall,

1996, 45). Worse, Bagnall observes, the parallel universe hypothesis does not deal with the dead grandfather paradox (i.e. that you go back into the past and kill your own grandfather): "Suppose we have, say, 100 parallel universes. Then, just as you pass from one universe to another, so will all the other "yous" – and they will all kill each other's grandfathers, bringing us back to square one." (Bagnall, 1996, 45).

In our opinion the causality violation problem cannot be escaped by the orthodox solutions. As one of us has argued elsewhere, time travel does involve inescapable logical difficulties (Smith, 1986b). This means that either Einstein's General Theory of Relativity is wrong – because it is causally and logically paradoxical – or else real contradictions can occur in reality as paraconsistent logicians such as Graham Priest suppose. (Priest himself has been strangely silent on the time travel issue.) All in all, as we have seen has occurred with advanced research in modern logic, a position of *self-undermining* or internal theoretical collapse has occurred, whether or not this is recognized by key researchers in the field (they are in fact not likely to recognize this or accept this, as it means a drastic lowering in epistemic status of their "hard science" disciplines would occur, in times which are far from sympathetic to pure and theoretical research). This confirms, in a most dramatic and ironic way the failure of the Enlightenment project. Although we are far removed from the extreme relativism, skepticism and nihilism of *some* interpretations of postmodernism, for we are not claiming that no *particular* logical, mathematical and physical knowledge claims can be validly made, the *universal* or *general* validity of such claims can be disputed. In other words, at the level of the most basic research into the fabric of reality and understanding, *universalism* is not merely false, but self-refuting and self-undermining. It is interesting to speculate ontologically and metaphysically about why this situation exists. In the light of work in logic and quantum mechanics, it seems plausible to us to suppose that our realist and monistic assumptions about the existence of "one world" are simply false, but we have no space here to pursue further metaphysical speculations.

THE STATE OF THE ARGUMENT

This chapter has attempted to demonstrate that universalism and cosmopolitanism fail at the most fundamental scientific level: the level of physics, logic and mathematics. We have attempted to show this without basing our critique upon any extreme form of skepticism, nihilism or relativism. Paradoxes and inconsistencies lie coiled in the heart of these basic sciences like a worm. If we are correct in our argument – and it is we believe virtually undeniable that universalistic principles often generate paradoxes – then we have good reason to reject universalism *simpliciter*, although it may prove to be the case that even this negative doctrine generates self-referential paradoxes.

We have now completed our epistemological and philosophical critique of Enlightenmentism. The remainder of the book makes implicit use of these skeptical arguments in undermining other politically correct sacred cows associated with the liberal internationalist and cosmopolitan worldview.

4　Coming Together and Falling Apart: The Failure of the One-World Dream

> Prejudice is good in its place. It makes people happy. It takes nations back to whatever is crucial to them; it ties them fairly and squarely to their roots; it enables them to flourish in their own proper manner. They become more passionate and therefore happier in whatever purposes or inclinations they may have. The most ignorant nation, the one most given to prejudices, is often, on that very score, preeminent. A period when people want to emigrate, when excessive hopes are entertained for foreign parts, is already a period of sickness and disorder. It is, as it were, a flabby and unhealthy time, presaging national death.
>
> – Johann Gottfried von Herder, *Une autre philosophie de l'histoire*
> (quoted in Finkielkraut, 1988, 24–5)

> The United Nations, founded to propagate the universalist ideas of Enlightenment Europe, now speaks on behalf of every ethnic prejudice, believing that peoples, nations and cultures have rights which outweigh the rights of man. The 'multi-cultural' lobby dismisses the liberal values of Europe as 'racist', while championing the narrow chauvinism of every minority culture; the advocates of ethnic identity attack the attempt of European peoples to retain their own identity. In the name of humanity the ideal of humanity is chased from its throne, and in the war against prejudice, the prejudice of others is exalted to a supreme authority. (Finkielkraut, 1988, back cover)

THE ONE-WORLD DREAM

Alain Finkielkraut in *The Undoing of Thought (La Défaite de la Pensée)* (1988), follows earlier writers such as Julien Benda (*The Treason of the Intellectuals/La Trahison des Clercs* (1969)) in revolting against the intellectuals who celebrate particularism over the eternal values of the Enlightenment. Multiculturalists are at fault, he argues, creating an opposition between "the higher life", the life of the mind on the one hand, and culture and custom on the other. Nationalists are also at fault, the followers of Herder, using cultural diversity to condemn the universal values of the Enlightenment. Finkielkraut also singles out the United Nations for special criticism in failing to support the universalistic one-world dream of the Enlightenment. UNESCO, the United Nations Educational, Scientific, and Cultural Organization, began with a critique of fanaticism following the Hitler era, and ended with a critique of Enlightenment-style thinking (Finkielkraut, 1988, 55). The UNESCO agenda, Finkielkraut observes, was to refute those who denied the unity of the human race. Thus in 1951 UNESCO commissioned Claude Lévi-Strauss to write "Race et histoire" which linked all differences between human groups to culture, rather than to race and biology. The result of this UNESCO-funded critique was to open the West to the culture of others, rather than to unite humanity under the banner of universalist Enlightenment values. Lévi-Strauss', work marked the beginning of the post-World World II rejection of the idea of progress and the shift in focus upon discontinuities in history rather than evolution. The idea of the Europeans as exploiters, projecting their own image upon non-European people, began its intellectual ascent: "We Europeans of the second half of the twentieth century were, it now transpired, not civilization itself, but just another culture, just one more fleeting and perishable human variety" (Finkielkaut, 1988, 196).[1]

Our philosophical position differs from Finkielkraut's. It is the so-called eternal values of the Enlightenment – of openness, objectivity, universality, promiscuous altruism (Hardin, 1982) and non-discrimination – which have led to the threat to the survival of European culture and civilization that Finkielkraut fears. Further, the United Nations is firmly enmeshed in the universalistic, naturalistic and humanist metaphysics of the Enlightenment. The United Nations is by its own Charter dedicated to humanistic principles and from its beginning, even in the Preamble to its own Charter, a "religious ideal" is expressed: "We the people of the United Nations determined to save succeeding generations from the scourge of war . . . have resolved to combine our efforts to accomplish these aims". Rushdoony notes that the phrase "determined to save" is an expression of a "religious ideal" (Rushdoony, 1970, 185). It is a theological necessity for every religion that it possess a unified godhead, and the United Nations is no different: "for the religion of humanity, as represented in the United Nations, the unity of mankind, without discrimination or subordination, is a necessity. The central sin becomes . . . everything that hinders the union and peace of the new god, humanity" (Rushdoony, 1970, 186). The purpose of the United Nations, expressed in the Preamble of its Charter, is to "save succeeding generations from the scourge of war" and to obtain, according to Chapter I, Article 1, 3, "fundamental freedom for all without distinction as to race, sex, language or religion". For this to be achieved, mankind must be united. This is the one-world dream. It is the aim of this chapter to show that this dream is flawed and unachievable. According to the present U.N. Secretary-General, Kofi Annan, "This is the age of the United Nations. There is light at the end of our century's dark and dangerous tunnel, and it is brightened by the hopes and dreams of all the world's people. The United Nations remains the one true and universal vessel of those dreams" (*Guardian*/Reuter, 1997, A13). Annan is correct in taking the U.N. to be symbol of the one-world dream; consequently the failure of the U.N. constitutes good inductive evidence to support the case that the one-world dream is also a failure.

The one-world dream has had its intellectual proponents over the centuries in one form or another, including the poet Dante (Dante Alighieri, 1265–1321), who favored the creation of a universal empire. Others include the poet Alfred Lord Tennyson (1809–92), Sigmund Freud (1856–1939), Albert Einstein, Nobel Prize-winning economist Jan Tinbergen, Lewis Mumford (1972, 142) and the philosopher Bertrand Russell (1946).[2] The writer H.G. Wells said in *The New World Order* (1940) that, "It is the system of nationalist individualism and unco-ordinated enterprise that is the world's disease, and it is the whole system that has to go" (Wells, 1940, 17). For human life to continue, the boundaries of existing sovereign states must be eliminated and merged in some large "Pax" (Wells, 1940, 17). Bertrand Russell likewise believed that the prevention of nuclear war could only be achieved by the creation of a militarily "irresistible" world government with a monopoly of armed force (Russell, 1946). The historian Arnold Toynbee also believed that atomic mass-suicide could only be prevented by the creation of a world state:

> The institution of war between states is a parasite on the institution of local sovereignty; a parasite cannot survive without its host; and we can abolish local sovereignty pacifically by voluntarily entering into a world-wide federal union in which the local states would surrender their sovereignty while continuing to exist as subordinate parts of the whole. This is the positive solution of the problem of war that Lionel Curtis advocated. One need not, and should not, be dogmatic about the details of a federal constitution for the World. But one should work for the achievement of this in some form or other. In the Atomic Age, this looks as if it were mankind's only alternative to mass-suicide. (Toynbee, 1969, 84–5)

This extract is from Toynbee's book *Experiences* (1969). Later in the same book Toynbee elaborated upon this theme:

We are now moving into a chapter of human history in which our choice is going to be, not between a whole world and a shredded-up world, but between one world and no world. I believe that the human race is going to choose life and good, not death and evil. I therefore believe in the imminence of one world, and I believe that, in the twenty-first century, human life is going to be a unity again in all its aspects and activities. I believe that, in the field of religion, sectarianism is going to be subordinated to ecumenicalism; that, in the field of politics, nationalism is going to be subordinated to world-government; and that, in the field of the study of human affairs, specialization is going to be subordinated to a comprehensive view. (Toynbee, 1969, 110–11)

Toynbee however never recognized the full significance of this advocacy of one-worldism. In his *A Study of History* (1960) he observed that declining civilizations tended to form universal states prior to their collapse. Such was Toynbee's fear of nationalist-inspired war that the possibility that modern civilization could collapse because of an impossible attempt at unification into a world state did not occur to him. Others such as Hilaire Belloc (1977)[3] and F.A. Hayek (1986), exercised more critical reasoning on this issue. For example F.A. Hayek in *The Road to Serfdom*, first published in 1944, is no friend of nationalism, maintaining that the resources of different nations should not be treated as the property of nations as a whole, but of individuals if friction between nations is to be avoided (Hayek, 1986, 163). But Hayek saw super-nationalism or one-worldism as posing even greater dangers than nationalism:

The problems raised by a conscious direction of economic affairs on a national scale inevitably assume even greater dimensions when the same is attempted internationally. The conflict between planning and freedom cannot but become more serious as the similarity of standards and values among those submitted to a unitary plan diminishes. There need be little difficulty in planning the economic life of a family, comparatively little in a small community. But as the scale increases, the amount of agreement on the order of ends decreases and the necessity to rely on force and compulsion grows. In a small community common views on the relative importance of the main tasks, agreed standards of value will exist on a great many subjects. But their number will become less and less the wider we throw the net: and as there is less community of views, the necessity to rely on force and coercion increases. (Hayek, 1986, 164–5)

The core problem with a world state in Hayek's opinion was that its reliance upon central planning necessarily committed it to an undemocratic rule by force:

> To imagine that the economic life of a vast area comprising many different people can be directed or planned by democratic procedure betrays a complete lack of awareness of the problems such planning would raise. Planning on an international scale, even more than is true on a national scale, cannot be anything but a naked rule of force, an imposition by a small group on all the rest of that sort of standard and employment which the planners think suitable for the rest. (Hayek, 1986, 165–6)

The same criticism has been also made on the left; Boris Frankel in *The Post-Industrial Utopians* (1987) gives a particularly clear expression of this objection to one-worldism:

> For generations, socialist and humanist have advanced the notion of global solutions to the irrationality and conflict induced by imperialist and nationalist institutions and practices. It was never quite clear how this world government, federation of councils, or other institutional arrangement could guarantee local grass-roots democracy while at the same time bringing order to the world through global planning. . . . the objective of continental central government (for example, one government for the whole of Europe), let alone world government, is an antidemocratic nightmare. Given the vital role which local, regional and national state institutions play in all facets of everyday life, it would be disastrous if these national institutions were replaced by even more supranational bureaucracies. Certainly, there is a pressing need for eco-socialists to organize co-ordinated institutional responses to political-economic, environmental and military problems. But supranational co-ordination and co-operation is *not* equivalent to the replacement of national and local governments by a world government. (Frankel, 1987, 248–9)[4]

Although the supporters of the one-world dream of the "universalist ideal of a single unitary system of government" (Scruton, 1982, 496) are numerous (Willkie, 1943; Bunge, 1985, 381–2; Hannerz, 1990; Korten, 1990; World Constitution and Parliament Association, 1991; Suter, 1992; Commission on Global Governance, 1995)[5], this "master objection" to one-worldism has never been satisfactorily answered and it cannot, in our opinion, because it is unassailable. We will see that the objection applies as well to the United Nations, an embryonic "world government".[6]

A CRITIQUE OF CONSPIRACY THEORIES

Before turning to our critique there is a preliminary topic to discussion: the question of a global *conspiracy*. Anyone writing on the topics discussed in this book is likely to be branded and smeared with this debate-stopping label – *conspiracy theorist* – so it is important to address this question. The world is awash with talk about conspiracies. For example, movie star Mel Gibson, star of the film *Conspiracy Theory* (1997), is quoted in the August 1997 edition of *Vanity Fair* as maintaining that the Fabian society and a conspiracy of international bankers is behind the (arguable) economic decline of Australia.[7] Australian-born journalist John Pilger in his documentary *The Last Dream* (1988), champions the idea that the CIA played a key role in the downfall of the Whitlam government in Australia in November 1975. Magazines and books are in abundance advancing conspiracy theories involving freemasonry (Knight, 1983), Rosicrucianism, Gnosticism, Hinduism, theosophy, the Illuminati, secret societies, Zionists, Adam Weishaupt, Jean Jacques Rousseau, occultists, Nazis, Neo-Nazis, international bankers and financiers (the Schiffs, Warburgs, Kahns, Rockefellers, Morgans, Rothschilds), the "Order", the "New Age", Knights Templars, environmentalism, UFOs, the Trilateral Commission, Council on Foreign Relations, Royal Institute for International Affairs and Satan![8] Material from the far right usually draws upon Carroll Quigley's *Tragedy and Hope* (1966), especially passages where Quigley admits the existence of a network of international financiers who seek to dominate the world economy (Quigley, 1966, 950) and invariably one finds the same extracts from the Council on Foreign Relations journal *Foreign Affairs* in the writings of the far left as well.[9] A similar mode of argument is employed by liberal writers as well as those of the left (Sklar ed., 1980; Gill, 1990; Chomsky, 1994).

A conspiracy is "a secret plan on the part of a group to influence events partly by covert action" (Pigden, 1995, 5). As far as a mode of historical and socio-political explanation goes, conspiracy theories do not enjoy academic respectability; they are regarded as "superstitions". Karl Popper in volume 2 of *The Open Society and Its Enemies* (1966), argued against the "conspiracy theory of society", claiming that as a mode of social explanation it was flawed as it merely required that the necessary and sufficient conditions for the explanation of social phenomena involved only the discovery of a group of planners and conspirators. Charles Pigden, in an article in the journal *Philosophy of the Social Sciences* (1995), points out that few if any conspiracy theorists hold that all social events are the product of a conspiracy. Indeed if they did their position would appear to be self-refuting because *their* own beliefs and theories are also a product of conspiracy. To maintain consistency, all the conspiracy theorist need propose is that *some* social events arise from non-conspiratorial causes (Pigden, 1995, 6). Further, a conspiratorial explanation, can be put forward as an empirically falsifiable hypothesis, thus meeting Popper's own methodological falsificationist standard of scientificity.

Conspiracy theories, following Charles Pigden's defense, need to be considered on their own merits. Some are true and some are false. But is there a global conspiracy? It is unquestionably true that globalist ideology has been propagated by every species in the power elite ecosystem – including think-thanks such as the Aspen Institute for Humanistic Studies, the Brookings Institute, Heritage Foundation, and Institute for Policy Studies. It has been supported by the Council on Foreign Relations, Trilateral Commission, Royal Institute of International Affairs, the Club of Rome and the Bilderbergers. Globalism has been advanced by international banking agencies such as the International Monetary Fund and World Bank and advocated by environmental groups such as the Sierra Club and Greenpeace. Humanistic groups such as World Vision and Amnesty International mother the causes of internationalism. Indeed, it is much easier to list the organizations and academics opposing globalism. Globalism is the status quo; it is the establishment position. Conspirators are much more likely to be anti-globalists; as Michael Douglas' character in the movie *Falling Down* (the story of the end of an America dominated by the white European male) puts it at the end of the movie, so "I'm the bad guy?". It is thus rather pointless to attempt to develop a global conspiracy theory. Globalization is simply the normal working of modern capitalism, the "business-as-usual" position. What the radical right view as secret "plotting" is nothing of the sort: it is merely the normal workings and unfolding of capitalism. Conspiracy theorists on the far right, such as the American-based John Birch society (Epstein and Forster, 1967), oppose global capitalism but happily accept national capitalism; the idea that there may be some fundamental flaw in the entire system is never examined as their entire universe seems to be composed of Christianity and smiling small business people. No serious attempt is ever made by the American far right to critically examine the philosophical roots of Christianity, a globalist and cosmopolitan religion *par excellence* and a religion which seems to have a "communal" or even communist foundation. To ask these sorts of questions would be like asking "mom" whether she washed her hands before making her all-American apple pie and quizzing her about its "secret" ingredients.

Global conspiracy theories are also highly simplistic: they are social theory on the cheap. For example some Australian conspiracy theorists argue that Australia's economic plight, its relative de-industrialization (Smith et al., 1997), is due to the operation of the *Lima Declaration* (United Nations Industrial Development Organization, 1975) which expressed the opinion that the share of the world industrial production by developing countries should be increased to at least 25 percent of total world industrial production by the year 2000 (Archer, 1992). However the transfer of resources, technology and jobs to developing countries has not been done in the main by national governments, but primarily by transnational corporations capitalizing on the geo-political-economic opening-up of the world. A sophisticated conspiracy theory could perhaps see this social process as conspiracy based, but use of Occam's razor would leave us with the underlying social processes. Conspiracy theories over-intentionalize social events; often the better scientific explanation makes reference to underlying social structural generative mechanisms, such as technological change. Cosmopolitans and international bankers could conspire all they want, but if the information-technological revolution did not occur, globalism would be stillborn. Conspiracy theorists from the right seldom critically examine the internationalizing power of modern technology.

Further, even if *some* globalist organizations and individuals are conspiratorial (and this we believe is undeniable) it is of the essence of a conspiracy that it be a *secret* plot. There is nothing secret about the globalist agenda – conspiracy theorists themselves fill entire books with quotations and extracts from the globalists who freely admit that they are working towards the breakdown of national sovereignty. And why shouldn't they admit this? It is their job, after all. The powerless do not know their exact fate, but again there is nothing odd about this, for all businesses must have their trade secrets and global business is no different. There may have been a globalist conspiracy once, but there is no longer. The secret is out.

Finally, conspiracy theorists often argue that the alternative to their position is the accidental theory of history: things just happen. They are right in opposing the chance theory of history as the aim of social-scientific explanation is to seek to find meaning and purpose in historical events if it exists at all. Often certain events may be due to chance, but it would be as irrational to assume that this was so at the beginning of inquiry as it would be to assume that a conspiracy exists prior to empirical examination. Often we may find that history is a vectorial product of conspiracy, non-secret intentional action, the unintended consequences of such action, chance events and natural and social structural causes. The theory of the breakdown of civilization proposed in this book and our other works is an example of this "eclectic" causal theory. It may also be the case that it seems as if a conspiracy exists in a certain situation when what in fact is the case is that the players are all operating on a similar game-plan having common philosophies and ideologies so that an emergent order arises, much in the way that consciousness is thought by (non-reductive) materialists to arise from the activity of neurons. If history is like this, then there does exist the possibility that the globalists could make fundamental mistakes and that critical instabilities could develop that could bring down the entire house of cards.[10] This is in fact the situation with the international community and it is seen most clearly in the case of the United Nations.

THE FAILURE OF THE ONE-WORLD DREAM

The U.N. Secretary-General in 1992, Boutros Boutros-Ghali, said that, "The centuries-old doctrine of absolute and exclusive sovereignty no longer stands, and was in fact never so absolute as it was conceived to be in theory" (Bellamy, 1996, 224). Javier Perez de Cueller also said in a speech to the University of Bordeaux, April 24, 1991: "We are clearly witnessing what is probably an irresistible shift in public attitudes towards the belief that the defense of the oppressed in the name of morality should prevail over frontiers and legal documents" (Bellamy, 1996, 224). The Australian policy consultant, Gary Sturgess (1996), ties together the philosophical threads of such comments. He observes that conservatives in Australia are concerned about the loss of Australian sovereignty through international treaties and the creation of an international bureaucracy. Sturgess notes that this is all part of being in a global village as "we are now dealing with rudimentary systems of supranational governance", which he quickly qualifies by saying, does not constitute a "world government" – as if there is a material distinction here. The loose and common term "world government" is usually used to refer to a system of supranational government. A full-blooded, rather than rudimentary system of supranational government would, for all effective purposes constitute a world government.[11] In this sense the United Nations has become a rudimentary world government but, we will see, a highly ineffective and flawed one (Helms, 1996). However it is not the iron-fisted, efficiently functioning elite dictatorship that the radical right and left fear, but a chaotic, bungling and disorganized dinosaur that is itself becoming increasing irrelevant and redundant in a world that is simultaneously retribalizing as well as globalizing. Contrary to the radical right, the United Nations rests upon a political foundation based upon the survival of the nation-state even though the nation-state in the United Nations' scheme of things has a sovereignty greatly reduced from the level that nationalists expect and love. The processes of globalization and retribalization, in breaking down the social cohesiveness of the nation-state, will also break down the social cohesiveness of any sort of one-world community based around the United Nations. This is but one argument against the United Nations as a globalist cosmopolitan entity, pursuing the ideology of the one-world dream. Here, we will show

how a growing body of criticisms of the United Nations can be systematically unified. But first, some preliminary conceptual spadework.

The United Nations Charter was signed in San Francisco on June 26, 1945 and it entered into force on October 24, 1945. Article 1 of the Charter puts the primary aim of the United Nations as the maintenance of international peace and security. The U.N. was also to aid in the development of friendly relations between nations and promote international cooperation in social and economic issues. The U.N. Charter provided for the establishment of six organs to achieve these aims: the General Assembly (Chapter IV), the Security Council (Chapter V), the Economic and Social Council (Chapter X), the Trusteeship Council (Chapter XIII), the International Court of Justice (Chapter XIV) and a Secretariat (Chapter XV). There is also a wide range of related organizations and programs from UNCTAD (United Nations Conference on Trade and Development) to independent specialized agencies such as the Food and Agriculture Organization (FAO).

It is well known that the United Nations has a perennial funding problem (Evans, 1993), and this problem is likely to continue in the future even given CNN Ted Turner's gift of one billion dollars. Running the bureaucratic machine that is the United Nations is very expensive. Gareth Evans (1993) discusses a number of proposals for U.N. funding, favoring a levy on international airline travel (Evans, 1993, 176). As far as we are aware, this proposal has not been taken seriously and in many respects is contrary to the spirit of internationalism and cosmopolitanism that Evans champions and defends. An increase in airline travel costs is most likely to have an adverse effect on international tourism and would penalize many poorer countries. Obviously if the United Nations is to expand its role in the global community, or even to function at its present level, the funding problem must be solved. This problem though is not the core problem facing the United Nations. The core problem, or set of problems, relate to its philosophical rationale. We will now consider a diversity of opinion ranging from the left, to moderates, to the right, all of which in essence note a fundamental flaw in the United Nations' rationale.

Michael Lind, who can hardly be dismissed as a right wing conspiracy theorist, believes that the U.N. "should be allowed to wither away into irrelevance" and that "George Kennan was right when he declared that the U.N. should have been buried stillborn at the Dumbarton Oaks conference" (Lind, 1995, 33). Lind gives a litany of woes associated with the U.N. For much of its history, before the collapse of the Soviet Union, the U.N. was the world's leading forum for anti-Western and anti-American propaganda by the Soviets and the Third World bloc. The General Assembly passed a "Zionism is racism" motion in 1975 (repealed in 1991) without condemning human rights violations by Arab nations (Lind, 1995, 30; Berman,

1997). South Africa's apartheid policy was condemned by the U.N., but the genocide in Rwanda, Burundi and human rights violations by most African governments were ignored. Idi Amin was warmly greeted by the General Assembly. A statesman with a Nazi past and Soviet sympathies became Secretary-General of the United Nations for two terms (Lind, 1995, 31). Lind believes that the U.N. is morally and politically corrupt and must be abandoned (Lind, 1995, 32). He points out, with irony, that the U.N. itself seems to support this conclusion: "In 1985, the U.N.'s own Joint Inspection Unit concluded a seventeen-year analysis of the organization with the prescription that the deteriorating world body be replaced by something new" (Lind, 1995, 32). In Lind's opinion, reforms, even to branches of the U.N. such as the Security Council will not work because the organization is itself fundamentally flawed. The U.N. did not and could not prevent the Cold War – and in may ways it inflamed it – and the U.N. is incapable of preventing a Cold War between China and the United States and Japan. Although the U.N. could play a role in mediating in lesser conflicts (and even here the U.N.'s record is poor), the U.N. fails when the stakes are high.

James Walsh in an article in *Time* (Australia) about the U.N. at 50, while believing that the U.N. has "universal moral legitimacy" (Walsh, 1995, 35) sees the organization's ambitions as "overblown" and "its bureaucratic arthritis embarrassing" (Walsh, 1995, 30–1; Hazzard, 1995). Richard Gott in an article in the *New Internationalist* (Gott, 1994) sees the U.N. as an organization serving the interests of global capitalism, and "the U.N. is not, and could never be, a democratic organization. If it were, the world would be run by the Chinese" (Gott, 1994, 26). Further, he argues, any attempt at producing a united world is wildly utopian because public opinion in the West "is utterly unprepared to accept losing its soldiers in foreign wars that it is in no way geared to comprehend" (Gott, 1994, 26). The Australian writer Frank Moorhouse (1996) also believes that the U.N. is doomed, because it is a "dangerously flawed institution" (Moorhouse, 1996, 164). There is little agreement about what it is supposed to do, how it decides what it is to do or objective judgement of its success. Moorhouse is particularly concerned, as are others, with the U.N.'s actions as an embryonic world government and globocop (Francis, 1992). The globocop role that the U.N. is taking under the heading of global justice and a safe world, has as its logical conclusion, armed intervention and "peace enforcement" on a massive scale. This produces a paradox of going to war to produce peace. Moorhouse rightly observes that this is certain to produce disaster. This is also well confirmed by the history of U.N. post-Cold War peacekeeping operations.

Moorhouse's skeptical claim may seem extreme, yet even an intelligent critic of nationalism such as Michael Ignatieff sees the U.N.'s post-Cold

War interventions as a "partial failure" (Ignatieff, 1995b, 22), and that the U.N. "is confronted with the accusation that its efforts have merely delayed the inevitable or prolonged the agony of those it sought to assist" (Ignatieff, 1995b, 22). This view is now receiving expression in popular publications such as the *Reader's Digest*, something which would have been unthinkable before the end of the Cold War (Van Atta, 1995a, b). The reason for this has been that apart from the Gulf War, operations in Bosnia (Lind, 1995; Bandow, 1996; Hawkins, 1996), Somalia and Rwanda have been failures (Kirkpatrick, 1994). In Rwanda for example, about a million people, mainly Tutsis but also Hutus, have died. The United States resisted further action after the Security Council withdrew the small peacekeeping force, and as Bellamy notes, "American diplomats were ordered not to describe the mass killings as genocide but as '*acts of genocide*', thus avoiding any legal obligation to do anything under the 1948 U.N. Convention" (Bellamy, 1996, 106).

The U.N. peacekeeping forces have also committed atrocities. In June 1993 U.N./Pakistani troops killed 14 Somalis, including women and children and wounded 20 others. Canadian, Belgian and Italian troops also engaged in murder and torture (*The Economist*, 1997b; Bates, 1997; Piotrowicz, 1997). This situation has occurred before. Michael Lind (1995, 30) mentions the U.N.'s Congo mission of 1960–64 as being the most disastrous intervention before the Balkans. Here U.N. troops backed up the Soviet-supported central government of the Congo. Belgium's King Baudouin announced independence for the Belgian Congo on June 30, 1960. The pro-communist Patrice Lumumba won the Congo elections. He unleashed a reign of terror, African-style, against the population. Moise Kapenda Tshombe declared Katanga's independence from the pro-Soviet Congolese regime; Tshombe was anti-communist and pro-Western but he was condemned by both American liberals and Soviet Communists. On July 14, 1960 the US and USSR supported a U.N. resolution for troops to be sent to the Congo. According to the Security Council resolution of August 9, 1960: "the United Nations force in the Congo will not be a party to or in any way intervene in or be used to influence the outcome of any internal conflict, constitutional or otherwise" (Document S/4426, paragraph 4). But by December 1961 a full-scale military offensive was conducted against the secessionist government of President Tshombe. The Congolese army, by virtue of U.N. support, were able to commit atrocities against the civilian population, such as the butchering of missionaries while U.N. bombs killed innocent people in the Prince Leopold and Shinkolobwe hospitals and the Reine Elisabeth Clinic. The attacks on these hospitals are often said to be a mistake due to lack of air photographs (Bellamy, 1996, 96). A document by 46 civilian doctors of Elisabethville, *46 Angry Men* (1962), who were Swiss, Hungarian, Brazilian and Spanish claimed that the hospitals were clearly marked with red crosses on their roofs and that the U.N. committed atrocities against innocent civilians. A documentary narrated by Congressmen Donald L. Jackson entitled, *Katanga: The Untold Story*, claims that the U.N. forces deliberately bombed hospitals, churches and schools in Katanga and that civilians, Red Cross workers and children were machine-gunned and bayoneted by U.N. troops. U.N. peacekeeping forces eventually forced Katanga back under communist rule. Further, as Lind correctly observes, "The U.N.'s bloody assistance to the central [Congo] government helped usher in one of Africa's most vicious kleptocrats, Mobutu Sese Seko" (Lind, 1995, 30). These are not the actions one would expect from an organization commanding "universal moral legitimacy" (Walsh, 1995, 35).

The "universal moral legitimacy" of the United Nations has been exercised in a number of ways that adds fuel to the fires of conspiracy theorists. Some examples will now be given. In May 1997 the U.N. announced that Australia had committed human rights violations against the "boat people" by holding these illegal aliens in detention. Countries between China and Australia had refused entry to the boat people without sanctions from the U.N. Another example concerns the Australian federal governments "Wik" native title legislation. Aboriginal activists told a conference on indigenous people in July 1997 that the U.N. should mediate a resolution of the Wik crisis. This call was made even though the Australian Prime Minister John Howard did consult with all interest groups in formulating his "10 point" response to the High Court's Wik decision. The Aboriginal activists disagreed with this response, but rather than try and win support from the Australian people for their cause they chose to use an international forum to override a national decision (Mitchell, 1997).

The United Nations Conference on Trade and Development (UNCTAD) has supported highly controversial sell-offs of Australian companies to foreigners. UNCTAD believes that governments around the world have recognized "the benefits of allowing rich transnational companies to invest in their countries" (Gazard, 1996, 4). The highly unpopular privatization contracting out and management of South Australia's water supplies and sewage services were supported by the World Bank. According to senior bank official Hoon Mok Chung this was a "well-timed and well-planned initiative" (Kelton, 1995, 2). However the initiative was forced through parliament in the face of strong public opposition, and allegations of government impropriety surfaced, only to be quickly "hosed down" (Baker, 1995). The inefficiency of the private corporation controlling South Australia's water and sewage was revealed in 1997 when a "great pong", arising from ineffective sewage treatment, filled Adelaide's air for several months. South Australia is the driest state in the driest inhabited continent on Earth. The state has experienced water crises in the past. Its water supply is under long-term threat by rising salinity in the Murray-Darling river system (Crabb, 1997). If the management of any re-source should be under government control – and hence (in principle) public scrutiny – it is the vital resource of water. There is perhaps no better example of how economic ideologies can cause ruling elites to lose contact with basic ecological reality.

The U.N. Human Rights Committee has also ruled against Tasmania's laws that prohibited sexual acts between men because these laws contra-vened the International Covenant on Civil and Political Rights to which Australia is a signatory. The Hawke government signed the First Optional Protocol in 1991 and the Keating government – although giving lip-service to concerns about Australian independence and sovereignty (provided that such concerns were Republican ones directed against the evil empire Brit-ain) – allowed complaints to be heard by other U.N. committees (such as the U.N. Committee on the Elimination of Racial Discrimination and the U.N. Committee Against Torture). Although these findings are alleged to be "advisory", there is great national and international pressure for offend-ing nations to accept these views and make domestic laws in accordance with them. In any case, if a U.N. Committee did decide that Australia, for example, was in breach of its international obligations, then the Federal Government is obliged to override State laws by virtue of the controver-sially interpreted external affairs power in the Australian constitution. Al-ready the High Court of Australia has been influenced by the moral opin-ions of the U.N. Human Rights Committee (Kemp, 1994). However these Committees do not meet fundamental standards of judicial objectivity and independence. The proceedings are conducted in private without the pos-sibility of public scrutiny. No cross-examination of witnesses occurs. There is no right of representation for the accused, no rules of evidence and no right of appeal. Further, members of the U.N. Human Rights Committee come from governments that are not democratic and even Jus-tice Elizabeth Evatt, a strong defender of the United Nations, has admitted in various media interviews that members of the U.N. Human Rights Committee are sometimes briefed by their governments about the stance which they should take on various issues. The independence necessary for judicial fairness is lacking so that the Committee becomes in effect a po-litically correct inquisition. In the case of Tasmania's anti-sodomy laws, members of the Committee came from nations that often had harsher laws than the very laws that they were asked to judge. The Tasmanian laws may have been "wrong" according to today's morality but they were not arbi-trary. The US Supreme Court has upheld that the prohibition of sodomy is constitutionally valid and approximately half of the United States has similar laws to those that Tasmania had. The majority of nations on Earth have similar and often harsher laws than the Tasmanian laws. These state laws were overridden by Federal law. Although there had been 46 convictions since 1985 under the Tasmanian sodomy laws there had been no prosecutions for consenting sex acts between adults in private. For example, one such case in August 1994 involved a homosexual man who had sex with two teenage boys. The tradition in the West has been that even if a community and nation is morally "wrong" in its laws and practices, democracy, education and the free exchange of information will allow a self-correcting educational process to occur. The top-down imposition of morality by the United Nations prevents this.

The Tasmanian example has wider implications, beyond Australia. Justice Michael Kirby of the New South Wales Court of Criminal Appeal said in April 1994 that the U.N. decision against Tasmania's anti-gay laws could compel other countries such as Romania and India to fall into line (Dow, 1994). Enlightenment values of tolerance and non-discrimination must triumph over traditional social and religious values, be they Christian, Judaic or Islamic (Magarey, 1994). In the case of Australia, the then Attorney-General Michael Lavarch stated in 1994 that he believed that the Australian Constitution breached Australia's international obligations because the monarchy discriminates on the basis of religion and sex as the line of succession goes to the eldest son who must be Anglican (Crouch, 1994). If the United Nations is prepared to interfere in the legal workings of a nation and is genuinely committed to the Enlightenment value of non-discrimination, then it will be interesting to observe its forthcoming moral crusade against the Vatican. Surely it is neglecting its moral duty until it ensures that there is a lesbian person of color in the Vatican as Pope!

Not only must democratic and politico-religious values be trumped by the global-citizen values of tolerance and non-discrimination, but so must historically and nationally-specific long-standing individual values, such as the value of individual self-protection with a firearm. The idea that the individual has a right to personal self-defense and protection is primeval and pre-dates the origins of civilization; if there is a candidate for a natural right it is surely this one, argue vocal firearms rights groups. For such a right to make sense an individual must have an effective means of self-protection and the mechanism of self-protection is historically and technologically relative. Once an individual needed to have access to a sword and shield, when aggressors had swords for attack. Today the most likely weapon of personal attack and defense is a firearm. So, defenders of this view argue, individuals (with qualification) should have access to firearms for self-defense. This style of argument is heard most frequently in societies which have a relatively recent "frontier" ethos, such as the United States and Australia, or where civilians feel that police forces cannot protect them against crime. Clearly the gun control issue is historically and nationally specific. Switzerland has no real problem, allowing most of its citizens to keep a fully-automatic rifle at home. This would be disastrous as a policy for other nations. Therefore the gun control issue needs to be decided by each nation for itself. The U.N. however has chosen to champion "microdisarmament", the elimination of civilian-owned firearms. The United Nations began a study of civilian-owned firearms in December 1995, prompted by concerns about a world-wide rise in violent crime associated with transnational criminal networks and drug trafficking. The U.N. solution to the problem is to remove the private ownership of firearms completely (even though the weapon of choice by most criminals is the pistol, not bolt action hunting rifles), by means of a proposed "Universal Declaration of Principles on Firearms" to be submitted to the Economic and Social Council and U.N. General Assembly by mid to late 1998 (Economic and Social Council, 1996a,b). The firearms issue is highly sensitive in both Australia and the United States. In Australia, the nation-wide surrender of all semi-automatic rifles and shotguns and pump action shotguns following the Port Arthur massacre in 1996, was achieved only by the Federal Government threatening relcalcitrant state governments with funding penalties if they did not comply with the surrender. Firearms owners were compensated for their weapons; the majority bought new legal long arms. However if one is to deal with the crime problem by eliminating one of the tools of crime rather than by attacking the socio-economic roots of crime, then more than the Australian scheme must be needed. To obtain all firearms, legal and illegal, will require an army to search every home, property and likely burial ground in the country. Then black markets and the creation of guns in secret underground workshops must be stopped. To effectively do this will require the creation of a police state. It is arguable that even an efficient police state would be incapable of controlling a black market in firearms if a strong desire for such weapons existed in society. Militia groups and radical right wingers would be certain to resist as their worst fears of tyrannical "global communism" would be realized. Increased terrorism may occur. In the meantime the drug problem is not solved. Here we have another example of the United Nations addressing an important issue by an entirely inappropriate mechanism that will divide communities (Sporting Shooters Association of Australia, 1997). Again, as in the case of Tasmania's anti-sodomy laws, the United Nations position may be correct (we take no position here) but it is *the means to achieving that end which are problematic.*[12]

IMPLICATIONS

It is time to draw together the threads of the argument of this section. We have outlined criticisms of the actions of the United Nations from a wide range of critics across the political spectrum. The criticisms all have a common core: the United Nations, in operating in an authoritarian top-down undemocratic fashion, has produced bungle after bungle. Rather than producing order, chaos has occurred. This is the case with cultural, political, economic and military interventions. Atrocities have been committed in the name of peace and world order. The United Nations has become an embryonic world government as the right has observed, but not the iron fisted efficient and disciplined one that they fear. Rather the United Nations has become something of a virtual super-nation, but a stumbling super-nation completely dependent upon the survival of the nation-state for sustenance and administration. It is doubtful whether the United Nations, even if it were given the monopolization of the planet's military weapons, could effectively manage such an armoury and coordinate their wise use. There is a built-in self-destruction mechanism inside such centralist strategies that will be explored in more detail with respect to the global economy in Chapter 5 of this book. In short, there are information-theoretic limits to centralism, and pushed beyond a certain threshold centralist structures begin to fail and forces begin to be generated which act to destabilize and undermine the structures. This occurred with the Soviet Union and it would *a fortiori* operate with any large globalist structure, especially one with delusions of grandeur of the world government scale. The critics of the United Nations are right in observing that this institution is doomed. It has committed itself to impossible universalist principles, which when operationalized generate a dialectic that ensures the failure of such principles. The reason why this is so has already been explained in this book. The United Nations is, or was intended to be, an embodiment of Enlightenment rationality. But as we have seen such rationality seems to be self-consuming and self-defeating. The failure of the United Nations and hence the failure of the one-world dream stems from this internal contradiction. As the United Nations is an exemplar of the one-world dream, we can conclude from the failure of the United Nations that the one-world dream is also a failure. In the final chapter of this book we will see that even the economic version of one-worldism is a failure.

5   Endtimes: Breakdown and Breakup

Where the sentiment of nationality exists in any force, there is a *prima facie* case for uniting all the members of the nationality under the same government, and a government to themselves apart. This is merely saying that the question of government ought to be decided by the governed. One hardly knows what any division of the human race should be free to do if not to determine with which of the various collective bodies of human beings they choose to associate themselves. But when a people are ripe for free institutions, there is a still more vital consideration. Free institutions are next to impossible in a country made up of different nationalities. Among a people without fellow-feeling, especially if they read and speak different languages, the united public opinion, necessary to the working of representative government, cannot exist.

– John Stuart Mill (1806–1873) (Mill, 1958, 230)

The extent of the power of money is my power. Money's properties are my properties and essential powers – the properties and powers of its possessor. . . . I am ugly, but I can buy for myself the most beautiful of women. Therefore I am not ugly, for the effect of ugliness – its deterrent power – is nullified by money. I, in my character as an individual, am lame, but money furnishes me with twenty-four feet. Therefore I am not lame. I am bad, dishonest, unscrupulous, stupid; but money is honored, and therefore so is its possessor. Money is the supreme good, therefore its possessor is good. . . . Do not I, who thanks to money am capable of all that the human heart longs for, possess all human capacities? Does not my money therefore transform all my incapacities into their contrary?

– Karl Marx (1818–1883) (Marx, 1972, 81)

The ultimate purpose of business is not, or should not be, simply to make money. Nor is it merely a system of making and selling things. The promise of business is to increase the general well-being of humankind through service, a creative invention and ethical philosophy. Making money is, on its own terms, totally meaningless, an insufficient pursuit for the complex and decaying world we live in. (Hawken, 1993, 1)

THINGS FALL APART: THE CENTER CANNOT HOLD

The tribes have returned, the American philosopher Michael Walzer notes, and across the globe "men and women are reasserting their local and particularist, their ethnic, religious, and national identities" (Walzer, 1994, 187). The "new tribalism" is not exclusively caused by globalization as secessionist movements have existed prior to this late twentieth century trend, but there is no doubt that the forces of globalization are fuelling the new tribalism and secession. *Secession* derives from the Latin word *secessionem*, meaning a withdrawal; it involves people within a state who identify as a "nation" by way of racial, ethnic, cultural and/or religious reasons, seeking by various means to establish a separate sovereign state of their own people in their own territory. As Premdas notes: "When a group of people come to view themselves consciously as being endowed with a unique language, race, religion or region and see that this is threatened . . . then . . . they become a 'nation' and 'an ethnic group' " (Premdas, 1990, 22–3). Secessionist and devolution movements exist in Canada, India, Sri Lanka, China, Europe, Australia and even the United States (Stumph, 1997). An important recent example of a successful devolution movement is the Scottish devolution referendum of September 1997, giving home-rule for Scotland, with tax-raising powers to Edinburgh. Indeed, separatist and secessionist movements exist wherever there is a danger of people becoming "minorities in their own land." With mass immigration, itself a product of the forces of economic globalization, no country is free from the challenge of separatism and secession (Smock and Smock, 1975; Esman, ed., 1976; Premdas, 1990). Internationalism, Kauffman notes, "the imposition of alien practices and cultural forms on native populations – deadens our souls, saps our vitality, and leaves us with lost and alienated men and women who feel as strangers in their own land" (Kauffman, 1997, 12).

A vast sociological and political literature exists on the topics of separatism and secession. (Morris-Jones, 1972; Beshir, 1975; Smock and Smock, 1975; Esman ed., 1976; Silverstein, 1980, De Silva, 1986; Wilson, 1988; Premdas, 1990; Premdas et al. 1990; Streeck, 1992; Broin, 1994). In this concluding chapter we shall consider the question of the "breakdown of nations" (Kohr, 1978) which the process of economic globalization is unintentionally exacerbating, and defend the right of the tribes to separate and preserve their racial, ethnic and cultural identities *if* they wish. The principal obstacle in the way of free secession is not philosophical or moral, but economic. Consequently this chapter will consider the work of theorists who have made contributions to secession and "tribal" theory in that direction. A small book such as this one can only present a Cook's tour of this field; however we believe that worthwhile contribution can be made by showing how work from both the left and the right can be synthesized into a coherent localist and particularist response to globalism and cosmopolitanism. We will show that however hopeless things look, there are still alternatives to the so-called "irresistible" trend of globalization.

Within contemporary American political philosophy, it is *prima facie* surprising to find defenses of both secession and the "new tribalism". We have already mentioned the case of Michael Walzer (1994). Walzer believes, and rightly so, that tribalism as such cannot be destroyed because tribalism "names the commitment of individuals and groups to their own history, culture, and identity, and this commitment (though not any particular version of it) is a permanent feature of human social life" (Walzer, 1994, 199–200). This particularism and parochialism is permanent, hence "it has to be accommodated, and therefore the crucial universal principle is that it must always be accommodated: not only my parochialism but yours as well, and his and hers in their turn" (Walzer, 1994, 200). Rather than supporting existing unions Walzer supports separation "whenever separation is demanded by a political movement that, so far as we can tell, represents the popular will. Let the people go who want to go" (Walzer, 1994, 197). Sunstein (1994) has recognized that there may be good political and moral reasons for secession, but he claims that there is insufficient reason for a constitutionally enshrined right to secede. Many American liberal philosophers have gone further than this though (Buchheit, 1978; Beran 1987, 1994; Buchanan, 1991a, b; Ewin, 1995). Typically the right to secede has been grounded on the liberal doctrine of political self-determination (Stewart, 1988; Nielsen, 1993; Gauthier, 1994; Neuberger, 1995; Wellman, 1995). Having criticized liberalism throughout this book, we have no further interest in this material beyond noting that those in the press who dismiss separatism as an "extremist" position are dismissing some of the best political and philosophical minds in America. For example, Robert H. Nelson in *Reaching for Heaven on Earth: The Theological Meaning of Economics* (1991) says that, "The right of free secession might . . . supercede economic principles of free trade, and other past freedoms in providing a founding principle for a postmodern economic order" (Nelson, 1991, 327–8). A world of smaller states would give each state the benefit of being a homogeneous society because states comprising a great diversity of people have internal flaws: "Political disagreements among groups in a diverse nation erode the moral capital and sense of community needed to make government work well. . . . A world of free secession would provide the alternative of dividing into smaller and more homogenous sovereign entities where there is much greater internal agreement on social goals" (Nelson, 1991, 329). Separatism and secessionism may also aid in the creation of a more stable world order or a new type of internationalism as Hans-Hermann Hoppe observes:

> Secessionism, and the growth of separatists and regionalist movements in Eastern and Western Europe, in North America as well as elsewhere, represent not an anachronism but potentially the most progressive historical forces. Secession increases ethnic, linguistic, religious and cultural diversity, while in the course of centuries of centralization hundreds of distinct cultures were stamped out. It will end the forced integration brought about as the result of centralization, and rather than stimulating social strife and cultural nivellation, it will promote the peaceful, cooperative competition of different, territorially separate cultures. In particular, it will eliminate the immigration problem increasingly plaguing Western Europe as well as the US. Presently, whenever the central government permits immigration, it allows foreigners to proceed – literally on government-owned roads – to any of its resident's doorsteps, regardless of whether or not these residents desire such proximity to foreigners. "Free immigration" is thus to a larger extent forced integration. Secession solves this problem by letting smaller territories each have their own admission standards and determine independently with whom they will associate on their own territory and with whom they prefer to cooperate from a distance. (Hoppe, 1996, 101)

Although Hoppe's essay from which the above paragraph is quoted occurs in the left wing journal *Telos*, Hoppe is not against economic integration and development. He looks forward to the creation of a world consisting of "small liberal governments economically integrated through free trade" producing "unprecedented economic growth and unheard of prosperity" – the Singaporization of the world. Libertarian economic writers such as the former *Economist* editor Norman Macrae in his book *The 2025 Report: A Concise History of the Future* (1984) also welcomes the coming of a world of "genuine pluralism", a new form of feudalism where trade flourishes, but where everyone is free to secede into small communities and "set up their own forms of very local government – communes, monasteries, profit-making local governments run by private-enterprise performance contractors, beach clubs on desert isles" (Macrae, 1984, 124 quoted from Nelson, 1991, 313). Surely this is better than a Bosnia in every city.

The idea that bigness is a cause of social misery is best known through E.F. Schumacher's *Small is Beautiful* (1973) but it had been argued for much earlier by Leopold Kohr in a paper published in the New York left-wing Catholic weekly *The Commonweal* September 26, 1941 under his brother's name Hans Kohr (Kohr, 1992).[1] Kohr had also used the phrase the "limits to growth" in articles published in 1956 and 1957 of the *Canadian Business Quarterly* (Palaver, 1992). Kohr maintained in his books *The Breakdown of Nations* (1978) and *The Overdeveloped Nations* (1976) that more is not necessarily better; beyond a certain point diseconomies of scale arise. Nature puts a stop to growth when things are large enough to fulfil their function (Thompson, 1942).[2] Applying this insight Kohr generalized on Malthus, arguing that there are limits to the size and complexity of societies because social problems grow at a geometrical rate while the human ability to cope, if at all, grows at an arithmetic rate. Anticipating modern chaos and complexity theory, he recognized that increasing complexity could lead to critical instabilities. Socially produced brutality "is largely nothing but the spontaneous result of the critical volume of power generated whenever the human mass reaches a certain magnitude" (Kohr, 1978, 34). Social misery can be prevented by keeping power-breeding social size at a sub-critical level. Kohr believed that a proposed "World State" will not reduce the prospects of war, but increase them and the United Nations, in his opinion, is not worth its price (Kohr, 1978, 56). He followed Toynbee's position in *A Study of History* (Toynbee, 1960), which sees the last stage of a civilization as characterized by political unification into a universal state, the state comprising all the members of a specific civilization. Kohr notes: "Today, pushed by the United Nations and their cultural agency, UNESCO, the Western universal state has advanced far beyond the dim outlines of an 'ideological premonition'; in fact, our statesmen seem to have nothing at all on their minds *except* our unification that will preserve our existence, but doom our civilization" (Kohr, 1978, 131). Kohr's books are instructive and contain fertile hypotheses, at the expense of lack of detailed argument, and over-generalization. The idea that scale is the cause of *all* social misery is not correct and meets the fate of all universal theories – openness to counter-examples. Social misery can surely arise even in a primitive tribal situation because of human folly and weaknesses. However, much social misery is a product of scale effects. A more rigorous develoment of Kohr's thesis was made by Kirkpatrick Sale in his book *Human Scale* (Sale, 1980, see also Winner, 1986, 85–97).

Secessionism and separatism have also been argued to be an outcome of the limits to growth and the transition to an ecologically sustainable society. On this Perelman has said:

... centrifugal forces increasingly challenge and strain the centripetal bonds of national and multinational interdependence. Just as dinosaurs were vulnerable to egg snatching by mammalian rodents, physical and social limits make giant organizations ever more vulnerable to the leverage of small groups. In confronting the mighty, the meek aspire to inherit not the whole earth but only small pieces of it: South Malucca, Eritrea, Croatia, Scotland, Quebec, Kurdistan, or (domestically) Maine (Indian lands), Michigan (the Upper Peninsula), Petaluma, or Martha's Vineyard. The way to diffuse the destructive potential of irreconcilable paradigm conflict is through division of territory. Historical examples are plentiful: the Biblical exodus, the division of the United States into slave and free states, the division of the Church into Eastern and Western branches, the creation of ghettos, the partitioning of Germany, Ireland, Cyprus, Palestine, India, and so forth. Clearly, territorial division is no panacea for conflict, but in many cases it probably has reduced or deferred some of the destructive consequences of profound conflicts. The impulse to separatism, localism, isolationism, and balkanization seems to be an inevitable feature of the coming transition to sustainable energy. (Perelman, 1980, 406–7)

Self-reliance and various forms of autarky have been supported by theorists such as John Galtung (1979, et al., 1980, 1982, 1986), W. Sachs (1986), Paul Ekins (1989), Tim Lang and Colin Hines (1993), H.E. Daly and J.B. Cobb (1989) and by the contributers to J. Mander and E. Goldsmith's edited volume *The Case Against the Global Economy and For a Turn Toward the Local* (Mander and Goldsmith eds, 1996). In general these theorists believe that an inevitable breakdown of the global economy will occur because of limits to growth considerations (Goldsmith, 1996a, 510). National self-reliance and/or national self-sufficiency should be adopted as a means of achieving ecologically sustainable development (Mosley, 1993, 1994). According to Mosley, national self-sufficiency "is a way of making human use of resources sustainable over the long term, maintaining a varied and viable environment, and giving people control of their destiny" (Mosley, 1994, 4). National self-sufficiency is not based on the principle of comparative advantage, but of comparative care and it seeks to substitute reliance on international trade by reliance on a nation's own productive resources, hence removing global free trade as a major source of ecological destruction (Mosley, 1994, 5; Batra, 1993; Gare, 1996; Smith et al., 1997).

The critics of autarky see such proposals as hopelessly anachronistic in a world of global capital flows where the virile, thrusting Asian tigers of capitalism have impregnated the world with the germ plasm of unprecedented economic growth (Lewis, 1992; Broderick, 1996). These critics see the juggernaut of global capitalism as unstoppable. This theme is best seen in our daily newspapers, and we for convenience will use Australian examples. Readers are free to substitute their local columnists. In the Australian print media B.A. Santamaria is one of the few to systematically challenge economic globalization in his columns in *The Australian* (Santamaria, 1994, 1995, 1996a, b, c, 1997a, b) (Allowing one resident heretic gives the illusion that a "free debate" on economic issues is occurring). Gerard Henderson, a columnist for *The Age* and *The Sydney Morning Herald* newspapers in Australia, has the self-appointed (we assume) task of exposing alleged conspiracies among the "lunar" (his favorite adjective) left, green, right or any group or person opposing the forces of global capitalism (cf also McGuinness, 1995; Warby, 1997). He is Executive Director of the Sydney Institute, a leading privately funded think-tank that has promoted the internationalization of Australia.[3] Henderson takes Santamaria to task, linking him and his Catholic-based organisation, the National Civic Council, with both left-wing and right-wing figures who embrace "isolationism"(Henderson, 1997a, b, c). This is almost as bad a sin as "racism" and "xenophobia" and indeed most globalists cannot resist linking these often disparate phenomena, whether there is reason to do so or not. Obvious this puts one's opponents at the business end of the politically correct spear. Now according to Henderson, "Australia cannot stand against the international trend to a freer movement in people and/or goods. Insularity will only breed contempt" (Henderson, 1997b, 15). In other words Australia should bow to the forces of international fear and blackmail. Further, we should enjoy this assault because free trade has meant that consumers can benefit from the importation of cheap Asian consumer goods. Henderson and his ilk are supporters of a doctrine, economic fundamentalism or rationalism, which declares "that when faced with the choice of a cheaper CD player and a son in work you must always choose the CD player" (Ellis, 1997, 15). Confronted with authoritative critics of economic fundamentalism such as John Ralston Saul (1997), William Greider (1997) and the New York-based investor George Soros (1997), Henderson takes the Voltairean position that the critics of the global economy may be wrong, but at least they should be heard. He does not attempt to show *why* these respective critics of globalization are wrong and why he is right. Sadly, a debate such as that would be too "heavy" for the intellectually lightweight newspapers that dominate the Australian print media. But even here, there are cracks in the armor of the true believer: "Recent election results the Western world over tell us that voters are not happy – even though economic data seem relatively satisfactory (apart from unemployment)" (Henderson, 1997c, 15) – as if unemployment was some insignificant detail! (Rodrik, 1997; Santamaria, 1997c; Wood, 1997). Economic rationalists/fundamentalists and globalists are committed to accepting that "open" economies like New Zealand must be "heaven on earth" (Nelson, 1991), even though New Zealand, which once had the third highest standard of living and the low unemployment rate of four percent, had by 1994 these economic data:

- The standard of living in New Zealand had plunged to 22nd in the world.
- Unemployment had risen to over 16% and would be higher if 120,000 people had not left the country to find work.
- The incidence of violent crime and youth suicide [per capita] was the highest in the world.
- Foreign debt had more than tripled to $70 billion. Public debt up 350% to $38 billion (although the reason for the reforms was said to be the debt!)
- Half the country's manufacturing jobs had disappeared.
- A 25% cut in welfare rates drove poverty rates up 40%.
- One in four children live in poverty and parents must now pay for part of their children's schooling.
- User fees are charged for medical treatment, so many poor people postpone getting care when they need it, and prescriptions go unfilled.
- Labour relations were deregulated. Unions no longer have any legal status.
- [A] fire sale of $19 billion in government owned assets included: Air New Zealand to Australians, telephone systems to Americans, government insurance to a private company. (Anonymous, 1996/97, 31)

Across the world people have become fearful about the dissolution caused by economic globalization (Hirst and Thompson, 1996), according to Hans-Peter Martin (whose book *The Global Trap* has sold 250,000 copies in the German speaking world and is being translated into 20 other languages (Martin and Schumann, 1997; Yallop, 1997)). Martin decided to criticize globalization after he attended a San Francisco seminar in 1995, along with 500 of the world's business and political leaders. These elites accepted that the world was heading towards the "20:80 society" where globalization and the new technologies would lead to 80 percent of the population being unemployed (Yallop, 1997). *The Economist* for example tells us that "the protection of workers in rich countries . . . is an economic mistake" (*The Economist*, 1997a, 90), confirming such fears. George Soros (1997), as we have already mentioned, fears that *laissez faire* capitalism – whose supporters believe that by an "invisible hand" the common good is best served by unrestrained, unregulated self-interest and greed – may break down unless it is "tempered by the recognition of a common interest that ought to take precedence over particular interests" (Soros, 1997, 48). Interestingly enough, even though Soros has opposed the social Darwinism of *laissez faire* capitalism (Soros, 1997, 52–3), Dr. Mahathir Mohamad, Malaysian Prime Minister, accused this financier of criminal activities in his speculative raids on ASEAN economies. At a speech opening the annual conference of regional foreign ministers of ASEAN in July 1997, Dr. Mahathir accused rogue currency speculators of attempting to wreck regional economies, and to force South East Asians to "submit to the dictatorship of international manipulators" (Baker, 1997a, B2). On July 27 1997 Dr. Mahathir compared the actions of Soros with those of drug traffickers: "as much as people who produce and distribute drugs are criminals because they destroy nations, the people who undermine the economies of poor nations [are too]" (Baker, 1997b, 38). The comparison is an offensive one for Mr. Soros. His activities in speculative raids are not illegal; indeed they are a sign of financial capitalist manhood. If Dr. Mahathir is prepared to accept the desirability of a world without borders, then finanical insecurity is the price his nation must pay. Soros' actions may be inconsistent with his published criticisms of the social Darwinism of *laissez faire* capitalism, but who said that logical consistency counted in the world of *realpolitik*?

Professor John McMurtry of the philosophy department at the University of Guelph has made the same point as Dr. Mahathir. He quotes from a leaked memorandum by the chief economist of the World Bank in 1991 that recommends that the less developed countries could achieve "welfare enhancement" by accepting "toxic wastes" and "dirty industries" (McMurtry, 1997, 4). The economic logic behind such reasoning, the World Bank's chief economist regards as "impeccable" (McMurtry, 1997, 4). We are in a situation, McMurtry writes with angst, "where the life of people, societies and the planet itself have been so subjugated to the rule of the money code that the most life-invasive and morally grotesque consequences of its reasoning appear "rational" and "impeccable" " (McMurtry, 1997, 4).[4] In examining the possibility of free secession, the creation of autarkic economies and effective opposition to economic globalization, we need to consider the value crisis of the global economy in more detail and whether there is in theory and practice a strategy or method of opposing it. We believe that in theory there is a way of countering globalization, but in practice it is most unlikely to succeed. Thus our opponents are right in arguing that the forces of globalization cannot be defeated. This in itself does not show that the critics of globalization are mistaken. In fact, both camps are right: globalization is inevitable but it also contains within its heart the seeds of its own destruction.

THE RULE OF THE RICH

> In the current phase of intellectual corruption, it must be stressed that, like democracy and human rights, the economic doctrines preached by the rulers are instruments of power, intended for others, so that they can be more efficiently robbed and exploited . . .
>
> - Noam Chomsky (1993, 100)

In his book *The Agenda* Washington Post correspondent Bob Woodward (1994) describes a meeting between President Clinton and his top economic advisors before his official inauguration in January 1994 (Santamaria, 1996c, 17). Woodward describes Clinton's introduction to the world of *realpolitik*: "At the president-elect's end of the table Clinton's face turned red with anger and disbelief: "Do you mean to tell me that the success of the program and my re-election hinges on the Federal Reserve and a bunch of fucking bond traders?" he responded in a half-whisper. Nods from his end of the table. Not a dissent" (Woodward, 1994, 84). The financial power of investment banks is both undeniable and well documented in the literature (Clarke and Tigue, 1975; Reinecke, 1988; Walter, 1989; Payer, 1991; Hirsh, 1994; Solomon, 1995). Pope Pius XI (1922–1939) recognized this in his encyclical *Quadragesimo anno* (May 15, 1931):

> It is patent that in our days not alone is wealth accumulated, but immense power and despotic economic domination are concentrated in the hands of a few, and that those few are frequently not the owners, but only the trustees and directors of invested funds, which they administer at their pleasure.
>
> This domination becomes particularly irresistible when exercised by those who, because they hold and control money, are able to govern credit and determine its allotment, for that reason supplying, so to speak, the life blood to the entire economic body . . .
>
> This accumulation of resources and power, the characteristic of the modern economic order, is a natural result of limitless free competition which permits the survival of those only who are strongest, which often means those who fight relentlessly, who pay least heed to the dictates of conscience. (quoted from Santamaria, 1996d, 260)

Louis Uchitelle, the financial correspondent of *The New York Times* wrote in the *International Herald Tribune* June 13, 1994 that "The American economy is governed by the bond market. [This is] a lose confederation of wealthy American bankers, financiers, money managers, rich foreigners, executives of life insurance companies, presidents of universities and non-profit foundations . . . and [the mutual] funds" (quoted from Santamaria, 1997b, 22). Santamaria observes that the funds of this financial elite are controlled primarily by Wall Street investment banks having the following market shares: Merrill Lynch (10 percent); Chase Manhattan (8 percent); J.P. Morgan (8 percent); Goldman Sachs (8 percent); Morgan Stanley (7.5 percent); First Boston (6 percent); Salomon Brothers (approximately 6 percent) and Lehman Brothers (5.75 percent) (Santamaria, 1997b, 22). The level of interest rates and capital flows throughout the integrated financial global marketplace ultimately rests in the hands of these investment banks through their determination of the level of interest rates on US bonds. Thus as the chief economist of New York's Chase Bank, Irwin Kellner, put it: "It is really the bond market that runs the country, not the President and not [Federal Reserve chairman] Alan Greenspan" (quoted from Santamaria, 1997b, 22). Supporters of the principle of national self-determination have objected to this "rule of the banksters", believing that usury will wreck any nation. William Lyon MacKenzie King, Prime Minister of Canada, 1935, put it as follows: "Once a nation parts with control of its currency and credit, it matters not who makes that nation's laws. Usury, once in control, will wreck any nation. Until the control of currency and credit is restored to government and recognized as its most conspicuous and sacred responsibility, all talk of the sovereignty of Parliament and of democracy is idle and futile" (quoted from Cameron & Finn, 1996, 2). In Australia, Professor Fred Argy, a leading financial theorist, said in 1996: "You've got to ask yourself whether it is not the lesser of two evils to have the guts to stand up to them [the financiers] – to tell them to go jump in the lake. They can put the government in a terrible corner, but provided the government has the economic fundamentals and the social priorities right, they can tell the financial markets to go to hell" (quoted from Santamaria, 1997b, 22). Santamaria, in reflecting on this advice recognizes that few people believe that this can be done, but that present policies are a "prescription for despair" (Santamaria, 1997b, 22). We will now argue that Professor Argy is wrong – the financiers are invincible – at least within the confines of a capitalist economy. The financiers cannot be told to jump in the lake because they own the lake! Further, various attempts to work out alternative economic strategies within the framework of a capitalist economy can be shown to be either theoretically flawed or without a chance of success.

In entering the field of alternative economists and monetary theory one enters a somewhat shadowy field, often dominated by cranks and anti-Semites, so one must be careful to watch where one puts one's feet lest one steps in something unpleasant. Conspiracy theories and conspiracy theorists abound. However, there are many sensible and reasonable publications. A small grassroots industry exists, attempting to show, usually by way of copious quotations, that banks "create money out of thin air" and that this is a crime of some magnitude (Kennedy, 1990; McLean and Renton, 1992; Stuart, 1992; Milne, 1993; Burgi, 1994, Hellyer, 1994). The Australian writer and industrialist John Iggulden observes that economics as a science does not question and indeed accepts as a *fait accompli*, "as an absolutely unchangeable given, one of the most questionable of all human practices: the creation of nearly all money, out of nothing and out of nowhere, as debts to be repaid with interest, by private commercial companies called "banks" almost all of which are operated solely for the purposes of private profits and private power" (Iggulden, 1988, 1). John Kenneth Galbraith in his book *Money: Whence It Came, Where It Went* gives a concise historical sketch of the origins of credit creation (for a detailed account consult Hilton, 1994; Zarlenga, 1996a, b)[5]:

> The process by which banks create money is so simple that the mind is repelled. Where something so important is involved, a deeper mystery seems only decent. The deposits of the Bank of Amsterdam . . . were, according to the instruction of the owner, subject to transfer to others in settlement of accounts. (This had long been a convenience provided by the Bank's private precursors.) The coin on deposit served no less as money by being in a bank and being subject to transfer by the stroke of a primitive pen.
>
> Inevitably it was discovered – as it was by the conservative burghers of Amsterdam as they reflected incestuously on their own needs as directors of the Dutch East India Company – that another stroke of the pen would give a borrower from the bank, as distinct from a creditor of the original depositor, a loan from the original and idle deposit. It was not a detail that the bank would have the interest on the loan so made. The original depositor could be told that his deposit was subject to such use – and perhaps be paid for it. The original deposit still stood to the credit of the original depositor. But there was now also a new deposit from the proceeds of the loan. Both deposits could be used to make payments, be used as money. Money had thus been created. The discovery that banks could so create money came very early in the development of banking. There was that interest to be earned. Where such reward is waiting, men have a natural instinct for innovation. (Galbraith, 1975, 29).

The great economist Joseph A. Schumpeter recognized that banks create credit (Schumpeter, 1976, 320) as did Irving Fisher (former Professor of Economics at Yale University) in his "100 percent money" plan (Fisher, 1936), a plan which Fisher thought would end the money-debt system (Hixson, 1991). The economist James Tobin remarks that, "Whatever their other errors, a long line of financial heretics have been right in speaking of "fountain pen money" – money created by the stroke of the bank president's pen when he approves a loan and credits the proceeds to the borrower's checking account" (Tobin, 1971, 272). Finally, one of the world's leading central bankers, Alan Greenspan, chairman of the US Federal Reserve, said in an address to the University of Leuven in Belgium on January 14, 1997 that, "Central banks can issue currency, a non-interest-bearing claim on the government, effectively without limits. . . . That all of these claims on government are readily accepted reflects the fact that a government cannot become insolvent with respect to obligations in its own currency" (quoted from Santamaria, 1997d, 23). For Greenspan, governments must find the proper balance between taxes, deficit funding and credit creation by the central banks, in paying for government programs.

The multiple creation of bank deposits is now textbook knowledge (Stanford, 1968, 1969; Dewald, 1969; Tsung, 1980). Some textbooks deny that individual banks can create credit, but recognize that the banking system as a whole can do so, expanding loans and investments by a multiple of additional reserves by a "multiplier effect" (Samuelson et al., 1975, 358). Other textbooks affirm, with careful qualification, that in a fractional reserve system, in general a bank in making a loan increases the money stock (Lipsey, 1969, 678–83; Fischer et al., 1988, 489). This debate, along with the precise operation of the money multiplier and complications such as capital adequacy ratios (at least in the Australian case), need not concern us here.[6]

We observe that the private creation of credit, as well as the entire fractional reserve banking system, have been criticized on a number of grounds. Economists such as Irving Fisher and economists in the "Sovereignty Movement" (including the late Professor John Hotson) have seen the fractional-reserve system as a cause of economic crises because the money supply of a nation, and the world, is grounded in debt. Banks issue credit to cover the amount of the loans, but they do not issue credit to pay the interest on it, so that the public increasingly falls into debt to the banking system. National and private debts as a whole will invariably rise (Hilton, 1994, 157). Hilton notes that if "real (bank) interest rates remain above real growth rates an intractable debt spiral will eventuate" (Hilton, 1994, 158). We will have more to say about the unsustainability of the fractional reserve/debt money system below. However some ecological critics, such as Garrett Hardin, have gone further and have argued that *usury*, the practice of lending money at interest, is ecologically flawed (Hardin, 1993). Usury was opposed by the early Christian Church until the 13th century, when "usury" was redefined as the charging of "excessive" interest (Sen, 1993). Hardin uses the term "usury" to refer to all positive rates of interest. The ecological problem with usury, in Hardin's opinion, lies with the nature of compound interest which one of the Rothschilds called the eighth wonder of the world. Compound interest makes money grow without limit, but from an ecological perspective this is arrogant nonsense in a world of environmental limits.

A bank account earning 5 percent compound interest per year doubles in value every 14 years. Compound interest is represented by a exponential growth curve, a curve which becomes steeper with the passage of time. Mathematically, a tangent to the curve becomes steeper, that is dy/dx tends toward infinity. Hardin illustrates the Rothschildian wonders of compound interest with this example. Two grams of gold, held in a bank at 5 percent compound interest growing for two thousand years produces the equivalent of 4.78×10^{42} grams of gold. The Earth itself has a mass of only 5.983×10^{27} grams so the bank owes 8×10^{14} solid gold Earths, that is 800 trillion Earths made of solid gold, a *reductio ad absurdum*.

The other side of the coin to this is that compound interest generates often impossible *debts*, because debt can approach infinity by the compound interest formula. Hardin concludes: "For six centuries 'informed opinion' has regarded the unlimited paying of interest on money as normal and generally desirable. People have assumed without question that material wealth can grow exponentially forever. Now we must admit that only debt can grow exponentially forever: that an exponential curve that soars off toward infinity can apply to nothing in the real world; and that such unpleasant events as inflation and debt repudiation are necessary correctives in a social system based on usury" (Hardin, 1993, 82).

There have been many critics of orthodox finance but their material has been seen by more modern writers as somewhat anachronistic, virtually held in suspended animation from the pre-World War II period.[7] Therefore let us consider some more modern proposals. The international Sovereignty Movement (which derives its name from the fact that countries lose their sovereignty when their finance is tied to the international financial markets), comprises the Canadian/North American Committee on Monetary and Economic Reform (COMER) as well as Economic Reform Australia (ERA) among other organizations. Their members include numbers of university based economists, bankers and business people (Hotson, 1993). By way of summary, these organisations are committed to reforming the unsustainable fractional reserve/debt money system the world currently uses. Both COMER and ERA support the concept of an ecologically sustainable society, and oppose unbridled "growth" economics, economic rationalism, the level playing field, and the current level of financial deregulation. They support a range of alternatives to debt-financing in both the public and private arenas. These include the creation of a significant proportion of the nation's money supply either as public credit without debt, or in the form of repayable loans at very low interest for voter-approved infrastructure projects via the Reserve or Central Bank. A financial steady state should be maintained by properly monitoring the movement of money within the entire economy, they believe. This will require adequate regulation of all financial institutions, with particular attention to the volume and cost of credit, in order to keep inflation under control. Governments must cease borrowing from private sources, particularly at high interest rates. This is essential if the massive build-up of foreign and internal debt is to be halted, and the financial system stabilized. Above all, these groups support financial decision-making which is in the interests of the welfare and happiness of all citizens. Professor Hotson believed that a sovereign government should never borrow any money from any private bank. It should either issue the required new money into circulation through its treasury, or else borrow from its Central Bank at very low interest rates, while restraining or wholly eliminating private bank creation and destruction of money. Far from being inflationary, low and noninterest loans generated by the Reserve or Central Bank will always be less inflationary than the interest bearing borrowings by which the Government currently pays for the budget deficit. This can increase initial project costs by up to 2–4 times.

The Sovereignty Movement's central argument relates to historical examples of the success of the scheme. Our first example comes from Australia. The Commonwealth Bank of Australia (CBA) opened for business in January 1913 and financed the Melbourne Board of Works with one million pounds at 0.5 percent interest instead of 4.5% quoted from English private banks. In 1914 the CBA lent £350 million at 0.5 percent for the national war effort. The private bankers were furious and a campaign started, which culminated in the 1924 Bruce-Page Government's CBA Amendment Act, which took control from the Governor of the CBA and placed it in the hands of a sycophantic Board of Governors. This ensured the demise of the People's Bank.

Another example often cited by monetary reformers is the case of Guernsey. The Channel Island of Guernsey emerged from the Napoleonic Wars impoverished and with an accumulated public debt of £19,137, costing £2,390 in annual interest payments. It had a total revenue of no more than £3,000. Dealing with this problem, a state parliamentary committee recommended the monetarization of some of the physical wealth of the society. This involved a state note issue of £6,000 to be used to meet various public expenses, including coastal preservation works, Torteval Church and a public monument. The issue was in 1816, and the money was to be redeemed "from taxes in three stages up to April of 1818, by which time the whole issue would be cancelled. . . . the scheme worked" (Stuart, 1983, 63). A further issue of state notes occurred in 1824, 1826 and 1929 until there was approximately £50,000 Guernsey pounds in circulation. The experiment did not generate wild inflation, as many allege that more

radical schemes such as social credit would do.[8] The state finance committee "apparently found no difficulty in redeeming note issues when their
particular purpose had been fulfilled. Usually this was done by retrospec-
tive taxation enacted to cancel a credit – which is a different thing from
financing a debt . . ." (Stuart, 1983, 66).

Although recognizing the plausibility of the Sovereignty Movement's
arguments and agreeing with their goals in principle, we do not believe that
this movement has any reasonable chance of success. In the United States,
the proposed State and Local Government Empowerment Act, championed
by Congressman Ray Lahood (legislation which would provide local governments with infrastructure funds through interest free loans for the
building of capital projects) has, as far as we are aware, not seen the light
of Congress' day. In Australia, Economic Reform Australia (ERA), of
which we are members, has done an excellent job of circulating literature
as far as a shoe-string budget allows, but so far this debate has not attracted
media and political attention. And it will not, we predict. The Sovereignty
Movement has underestimated first the power of the international financiers and the weakness and growing economic impotence of the nation-
state and national economies. Although the economists associated with
COMER and ERA maintain a politically correct front by distancing themselves from social credit proposals, these organizations, even though they
are broadly left wing based, share the same philosophical base as Major
Douglas, believing that politicians of the nation-state can implement economic nationalist policies. However there does not seem to be the political
will to do this. In Australia for example, Economic Reform Australia,
dominated by the left, refuses to associate with nationalist parties such as
Australia First (with the sitting member, Graeme Campbell) and One Nation (with the sitting member, Pauline Hanson) because such individuals
are regarded as politically incorrect. On the other hand, as far as we can
ascertain as outsiders, neither of these political parties, although opposing
economic rationalism, has shown much capacity to foster deep fundamental economic thinking or even to capitalize on the Sovereignty proposals. It
seems to us, then, that economic nationalism has been defeated by economic globalism.

However, before the economic globalist celebrates final victory, we
need to back-track in our argument. The Sovereignty economists did not
advance their proposal as an optional extra, something which would be
nice to try. The proposal was advanced out of a sense of recognition of
economic and environmental necessity. This sense of urgency can be captured by many quotations that can be taken from ecologists and environmentalists (Earle, 1997; Gore, 1997; Hajari, 1997; Hallowell, 1997; Linden, 1997; Serrill, 1997; Thompson, 1997). But instead, let us quote the
words of a US industrialist, Bob Shapiro, CEO of the chemical and life

sciences company, Monsanto: "None of us today, whether we're managing a house or running a business, is living in a sustainable way. . . . If economic development means using more stuff, then those who argue that growth and environmental sustainability are incompatible are right. And if we grow by using more stuff, I'm afraid we'd better start looking for a new planet." (quoted from Gilding, 1997, 6). One of the core arguments for the Sovereignty proposal is that low interest loans would enable a financing of sustainable development to occur (Hotson, 1993). Many Western governments are failing to adequately address global environmental problems. Australian total greenhouse emissions by the year 2000, for example, are expected to be at least 50 percent higher than 1990 levels (*Environment South Australia*, 1997, 35). The Sovereignty proposal would enable economically-pressed governments to undertake major environmental repair programs, which private corporations are unlikely to do because of a lack of short-term profitability. These programs are necessary for the survival of civilized life (including the existence of the global economy itself). As Hotson puts it: "Could anything be more insane than for the human race to die out because we "couldn't afford" to save ourselves?" (Hotson, 1993, 171). Yet apart from the protests of a few environmentally aware industrialists and the familiar faces in the ecology/environmental movement, this is precisely what is being allowed to occur, and our pathos is greater given the economic unsustainability of our present financial system. We have already touched on this point; Professor Hotson outlines why this is so in more detail:

Why is the fractional reserve/debt money system unsustainable? With present institutions, prosperity, growth and ecological viability are not sustainable in the long run because of the excessive growth of debt and interest on debt. Throughout recent centuries the following pattern has manifested itself: real output only grows in years in which aggregate demand grows, demand only grows when the money supply grows, the money supply only grows when debt grows. The longer output, demand, money supply, and debt grow the higher the rate of interest becomes and the more excessive the growth of interest and debt. This pattern presents itself internationally as well as nationally, as unpayable Third World interest must either be added to unpayable Third World debt in ever greater resort to "Ponzi finance," (borrowing to pay interest) or the leading banks of the world must be declared insolvent.

If, in the attempt to arrest the price inflation resulting from the excessive rate of debt formation, the monetary authorities raise the rate of interest still higher the result is a financial panic. The panic, or potential panic, then requires monetary authorities to reverse themselves to bail the system out through greatly increased bank reserves, while governments are required to increase the public debt. The resulting inflation and deficits have too often been seen as "the" problem for decision makers to focus upon, rather than upon the far greater challenges of ecological breakdown, and the major changes humanity as a whole must make to achieve sustainable development. (Hotson, 1993, 173)

As we said earlier, debt and the interest on debt grows faster than the income available to repay the debt, so debt repudiation depressions (George, 1990; Adams, 1991) and economic crashes are an inevitable part of this system (Hotson, 1993, 174; Figgie and Swanson, 1993). Robert H. Hemphill of the Federal Reserve Bank of Atlanta in the 1920s and 1930s recognized this and said in the foreword to Irving Fisher's *100% Money*: "When one gets a complete grasp of the picture, the tragic absurdity of our hopeless position is almost incredible, but there it is. It is the most important subject intelligent persons can investigate and reflect upon. It is so important that our present civilization may collapse unless it becomes widely understood and the defects remedied very soon (quoted from Fisher, 1936, ii). The defects noted by Hemphill and Fisher have not been remedied, but rather have been intensified and globalized so that now instead of us having to worry about a national economic collapse, our concerns must be directed towards *global* economic collapse. If the Sovereignty argument is correct, this is our fate, although we cannot predict when.

We have argued in *The Bankruptcy of Economics* (Smith, et al., forthcoming) that there are other reasons for supposing that the global economic system is not sustainable (see also Smith, 1991a, b). These reasons relate to the theoretical and empirical inadequacy of the economic theory (not merely financial theory) – the neoclassical synthesis – upon which the operation of the global economy depends. There is an extensive literature documenting the theoretical inadequacies of neo-classical economics as a social theory attempting to supply a realistic model of the operation of economies (Sraffa, 1926; Bharadwaj, 1978; Boulding, 1978; Christensen, 1991; Cowen, 1993). Most importantly, the *laissez faire* idea that free markets lead to an optimum allocation of resources depends upon the idea that markets tend towards equilibrium and this idea has been challenged from a number of directions. The financier George Soros, for example, has argued that in financial markets (and these are highly important markets for the allocation of resources) the shape of supply and demand curves cannot be assumed to be given "because both of them incorporate expectations about events that are shaped by those expectations" (Soros, 1997, 48–50).[9] In financial markets, Soros observes, prices do not tend towards equilibrium, but are "chaotic" functions of the expectations of buyers and sellers. There are in fact "prolonged periods when prices are moving away from any theoretical equilibrium", and even if prices reach equilibrium, "the equilibrium is not the same as it would have been without the intervening period" (Soros, 1997, 50).

The dynamics of complex non-linear sytems and the abandonment of the equilibrium concern of neo-classical economics also characterizes *ecological* economics (Christensen, 1991). One major theme in ecological economics is the limits to growth, in particular that many economic models are incompatible with the laws of thermodynamics (Smith et al., 1997). Ecological economists have criticized neo-classical economists for their lack of concern about the interdependence between economic and ecological systems (Perrings, 1995) and their failure to recognize that an unregulated market economy has no mechanism or "invisible hand" capable of achieving ecological sustainability. In fact, there is a substantial literature indicating that the global economy is ecologically unsustainable because it has already overshot the carrying capacity of the planet (Smith, et al., 1997). Accepting the short-term *inevitability* of economic globalization as well as its long-term *unsustainability* leaves us with the necessity of accepting that a global economic collapse (Davidson and Rees-Mogg, 1992, 12–13) and an ecological collapse are unavoidable. Certainly the financial and alternative economic solutions based upon the economic and political viability of the nation-state are unsatisfactory given the virulence of the forces at work producing a "global meltdown" (Smith et al., 1998b). Our search for a sustainable economic basis for human society must be elsewhere.

THE ECONOMY OF THE TRIBE

F.A. Hayek, a famous economic libertarian and apostle of *laissez faire* (Soros, 1997, 48) alleges that continuous bouts of acute inflation and deflation are caused by the government monopoly of money as are "recurring waves of depression and unemployment" (Hayek, 1976a, 2,b). According to Hayek the government monopoly over the control of money has also meant a relaxing of the necessity of governments to keep their expenditure within their revenue, resulting in large historical increases in government expenditure. Hayek is strongly opposed to economic nationalism and supports the free mass movement of people over the globe: "Abolition of the monopoly of money would make it increasingly impossible for governments to restrict the international movement of men, money and capital" (Hayek, 1976a, 2). Here we have an excellent example of the triumph of ideology over science. Hayek starts with an anti-government pro-individual position (and there is nothing wrong with that provided one's value of commitments are open, which in this case is not so) and seems blinded to the fact that the control of credit is in *private* hands – private monopolies. The Bank of England and the Federal Reserve are *private* organizations which have a special relationship with their respective governments. Hayek, if he is to be consistent, must object to the monopolization of credit creation in general, whatever the source. His claim that "recurrent periods of depression and unemployment, are a consequence of the age-old government monopoly of the issue of money" (Hayek, 1976a, 2), is in fact an objection to monopolization in general. Indeed, Hayek himself notes that "bank deposits subject to cheque, and thus a set of privately issued money, are today of course a part, and in most countries much the largest part, of the aggregate amount of generally accepted media of exchange" (Hayek, 1976a, 18). Hayek rightly sees money as a cultural product like morality, language and law, which "emerge spontaneously" and therefore do not have to be "created" legal tender by governments. We will follow up Hayek's point about the social construction of money shortly. First however, we will elaborate upon the nature of this paradox seen in Hayek's position, and in economic libertarianism and globalization.

Economic libertarianism and *laissez faire* economics are opposed to legal and social restraints on individual economic freedom. According to this ideology, economic welfare is best produced by the unrestrained pursuit of individual self-interest. But what this ideology ignores is that even if all of this is true for a hypothetical world of libertarian atoms on a level playing field, it is not true of the real world. Individual differences soon produce inequalities. Individuals of almost all ethnic groups – excluding those of Anglo Saxon stock, who believe their own philosophical myths – tend to hunt best in tribes, and nepotism ensures advantages in the game of capitalism over those who play by the Marquis of Queensberry rules of individual isolation, obedient to the letter of the law and the WASP ethic of hard work. Those who play by the rules of individualism can be easily defeated by collective ethnic and tribal cooperation. Many of the recent migrants to Anglo Saxon countries, especially from Asia, soon learn (if they don't already know) that the way to succeed is to work together, to help one another, often developing an ethnic cash-in-hand economy which minimizes tax. Operating in this way, fortunes can be quickly made, real estate can be acquired and the stranger soon becomes the landlord and lord of the land. We are not making some moral judgment about this nepotism and tribalism; on the contrary it is a naturally superior way to operate and it is Anglo Saxons, not migrants who are deluded about the nature of the *realpolitik* of the workings of the world. Our point is that economic libertarianism is blind to the realities of race, religion and ethnicity, and will fail for this reason. Natural selection in the economic sphere will destroy those who follow the way of economic libertarianism, where others do not.

For the same reason, at the corporate level, a *laissez faire* economy is unstable in an evolutionary sense. The Darwinian game of competition soon leads to selection against companies as the stronger and the smarter defeat them, instigating amalgamations and takeovers. The principle of unrestrained greed and profit maximization soon puts selected firms on the path to market domination, and market domination is by definition the most secure way of maximizing profits. However efficient a firm operates, as long as a competitor exists, there are always profits that go to that competitor that could in principle go to the originally considered firm. Hence the evolutionary rise to dominance of today's Transnational Corporations (TNC) and their oligopolistic and sometimes monopolistic control of the global economy. Today's economic world is a far cry from the world of capitalism of Adam Smith, and yet the seeds of global economic domination are already present in the economic libertarianism of Smith. Even a phenomenon such as privatization – allowing private enterprise to perform some of the functions of government – is essentially a move towards the private monopolization of resources. The firms which usually succeed in obtaining government out-sourcing contracts or buying once-public amenities are large Transnational Corporations, which because of their size and economic strength, beat local firms. If they don't win, the option always exists for "swallowing whole" the local firm later by a takeover (Smith et al., 1997).

Deregulation, privatization and the elimination of protection are inevitable outcomes of the operation of the capitalist system, Ted Trainer (1997) has rightly argued. Marxists have believed that there is a tendency for the rate of profit to fall in capitalism, and Trainer believes this himself. It is not necessary to hold to this contested position to see that a capitalist economy invariably must evolve into a deregulated globalized system. Capitalism is committed to the search for ever-increasing profits – recall from neoclassical economics that the firm engages in profit-maximization. Ultimately all barriers to markets and resources must be dropped because such barriers stand in the way of profit maximization. Individual consumers are utility-maximizers and they must not oppose this process of economic penetration. The consumer does not receive as a reward thirty pieces of silver, but rather cheaper consumer goods which can be purchased while he/she still has a job. Deregulation naturally arises in a system where Transnational Corporations wish to gain access to resources and markets.

Earlier we promised to return to Hayek's observation that money is a social construction. In this we believe lies the key to the construction of an effective lifeboat for the tribes to survive the economic, social and environmental anarchy which the global economy is bringing and is set to bring increasingly to the world. Richard Douthwaite in his book *Short Circuit: Strengthening Local Economies for Security in an Unstable World* (1996) and Ted Trainer in his books *The Conserver Society* (1995) and *Towards a Sustainable Economy* (1996) have presented comprehensive surveys of grassroots economic strategies which communities can use to create a buffer against the *sturm und drang* of the global economy. Douthwaite and Trainer both summarize a wealth of material from anarchist environmentalist, devolution and "small is beautiful" traditions by which community economic self-reliance can be obtained and the global economy in turn "short circuited". The idea here is to build independent but parallel economies, where families and communities own their own means of livelihood. In other words, almost in a parody of Hayek, economic privatization is taken to its logical conclusion. Resources should be used to meet community needs rather than far-off markets so that the global economy does not decide what is produced. In general this involves: (1) the establishment of an independent currency system; (2) development of an independent banking system; (3) locally produced energy; (4) the local production of basics such as food, clothing and shelter, and (5) the recognition of the need to abandon the ideas of affluence and the growth economy and the acceptance of the ideal of "living within limits" (Hardin, 1993). In short:

> A sustainable world will not be one dominated by large companies and run according to the conditions necessary for maintaining international competitiveness and speeding economic growth. It will be one of small communities that run their own affairs and that, rather than trading across the globe, meet or make most of their requirements from their local resources. For it is only if communities develop cultures that enable them to live indefinitely within the limits of their own places that humankind as a whole will be able to live sustainbly within the limits of the natural world. (Douthwaite, 1996, 59)

Douthwaite and Trainer both document a number of ways in which communities can establish their own currency system, which have been tried and have proven successful, such as the LETS (local exchange/employment trading system), the biggest LETS system of which is in Australia. Other systems of decentralized banking have been tried in the past at various times and may be reimplemented (Ekins ed, 1986; Turnbull, 1986; Dauncey, 1988). Trainer in many respects goes further than this, documenting how self-sufficiency is possible to a much greater degree than at present at the family and individual level – green-left survivalism if you like. As people are chewed up and spat out of the mouth of the beast of the global economy, people will need to live simpler, much less materially affluent life styles as a matter of necessity rather than choice. This "downshifting" can be done and many people are now doing it. Necessity is a fertile womb.

The hope of the environmentalists who have developed the concept of a conserver society is that people by education will come to freely adopt ecologically sustainable lifestyles just in the nick of time to save humanity from environmental collapse and global anarchy. We do not believe that this hope is a realistic one (Smith, et al., 1997). A crash is inevitable and civilization as we know it cannot survive. This does not mean that the extinction of the human race is at hand, although this has been argued to be so (Leslie, 1996). The unit of human survival is the tribe, rather than the isolated individual; as Trainer observes: "The most secure people are those who have a tribe – many people close by who value them and who will give unquestioning material and emotional support the moment it is needed" (Trainer, 1995, 135). The survival of the tribes thus is intimately connected with the achievement of conserver life styles, and the construction of a conserver society ultimately depends upon the survival of the tribes, of racial, ethnic, religious and cultural diversity embodied in distinctive communities. It is the only remaining possibility for human survival against the coming ecological and economic tsunami.

Notes

CHAPTER 1: RAGNAROK! RACE, PLACE AND GLOBAL
ANARCHY AT THE END OF THE MODERN AGE

1. For more on this theme by the same core research team cf (Sauer-Thompson and Smith, 1996; Tanton et al., eds, 1996; Lyons et al., 1995; Smith, 1991a, b).

2. Whether the end of civilization is a good or bad thing is a philosophical problem in its own right. Ibn Khaldun in *The Muqaddimah* (i.e. *The Introduction* to his *Kitab al'ibar* or *History of the Arabs*), like a number of Western continental philosophers, sees civilization as a type of physical and spiritual "corruption":

> The goal of civilization is sedentary culture and luxury. When civilization reaches that goal, it turns toward corruption and starts being senile, as happens in the natural life of living beings. Indeed, we may say that the qualities of character resulting from sedentary culture and luxury are identical with corruption. Man is man only in as much as he is able to procure for himself useful things and to repel harmful things, and in as much as his character is suited to making efforts in this effect. The sedentary person cannot take care of his needs personally . . . He has no courage as a result of luxury and his upbringing under the impact of education and instruction. He has become dependent upon a protective force to defend him. He then usually becomes corrupt with regard to his religion, also . . . When the strength of a man and then his character and religion are corrupted, his humanity is corrupted and he becomes, in effect, transformed. (quoted from Brown, 1963, 466–7).

3. The work of Huntington and Harries has been criticized by defenders of the cargo cult of Asianization in the Australian print media.

121

The intellectual quality of the criticisms is embarrassingly poor. Richard Woolcott (1993) addresses Owen Harries' criticisms of Asianization by bluntly asserting that Australia must live with Asia for the rest of time because of the "inescapable reality of our geography". But he cannot maintain consistency for long, admitting that Asia is simply a "geographical term to describe an enormous part of the world" (Woolcott, 1993, 8). He then says that all countries' foreign policies are determined by the countries in question by decisions about how best to advance their national interests. All, except Australia's, of course. According to Woolcott, Owen Harries is talking nonsense that "could feed those dark fears and prejudices of racists who still look back with nostalgia to a white, essentially Anglo-Celtic Australia" (Woolcott, 1993, 8). Readers in countries other than Australia may be interested to know that Woolcott's style of argument, using "Racist!" as a debate stopper, is typical of the level of public policy debate in the Australian print media. Woolcott is a former secretary of the Department of Foreign Affairs and Trade and Ambassador to the United Nations and one would have expected a higher quality of debate. Much the same can be said about Greg Sheridan, *The Australian's* foreign editor, in his response to Owen Harries (Sheridan, 1993). Some "traditional-minded strategic thinkers" have become "unhinged" according to Sheridan. This is the fate of Owen Harries. In fact, Sheridan argues, the Harries/Huntington thesis is "farcical" because of conflicts *within* civilizations (Sheridan, 1996). This in itself does not refute the Harries/Huntington thesis, but it does undermine Sheridan's own cornucopian globalism which holds that there is nothing in the universe that can stop the growth of the Asian economies. God is alive and well and *is* Asia for Sheridan. But not only could Harries and Huntington give weaponry to the racists and the dying Anglo-Celtic culture of Australia, but they are advancing a "conspiracy" theory. At this point all debate must end: that is how things are done in Australia today.

Gerard Henderson (1997c) is equally contemptuous of Huntington's book. In particular he regards Huntington's claim that Australia's elites chose to "defect from the West" and Asianize as absurd. All that has occurred is that governments have worked to develop trade relationships with nations of the Asia-Pacific. Absurdity though lies on Henderson's, not Huntington's side of the fence. There is an enormous body of evidence indicating that Australia's business and intellectual elites have "defected from the West" and are quite content to abandon the old Australia which they look upon with contempt (Smith ed., 1991). A special edition of the American journal *The Social Contract*, forthcoming in 1998, will deal with this issue of Australia's identity crisis in depth.

It is worthwhile to mention these Australian media attacks on Huntington, who another Australian academic critic has described as "one of the world's most respected political scientists" (Catley, 1997, 75), because these attacks are symbolic of the poor quality propaganda and repressiveness of the Australian print media which regards any critic of the ruling elite's ideologies as an enemy to be smeared and destroyed at all costs. Fair deals are seldom given. We invite our overseas readers in the "international community" to investigate this matter and monitor the Australian press to confirm the truth of this claim.

4. Almost all societies in the modern world have been "multicultural" and "multiracial" in the sense of containing ethnic and racial minorities. Usually these minorities have been in small numbers and rightly or wrongly have existed on the margins of society. Modern Western multicultural and multiracial societies consist of large numbers of racial and ethnic groups, the total members of which constitute a significant proportion of the population, if not the majority statistically.

5. There is a growing body of literature in philosophy and socio-political theory on the nationalism question. A brief reading guide now follows: (Randle, 1970; Shafer, 1972, 1982; Ronen, 1979; Walzer, 1980a; Arndt, 1981; Anderson, 1983; Beitz, 1983; Gellner, 1983; Nielsen, 1983; Shue, 1983, 1988; Smith, 1983, 1988, 1994a; Cohen, 1984; James, 1984, 1989; Lohrey, 1984; Archer, 1985; Breuilly, 1985; Milner, 1987; Williams, 1987; Frankel, 1988; Miller, 1988, 1995; Stewart, 1988; Barth, 1989; Barry, 1989; Meadwell, 1989; Nathanson, 1989; Ward, 1989; Williams, 1989; Arnason, 1990; Bauman, 1990, 1992; Gilbert, 1990; Hoey, 1990; Jenkins, 1990; Turner ed., 1990; Wallerstein, 1990; Lind, 1991; Cantell and Pedersen, 1992; Hobsbawn, 1992; Pogge, 1992; Lukacs, 1993; Matustik, 1993; Dunn, 1994; Gilbert and Gregory eds, 1994; Gomberg, 1994; O'Neill, 1994; Rickard, 1994; Rorty, 1994; Verdery, 1994; Archard, 1995; Bader, 1995; Ignatieff, 1995; Jenkins, 1995; Lustick, 1995; Philpott, 1995; Rosas, 1995; Tamir, 1995; Thornton, 1995).

6. A recognition of the dilemmas of mass, non-discriminatory immigration to the West is now well entrenched in the academic literature (Hull, 1983; Barkan, 1992; Loescher ed., 1992; Black and Robinson eds, 1993). Marilyn Hoskin in her Book *New Immigrants and Democratic Society* (1991) summarizes the immigration dilemma as follows:

Signs that new immigrants are an increasingly significant feature
of contemporary life are everywhere. Ethnic-towns, once a
mainstay of large cities only, are appearing in small towns and
suburbs. Areas which had never witnessed cultural fairs or cele-
brations have been treated to demonstrations of international diversity. At the same time, neighborhoods which were once calm
and relatively homogeneous have begun to experience competition, tension, and even violence over foreign-owned businesses.
Schools are struggling to meet the linguistic and social needs of
children of foreign families. Nations which had prided themselves on their "open" societies have been stunned by the hostility with which immigrants have been met, and have found solutions to be elusive. (Hoskin, 1991, ix)

7. Ancient Egyptian painters and sculptors recorded, usually in color,
    the physical appearance of their rulers and people, and foreigners.
    Scores of Egyptian mummies and skeletons are also in the posses-
    sion of museums and scientists. All of this data reveals that the
    people of ancient Egypt were racially diverse, but with respect to
    generalizations many of the Egyptian upper class of ancient times,
    such as officials, courtiers and priests, look much like modern
    Europeans (Coon, 1939, 96). The skin pigmentation of ancient
    Egyptians was typically "brunet white", usually with brown eyes
    and dark brown or black hair. Queen Hetep-Heres II of the Fourth
    Dynasty, daughter of Cheops the builder of the great pyramid was
    blond and of Nordic appearance and her skin is portrayed as white
    in the colored reliefs of her tomb (Coon, 1939, 98). Later Egyptian
    reliefs also had representations of negroes but it is absurd to con-
    clude from this that the ancient Egyptians were "black". Of course
    this reasoning and source-reference are "Eurocentric" and "racist",
    but since we are all socially determined to believe what we believe,
    according to postmodernism, how could it be otherwise!

8. The reason why, if modern civilization collapses it will not rise
    again, has been given by Hoyle in his book *Of Men and Galaxies*
    (1964):

    It has been often said that, if the human species fails to make a
    go of it here on Earth, some other species will take over the
    running. In the sense of developing intelligence this is not cor-
    rect. We have, or soon will have, exhausted the necessary physi-
    cal prerequisites so far as this planet is concerned. With coal
    gone, oil gone, high-grade metallic ore gone, no species how-
    ever competent can make the long climb from primitive condi-

tions to high-level technology. This is a one-shot affair. If we fail, this planetary system fails so far as intelligence is concerned. The same will be true of other planetary systems. On each of them there will be one chance, and one chance only. (Hoyle, 1964, 64)

CHAPTER 2: THE FAILURE OF THE ENLIGHTENMENT PROJECT: THE BALKANIZATION OF EVERYTHING

1. Others have also recently proclaimed the death of Enlightenmentism. For example John Carroll in his book *Humanism: The Wreck of Western Culture* (1993) begins his text with these words:

    We live amidst the ruins of the great, five-hundred-year epoch of Humanism. Around us is that "colossal wreck". Our culture is a flat expanse of rubble. It hardly offers shelter from a mild cosmic breeze, never mind one of those icy gales that regularly return to rip men out of the cosy intimacy of their daily lives and confront them with oblivion. Is it surprising that we are run down? We are desperate, yet we don't care much any more. We are timid, yet we cannot be shocked. We are inert underneath our busyness. We are destitute in our plenty. We are homeless in our own homes.

    What should be there to hold our hands, is not. Our culture is gone. It has left us terribly alone. In its devastation it cannot even mock us any more, sneer at the lost child whimpering for its mother. That stage too is over. Our culture is past cruelty. It is wrecked. It is dead. (Carroll, 1993, 1)

2. Gray (1995, 193) quotes an insightful passage from John Lukacs' book *The Passing of the Modern Age* (1970) which illustrates our postmodern predicament:

    Centuries ago the Middle Ages were passing, without people noticing what was passing. The very term "Middle Ages" and the division of history into Classic-Middle-Modern Age did not become accepted notions until at least two hundred years after the waning of the Middle Ages. To us, the passing of the Modern Age and the recognition of its passing are much closer, at times so close as to be almost simultaneous. (Lukacs, 1970, 13)

3.   Janna Thompson in her book *Justice and World Order* (Thompson, 1992) sets out to present a philosophical account of international justice from a cosmopolitan perspective and this work provides a clear exception to Pogge's rule that modern moral philosophy takes the unit of evaluation as the individual. However Pogge's claim remains as a statistically true generalization rather than a universally true generalization. (Using quantifiers the difference is between "most *x*" and "all *x*"). Thompson is sympathetic to the idea of a world state or government (Thompson, 1992, 92) but ultimately embraces in her ideal world order a "world society of interlocking communities" (Thompson, 1992, 187) that could evolve into a world government in much the same way that nations evolved (Thompson, 1992, 92–4). There are many conceptual obstacles in the way of such a cosmopolitan theory. The first is *political realism* that sees the world as a conflict with states in competition for survival. According to the political realist, without a world government (and most political realists believe that a world government is impossible precisely because of the conflict of states) each state must look after itself. The Greek historian Thucydides expressed the political realist sentiment as follows: "they that have odds of power exact as much as they can, and the weak yield to such conditions as they can get" (Thompson, 1992, 2). Modern defenders of such a position often base their accounts on sociobiological accounts of innate human aggression. Thompson is skeptical about the evidential support of such theories but does recognize their explanatory attractiveness:

> What makes theories about the biological or psychological basis of human aggression and domination perennially attractive, in spite of their questionable scientific basis and their controversial nature, is the persistence not only of conflict and injustice, but of what can only be described as irrational hatred, blind ambition, ideological madness; and nowhere is human perversity more prominently displayed than in international affairs. (Thompson, 1992, 7–8)

The other major problem facing Thompson's cosmopolitanism is postmodern and communitarian critiques of universalistic morality that see the moral point of view as tied to local traditions, so that the independent standards sought by the cosmopolitan and universalist do not exist. She notes that communitarians and postmodernists usually accept a principle of tolerance, to accept difference and incommensurability, but she recognizes that if communitarians and postmodernists hold to a strong incommensurability thesis, then a theory of inter-community justice is impossible. She suggests that the world as a whole could be regarded as a community, as Walzer does in his book *Just and Unjust Wars* (1980b). The considerations of the present book refute, we believe, Thompson's latter suggestion. She does not succeed or even attempt the task of refuting political realism, communitarianism and postmodernism, which obviously would be too large a task for her book.

4. The literature on Nietzsche, nihilism and perspectivism/relativism is vast. For a sample consult (Pfeffer, 1965; Aschenbrenner, 1971; Wilcox, 1972; Schacht, 1973; Newman, 1982; Stack, 1982; Magnus, 1983; Schacht, 1983; Schutte, 1984; Nehamas, 1985; Bearn, 1986; Gilfedder, 1986; Janover, 1986; Stewart, 1986; Crittenden, 1988; Freeman, 1988; Fuchs, 1988; Holbrook, 1988; Mickunas, 1988; Williams, 1988; Martin, 1989; Norris, 1989; Ansell-Pearson, 1990; Basinski, 1990; Fowler, 1990; Koelb, ed., 1990; Poole, 1990, 1991; Wood, 1990; Aloni, 1991; Warren, 1991; Seigfried, 1992; Acampora, 1994; Ibanez-Noe, 1994; Owen, 1994; Berkowitz, 1995; Havas, 1995).

Nietzsche is often criticized by analytic philosophers for downgrading reason in human affairs and elevating the will to power as the redemption of mankind and the highest "reality" (Aschenbrenner, 1971, 103). In the context of the criticism it is interesting, and perhaps ironic to observe that one of the founding fathers of analytic philosophy (and a critic of Nietzsche), Bertrand Russell, accepts a similar view. In Russell's *Power: A New Social Analysis* (1975 – originally published 1938) power is seen as the engine of history; the fundamental motivations of human beings beyond a certain level are not economic or material (which are finite desires), but are based on the lust for power, an infinite desire. The ultimate human wish is for omnipotence. Consequently, the "laws of social dynamics are laws which can only be stated in terms of power . . ." (Russell, 1975, 9). Russell observes that reason and science "gave the white man the mastery of the world" and then makes a general point that reason itself is acceptable ultimately because of power:

> From this example, something may be learnt as to the power of Reason in general. In the case of science, Reason prevailed over prejudice because it provided means of realising existing purposes, and because the proof that it did so was overwhelming. Those who maintain that Reason has no power in human affairs overlook these two conditions. If, in the name of Reason, you

summon a man to alter his fundamental purposes – to pursue, say the general happiness rather than his own power – you will fail, and you will deserve to fail, since Reason alone cannot determine the ends of life. And you will fail equally if you attack deep-seated prejudices while your argument is still open to question, or is so difficult that only men of science can see its force. But if you can prove, by evidence which is convincing to every sane man who takes the trouble to examine it, that you possess a means of facilitating the satisfaction of existing desires, you may hope, with a certain degree of confidence, that men will ultimately believe what you say. This, of course, involves the proviso that the existing desires which you can satisfy are those of men who have power or are capable of acquiring it. (Russell, 1975, 95)

If it were possible to satisfy all human desires by prayer and magic, there would be little point in learning science and developing technologies. Russell having made this insightful observation then goes on to criticize power philosophies such as pragmatism, which he absurdly characterizes as the position that a belief is true if its consequences are pleasant (Russell, 1975, 175). It is of course easy to refute such a position as there can be unpleasant but "true" beliefs. Pragmatism is more accurately defined as the view that the criterion of truth is practical success.

5.   The problem of evil in a super-ultimate sense is an outstanding problem for Christian theology as well, although the problem is seldom examined in the necessary depth. Assuming that human freewill exists and that hard-determinism and fatalism is false – a large philosophical assumption (Thorp, 1980; Nozick, 1981, 291–397; Watson ed., 1982; Honderich, 1988a, b) – Christian philosophical apologists have attempted to show, with great ingenuity, that there is no logical inconsistency between the postulation of the existence of an omnipotent all-knowing, all-good God and the existence of evil. This is due to the freewill of humans, bringing about the Fall and the coming-into-being of natural evils such as sickness, death, entropy and biological systems based upon "survival of the fittest". Further back in time, the freewill of Lucifer is postulated to account for other evil. Now, the traditional *Genesis* story of the Fall cannot in itself explain away the existence of evil because of Adam and Eve's freewill because Eve ate from "the tree of the knowledge of good and evil", so logically before doing so she was morally innocent; after all, Adam and Eve did not notice each other's nakedness. Why would an all-loving father punish an innocent child for an act

of disobedience initiated in any case by an infinitely deceptive be-ing? Isn't it going overboard, if punishment is justified to condemn such beings to suffering and death? Why is it that Lucifer, for an act of rebellion is expelled from Heaven to become the negation of God in Hell? Why does an act of rebellion result in Lucifer, once an an-gel of light becoming *infinitely* evil? It may be true that the "higher they soar, the lower the fall, when they fall" but this would not ex-plain why Lucifer became infinitely evil nor does it give a genera-tive mechanism for this event. It cannot, under pain of contradiction be caused by an all-good God. Nor does this evil arise merely from the exercising of the power of freewill. Freewill merely means that the agent is not externally deterministically caused to do what she/he does. It is logically possible for an agent to have freewill, but even though of finite power, choose not to sin, disobey or rebel. The Catholics believe that the Virgin Mary is such a person. So the problem of evil cannot be explained by the postulation of freewill; it does not explain Lucifer's initial rebellion or Eve's fatal choice. It is not the capacity to freely choose which is the problem here, but the background causes. Why did Lucifer have the nature that he did? If he was the highest angel, then surely, even given his free-will, he had a design fault. The problem of evil lies in Lucifer's re-bellion, *not* in his freedom to rebel. This super-ultimate problem of evil is an outstanding problem for Christianity. There are of course other "problems" for the Christian, hoping to blend traditional Christianity (Heaven and Hell and all of that) with the politically correct ideologies of today, as Fleming observes:

> even a cursory inspection of the old Testament reveals a hair-raising series of murders and massacres apparently decreed by the Almighty himself. The worst war crimes of which the Serbs are accused are pretty small stuff compared with the treatment of the Sodomites who were evaporated simply for expressing their sexual diversity, or the Canaanites who were slaughtered as aliens in their own land (Fleming, 1996, 10)

For example, King David, a slayer of the enemies of the Lord, once massacred two hundred Philistines, castrated them and presented a pile of their mutilated genitals to their king, with the Lord's ap-proval.

The Old Testament asserts that there is an exclusive covenant between Yahweh and the children of Israel, and human history will be its testing ground, a claim which George Steiner believes is the "most stunningly audacious statement in the entire history of religion" (Conway, 1992, 32). Whether this is so or not, the Old Testament is a form of ethical particularism of a highly ethnocentric or "racist" nature (Exodus 19:5; 33:16; 34:16; Deuteronomy 7:1; 7:6; 14:2; 28:1). The New Testament itself, despite its cosmopolitan dressing given by St. Paul, is highly discriminatory as well: the "righteous" will receive "life eternal", disbelievers "everlasting punishment" (Matthew 25:46). This naturally leads to the interesting theological question: what is at fault, this ancient text and its teachings (which must be dismissed as sheer racism, dogmatism and bigotry) or the modernist and cosmopolitan standards of rightness that are smuggled into these arguments?

6. The "international" media were strangely silent – with but a few local exceptions – about the crimes against other blacks committed by the ANC in South Africa, including whippings and "necklacings". In a "necklacing", a motor tyre was placed around the neck of a black who did not support the ANC and the poor fellow was then burnt to death. The whipping of blacks by cruel white police under the Apartheid regime was rightly condemned, but not the whippings *allegedly* conducted by Winnie (Madikizela) Mandela (Reuters, 1991). Indeed, in September 1997 the British politican Emma Nicholson and the Scottish journalist Fred Bridgeland alleged that Nelson Mandela conspired to protect Winnie from charges of kidnap and murder (O'Loughlin, 1997). The international media were also silent about the rape of 48 schoolgirls in Soweto in 1990 (Barnard, 1991). Western liberals did not object to President Nelson Mandela's welcome to South Africa of Minister Louis Farrakhan, leader of the "Lost-Found Nation of Islam in the West", who was treated like a visiting Head of State. Farrakhan supports the creation of a separate African state as a homeland for African-Americans, out of the present United States. He wishes to see African-Americans become masters of their own destiny rather than a marginalized people. The idea that different racial and ethnocultural groups should have their own geographically, separate homeland was known in South Africa as *apartheid*, the policy of the Conservative Party of South Africa. Apartheid in this sense was never introduced into South Africa; instead of separate and equal development, ruling whites of the time pursued a policy of running a multiracial state on a "non-democratic" "inegalitarian" basis. "International opinion" concentrated its fire on the issue of race and ethnic separatism, giving the social economic conditions of blacks secondary concern. No comparison was ever made about human rights and economic conditions in the rest of Africa or the consideration of black tyranny in Africa (Ayittey, 1990). Moral condem-

nation by "international opinion" is, it would seem, arbitrarily selective (Conway, 1992, 172).

Marlene Goldsmith explores this issue in some depth in her controversial book *Political Incorrectness: Defying the Thought Police* (1996b). Apartheid was a "fashionable worry" but women and genocide don't seem to matter. She notes that "racism", compared to other human rights issues, is an odd issue to be singled out for special moral condemnation such as by sporting boycotts. But China brutally discriminates against its largest minority, women: "in China, independent women's organizations are banned, [many] women lead lives of misery and degradation in slave labor camps, sexual abuse is endemic in the army, free speech and political dissent are denied and result in imprisonment, and women are denied reproductive rights" (Goldsmith, 1996b, 34). She notes that the U.N. Fourth International Conference on Women was held in Beijing in 1995 but the U.N. urged the International Olympic Committee (IOC) to expel Rhodesia from the 1972 Olympic Games because Rhodesia was "racist". (Goldsmith, 1996b, 34). It is also worth mentioning the missing 600,000 Chinese baby girls per year who are probably missing because of female infanticide (Lewis, 1992, 206). As well, both the U.N. and the IOC were silent about the genocide occurring in Pol Pot's Kampuchea, now Cambodia:

> Following the Khmer Rouge seizure of power in 1975 and murder of more than one million people, the United Nations Human Rights Commission stated that the regime had carried out, in the words of Alex Mitchell, 'the worst genocidal crimes to have occurred anywhere in the world since Nazism'. The U.N. has now eliminated reference to the Khmer Rouge genocide and refers only to 'policies and practices of the recent past'. This is hypocrisy at its worst. What was genocide in 1975 is still genocide, and the Khmer Rouge is still the Khmer Rouge. (Goldsmith, 1996b, 34–5)

7. Adam Smith in *The Theory of Moral Sentiments* captures in an insightful paragraph one of the basic proposals of biological particularism, that contrary to universalism the degree of sympathy at least *prima facie*, rapidly diminishes with distance

> Let us suppose that the great empire of China, with all its myriads of inhabitants, was suddenly swallowed up by a earthquake, and let us consider how a man of humanity in Europe, who had no sort of connexion with that part of the world, would be af-

fected upon receiving intelligence of this dreadful calamity. He would, I imagine, first of all, express very strongly his sorrow for the misfortune of that unhappy people, he would make many melancholy reflections upon the precariousness of human life, and the vanity of all the labours of man, which could thus be annihilated in a moment. He would too, perhaps, if he was a man of speculation, enter into many reasonings concerning the effects which this disaster might produce upon the commerce of Europe, and the trade and business of the world in general. And when all this fine philosophy was over, when all these humane sentiments had been fairly expressed, he would pursue his business or his pleasure, take his repose or his diversion, with the same ease and tranquility, as if no such accident had happened. The most frivolous disaster which could befall himself would occasion a more real disturbance. If he was to lose his little finger tomorrow, he would not sleep tonight; but, provided he never saw them, he will snore with the most profound security over the ruin of a hundred million of his brethren, and the destruction of that immense multitude seems plainly an object less interesting to him, than this paltry misfortune of his own. (Smith, 1976, 136–7)

8.   Although Singer's universalistic utilitarian ethics seem non-discriminatory and otherwise politically correct, there are problems facing utilitarianism with respect to universal holocaust production. *Positive utilitarians* – who believe that the goal of ethics is utility or happiness production – must show what is wrong with the position of *negative utilitarianism* – that the goal of ethics is unhappiness-elimination. John Leslie, in various articles and especially in his book *The End of the World* (Leslie, 1996), has thrown down the challenge to utilitarians to show, from a negative utilitarian perspective, what is wrong with the *painless* genocide of the human race, which certainly seems to solve the problem of unhappiness-elimination albeit in a most radical way.

9.   Liberalism and left thought are concerned with freedom from domination and exploitation and the desire for a "powerless" world. Roger Scruton has argued that this quest is incoherent: "The condition of society is essentially a condition of domination, in which people are bound to each other by emotions and loyalties, and distinguished by rivalries and powers. There is no society that dispenses with these human realities, nor should we wish for one since it is from these basic components that our worldly satisfactions are composed" (Scruton, 1985, 193–4). Scruton quotes Kenneth Minogue on this point: ". . . the worm of domination lies at the heart of

what it is to be human, and the conclusion faces us that the attempt to overthrow domination, as that idea is metaphysically understood in ideology, is the attempt to destroy humanity" (Minogue, 1985, 226).

CHAPTER 3: SHIPWRECKED BY THE LAUGHTER OF THE-GODS: THE EPISTEMOLOGICAL LIMITS OF UNIVERSALISM

1. This chapter reworks and updates material which first appeared in *The Bankruptcy of Economics* (Smith et al., 1998a). We cannot address here in any useful depth the multitude of metaphysical, ontological and epistemological problems, all unsolved and probably unsolvable, in the foundations of logic and mathematics. See: (Quine, 1963; Loux, ed., 1970; Linsky, ed., 1971; Lewis, 1973; White, 1975; Geach, 1976; Armstrong, 1978a, b; Parsons, 1979, 1980; Sellars, 1979; Field, 1980; Platts, eds, 1980; Salmon, 1981; Kitcher, 1983; Zalta, 1983; Neale, 1990; Luntley, 1991; Casati and Varzi, 1994; Mühlhölzer, 1995).

2. Read (1988) defines *relevant* as follows: two propositions are logically relevant if the *fusion* of one with the contradictory of the other cannot both be true (Read, 1988, 135). The fusion relation binds two propositions together in a way more intimately than extensional conjunction. Thus Read must characterize this relation in ways distinct from "&". To do this by means of implication, taking "A X B" (read: A fusion B) to be equivalent to "$\sim (A \rightarrow \sim B)$" is circular. Read believes that fusion should be characterized relative to an algebraic operation on premises satisfying various structural conditions. This theory is not developed in sufficient detail to assess whether or not it provides a satisfactory general account of the concept of "relevance" or "relevant".

3. L.F. Johnson in his book *Focusing on Truth*, says about Tarski's semantic conception of truth:

> The semantic definition of truth does not give us a criterion of truth, and it is not intended to. In a sense, we might say that it does not even give us a definition of truth. Rather, *we* give it a definition of truth, which we build into the satisfaction-specifications. We specify that 'x is white' is satisfied by sequences starting with snow and not those starting with coal, because snow is white and coal is not. This is *not* to say that we presuppose some definition of truth on the basis of which we find that 'Snow is white' is true. Instead, Ramsey-like, we de-

pend on our knowledge of snow and coal, which includes knowing that one is white and the other is not. It is out of such bits that we construct our definition of truth. (Johnson, 1992, 97)
Unfortunately on the standard account of "knowing", knowing that snow is white presupposes the truth of the proposition that snow is white, so the semantic definition of truth on Johnson's account does not give us a definition of truth.

CHAPTER 4:   COMING TOGETHER AND FALLING APART: THE FAILURE OF THE ONE-WORLD DREAM

1. Finkielkraut observes that UNESCO's opposition to "racist" thought went so far as to reject *a priori* any thought giving any serious cognitive attention to race. In 1971 at a UNESCO conference to open the international year for the struggle against racism, Lévi-Strauss again argued that race depended upon culture. However even this was enough to condemn him of heresy by the gathered politically correct, because he was allegedly letting the wolf in by the back door (Finkielkraut, 1988, 78).
2. Other examples of advocates of the one-world dream have been mentioned in chapter 2 of this book.
3. Belloc, like James Burnham (1941), saw the formation of a "managerial state" or "servile state" producing a society with a more powerful capitalist class than existed previously and where ordinary people have lost their legal freedom and become subject to compulsory labor, that is slavery (Belloc, 1977, 28). Robert Nisbet notes in his introduction to Belloc's book that, "Such a state rests economically only upon its capacity for taking wealth from large numbers of people as the means of supporting . . . the rising number of those who are in a real sense parasites" (Belloc, 1977, 24).
4. In general, nationalism and Marxism are philosophically incompatible (Connor, 1984, 5). Unless it suits the ends of power politics (Stalin, 1945), nationalism has been seen by Marxists as a bourgeois ideology used by the ruling class to divert the working class from realizing its class interests. This claim is not carried to its logical conclusion and made against internationalism; socialists of all shapes and colors look forward to the withering away of nationalism and the internationalization of culture and social life (Tamedly, 1969; Smith, 1990) provided that this process occurs in the evil West. The left and socialists though have often been strong

supporters of nationalist movements in the Third World, completely ignoring the excesses of any such movements.

5. According to F. Knelman in *Anti-Nation* (1978), a sustainable society is "anti-nation", "Including in its organizational structures, built-in mechanisms to ensure the ultimate withering away of its own national identity and its merging into an inter-and trans-national global community" (Knelman, 1978, 135). Further, "Anti-nation is a state which espouses powerlessness, which divests itself of flags and anthems, armies and "intelligence" services, which disposes of class power, male power, money power and white power" (Knelman, 1978, 136). We welcome Knelman and his ilk to be the first to live in such a "State".

6. The philosopher Joseph Agassi (1990) sees the need for an organization which would decide which disputes are legitimate and which are not, and when it declares a disagreement illegitimate, the dispute loses its credibility (Agassi, 1990, 217). Agassi has spent much of his time developing and defending the work of the philosopher of science Karl Popper, supporting critical reason, falsificationism and open debates. Where is this concern here? How can any public body decide which disputes are legitimate and which are not, thereby ruling-out of court, by definition, continual rational assessment by present and future humanity?

7. Henderson (1997a, 24) is easily able to destroy Mel Gibson's claim, rightly observing that the Fabian society has trouble keeping itself together. More sophisticated conspiracy theorists have used former Australian Prime Minister Paul Keating's address to the Victorian Fabian Society (November 11, 1987) as evidence of a Fabian-caused conspiratorial decline of Australia. Keating said: "Within my portfolio eventual party support for financial deregulation, the float of the dollar and foreign bank entry stand out as relevant examples. These were measures undertaken not to make some foreign exchange dealer a big salary or to fatten the balances of entrepreneurs. *They were taken to integrate the Australian economy with the rest of the world*" (Lee, 1991, 44 emphasis added). The sophisticated conspiracy theorist could argue that it is Fabian *principles* rather than the actual Fabian *society* which play the role that Gibson identified. Obviously enough, making this debating point does not commit us to accepting Gibson's conspiracy theory.

8. A small sample of the literature of conspiracy from extreme left to moderate to extreme right includes (Barruel, 1797–1798; Robison, 1798; Webster, 1919, 1921, 1924; Schwartzchild, 1947; Skousen, 1958, 1970; Kelly, 1969; Allen, 1971, 1987; Davis ed., 1971; Billington, 1980; Eringer, 1980; Ferguson, 1980; Sutton, 1985;

Wurmbrand, 1986; Perloff, 1988; Still, 1990; Davies, 1992; Crozier, 1993; Guyatt, 1996; Icke, 1996). The definitive book on conspiracy theories has yet to be written.

9. The most quoted extract in the global conspiratorial literature may
well be Richard Gardner's claim that to build a new world order "an
end run around national sovereignty, eroding it piece by piece, will
accomplish much more than the old-fashioned frontal assault"
(Gardner, 1974, 558).

10. The literature on the alleged global conspiracy is typically produced
by American fundamentalist Protestants. Although it would seem at
first glance that a conspiracy theory would allow room for intervention by human action, within the tight self-reinforcing structure of
their theories, there is no hope for change apart from divine intervention. The reason seems to be because the grand conspiracy is a
conspiracy by Satan against God. The coming collapse, predicted in
this book (and argued to be due to material forces) is really only the
coming of the horsemen of the apocalypse. This millenarian position, judging from comments on the Internet, holds that all of this
will unfold in the next two years, and God, a lover of special numbers, will bring about an end of human history in the year 2000.
Some millenarianists claim that Christ will reign on Earth for one
thousand years, after which another cosmic battle between good and
evil will occur, and then the human story will end (Cohn, 1970,
1993). The interesting thing about this hypothesis is that it has a
"use-by" date and is thus falsifiable. It is of course always possible
to explain away the failure of the Second Coming by any number of
ad hoc hypotheses but not without considerable embarrassment.
Fundamentalists, mystics and prophets will be severely tested
within the space of the next two years.

11. Sturgess notes that migration and tribalism have themselves played
an important role in diminishing the geo-political significance of the
nation-state:

> Joel Kotkin has written about the "global tribes" – transna-
> tional economic networks built on a sense of ethnic and relig-
> ious solidarity – which have played a vital role in the creation of
> a global economy. Joseph Assaf, managing director of Sydney-
> based Ethnic Communications, has spoken of these networks as
> "cultural States" – "global confederacies which transcend tradi-
> tional political and tribal confines".
>   One of the reasons why Sydney is Australia's global city is
> because of these confederacies. For example, they were ex-
> ploited (successfully) in Sydney's bid for the 2000 Olympics.

These developments have led to a great deal of speculation about the future of sovereign nation-States. And it is certainly true that we are rethinking the traditional concept of sovereignty as it relates to the nation-State. (Sturgess, 1996, 13)

12. The same argument can be made regarding the United Nations Convention on the Rights of the Child, which pro-family and conservative Christian groups across the globe have attacked on the grounds of being anti-family and disruptive of parental authority and discipline. Conservatives such as Professor L.J.M. Cooray see the Convention "as a whole biased towards the rights of children as against the duties and responsibilities of parents in rearing their children in a caring atmosphere" (Cooray, 1989, 10).

CHAPTER 5: ENDTIMES: BREAKDOWN AND BREAKUP

1. Echoes of the theme that the cause of social misery is bigness can also be found in Ralph Waldo Emerson's essay "Self-Reliance." In attacking the cult of travelling, Emerson defends the local against the cosmopolitan:

   ... the rage of travelling is a symptom of a deeper unsoundness affecting the whole intellectual action. The intellect is vagabond, and our system of education fosters restlessness. Our minds travel when our bodies are forced to stay at home. We imitate; and what is imitation but the travelling of the mind? Our houses are built with foreign taste; our shelves are garnished with foreign ornaments; our opinions, our tastes, our faculties, lean and follow the Past and the Distant. The soul created the arts wherever they have flourished. It was in his own mind that the artist sought his model. It was an application of his own thought to the thing to be done and the conditions to be observed. And why need we copy the Doric or the Gothic model? Beauty, convenience, grandeur of thought, and quaint expression are as near to us as to any. (Emerson, 1911, 62)

2. D'Arcy Wentworth Thompson in his classic *On Growth and Form* formulates the "scale/size" principle as follows:

   The effect of *scale* depends not on a thing in itself, but in relation to its whole environment or milieu; it is in conformity with the thing's "place in Nature," its field of action and reaction in the Universe. Everywhere Nature works true to scale, and everything has its proper size accordingly. Men and trees, birds and fishes, stars and star-systems, have their appropriate dimensions, and their more or less narrow range of absolute magnitudes. (Thompson, 1942, 24)

3. The role of right wing economic think-tanks in the promotion of economic rationalism and globalization is discussed in detail by Richard Cockett in *Thinking the Unthinkable: Think-Tanks and the Economic Counter-Revolution — 1931–83* (1994).

4. The top Asian banker Philip Tose, chairman of Peregrine Investments (Asia's largest investment bank outside of Japan), caused outrage, in a speech delivered to an audience of Harvard Business School alumni at a Hong Kong conference when he said that democracy was the reason why India has failed to achieve its economic goal of becoming a regional superpower, whereas China had succeeded. Democracy is bad for the economy. Similarly he argued that the introduction of universal suffrage in the United States in the 1960s through Lyndon Johnson's civil rights legislation had weakened the US economy (Sheridan, 1997). This type of anti-democratic "racist" thinking is apparently common among senior businessmen and government leaders in Asia. Yet we in Australia are told by our elite that we cannot have a debate about immigration, multiculturalism and Asianization (let alone do something about them) as it may offend our sensitive Asian neighbours. Hypocrisy is one ingredient which is not scarce in our global village.

5. The Latin word for money is *pecus*, meaning cattle (from the Latin *pecus* comes the modern word *pecuniary*). Money at the dawn of civilization was originally issued in ticket form using leather discs. However, later in history rare metals such as gold and silver came to be regarded as wealth. They were deposited with goldsmiths for safe keeping. The goldsmith in return issued receipts against these deposits. People found that it was more convenient to do business with the receipts themselves rather than to draw the gold or silver out of the goldsmith's safe. The receipts themselves became money because people had faith that at any time they could recover their gold or silver from the goldsmiths. In time the goldsmiths found that because some people left their precious metals with them indefinitely it was possible to issue more receipts than the wealth deposited with them: that is, they could create money. All would go well providing a safety margin of precious metal was kept in the vaults adequate to cope with the demands of withdrawals (Hilton, 1994).

6.   In August 1988 the Reserve Bank of Australia established capital adequacy requirements to ensure stability in the Australian banking system by requiring that an adequate level of capital is maintained so that banks can deal with losses, especially from credit risks, consistent with the international standards of the Basle Committee on Banking Regulations and Supervisory Practices. Australian banks are required to have a ratio of capital (consisting of "Tier 1" and "Tier 2" capital) to risk-adjusted assets and off-balance sheet exposures, on a risk-weighted basis of 8 percent. At least half of this must be Tier 1 capital consisting of ordinary capital, paid-up non-cumulative irredeemable preference shares, retained earnings, reserves (other than asset revaluation reserves), minus goodwill and other intangible assets. From September 30, 1992 Tier 1 capital also must include net future income tax benefits if the future income tax benefits are greater than deferred income tax liability. Tier 2 capital comprises asset revaluation reserves, a general category for doubtful debts, hybrid debt/equity instruments and subordinated term debt having an original maturity of at least 7 years (paraphrased from National Australia Bank, 1992, 103). From both Tier 1 and Tier 2 capital are deducted net assets in "non-consolidated" controlled entities and the holdings of other banks' capital instruments. The situation then is more complex than that popularized by monetary heretics from both the left and the right who have as their motif that banks "create money out of nothing."

7.   Frederick Soddy, Nobel Laureate in chemistry (1921), saw the threatened collapse of Western civilization as arising from its false money system (Soddy, 1926, 1931, 1934). Although a brilliant scientist, Soddy's economic works were bitterly resented by economists of his time and he was regarded by them as a heretic and a crank. However his work has been rediscovered by ecological economists (Daly 1980; Kauffman ed., 1986; Hattersley, 1988, Martinez-Alier, 1993) where it is beginning to receive a sympathetic reading.

Soddy begins his critique of the economic system with the idea that the problem of producing wealth has been solved by modern technology. The problem which has not been solved is that of distributing wealth. Money distributes wealth in the community. Yet the monetary system in Britain in the 19th century went from a public system with the Realm having supreme authority in the creation of credit to a system of privatization with money being created by private entities and lent at interest, Soddy says. The private creation of wealth, according to Soddy "represents a debt of goods owed to the individuals who own it, by the nation, enforceable by the law, which has, without the sanction of any national authority, been quietly added to the burdens of the nation by methods that resemble the tricks of the conjuror" (Soddy, 1926, 20). The real nature of wealth is material, things that can be used and consumed rather than abstract things that can be lent at interest. Wealth is subject to the operation of the second law of thermodynamics and is capable of being degraded and destroyed. Debts are immortal until repaid; they are legal claims to future wealth. What is taken as wealth by orthodox economists is often a form of communal debt (Soddy, 1926, 27); in fact defining "wealth" by means of the term "money" is logically circular. For Soddy a definition of "wealth" in the first instance must be based on those physical requisites which enable human life to exist. Soddy then attempted to produce a biophysical foundation for economics which anticipated some of the work done by contemporary ecological and environmental economics (for more details: Smith et al., 1997).

C.H. Douglas and the Social Credit school have been even more strongly criticized by orthodox economists and in many respects their technical objections to Douglas' work have been correct. Galbraith notes that Major Douglas anticipated Keynes, as Keynes himself observed (Galbraith, 1975, 236). (The reader may also be interested in Galbraith's observation, following Joan Robinson that "Hitler had already found how to cure unemployment before Keynes had finished explaining why it occurred" (Galbraith, 1975, 238) – the cure being building up a destructive military machine!) We offer a brief account and evaluation of Social Credit here (Douglas, 1974, 1979a, b)

Douglas claimed to have identified an important defect with the production system. There are really only three alternative policies with respect to a world economy:

(1)   It is an end in itself for which man exists.
(2)   While not an end in itself, it is the most powerful means of constraining the individual to do things he does not want to do i.e. it is a system of government.
(3)   Economic activity is simply a functional activity of people in the world; that the end of man, while unknown, is something towards which most rapid progress is made by the free expansion of individuality.

The first two policies appear to predominate in today's world. Considered as a means of making people work the existing financial system is probably nearly perfect. Its banking system, methods of taxation and accountancy counter every development of applied science, organisation and machinery, so the individual, instead of obtaining the benefit of these advances in the form of higher civilization and greater leisure, is merely enabled to do more work if she/he has a job at all. Considered as a mechanism for distributing goods, however, the existing financial system is radically defective, Douglas said. In the first place it does not provide enough purchasing power to buy the goods which are produced. Industry, in the process of production, does not distribute sufficient money to buy back its total product. The deficiency of purchasing power must progressively increase for three reasons, Douglas believed. The three reasons are:

(1) Interest is charged on money at its point of creation.
(2) The increasing complexity of products requires greater numbers of successive production stages, and therefore money cycles.
(3) Increasing mechanization reduces the wages paid.

From point (3) Douglas saw that increasing unemployment is a natural consequence of the system, and that the concept of "full employment" is clearly ludicrous.

Social Credit is a Christian economic philosophy. Under Social Credit, money must have a life and death cycle that reflects the reality of physical production, in order that man might live in harmony with God. In a Christian economy money is brought into life to finance production and cancelled out of existence when production is consumed. If money is to serve ultimate reality, and become a means of allowing each individual access to that ultimate reality, *it must be created free of debt.*

The only possibility of liberating people from the soul-destroying burden of useless routine labor or mechanical work better done by machines, and the even more soul-destroying burden of unemployment, is by distributing the "wages of the machine" to all, as our share in the cultural inheritance – Douglas' national dividend. This would require the use of debt-free credit, not in unlimited amounts, but precisely to the amount required for the cancelling of debts and which would otherwise be met by borrowing, expenditure cuts and retrenchments.

Douglas stipulated the following principles which must govern any reform of the financial system:

(1) That the cash credits of the population of any country shall at any moment be collectively equal to the collective cash prices for consumable goods for sale in that country.

(2) That the credits required to finance production shall be supplied, not from savings, but by new credits relating to new
production.

(3) That the distribution of cash credits to individuals shall be
progressively less dependent upon employment. That is, the
dividend shall progressively displace the wage.

The major theoretical defect in the Douglas Social Credit system (apart from its philosophical basis being unrealistic for a
"fallen" world) relates to Douglas' justification of the claim that
people suffer from a deficiency of purchasing power. This is not
caused merely by the private banks' monopolization of credit, but
stems from Douglas' infamous A + B "theorem". The A + B
"theorem" is an argument as to why income distributed with respect
to production over a given time period cannot buy the whole of
production, so that the total purchasing power is always less than
the whole of production. Consider a firm F. Costs are assumed to be
wages, salaries and dividends (A) plus depreciation of the industrial
base (B). A is income, purchasing power is A–B, so purchasing
power is insufficient to discharge the cost (Monahan, 1967, 35).
Douglas believed that this deficiency in purchasing power led to inflation of costs and prices and to wage and salary increases
(Monahan, 1967, 35), but there is no reason an alleged deficiency in
purchasing power would be inflationary if it exists in every sector of
the economy, which Douglas said it did. Further the claim that A
will not buy A + B for one factory, is not necessarily true of the
economy as a whole, especially when postindustrial services are
considered. Douglas seems to have committed the fallacy of com-
position. As well, so what if A will not buy A + B – a factory with
few workers and robots could produce enormously valuable technologies that the workers could not buy and would not need to buy.
As the A + B theorem is the basic technical result of the Douglas
system, its rejection means that Social Credit should be rejected in
its classical form (Colebatch, 1932; Lewis, 1935; Hiskett and
Franklin, 1939). Many of its insights could be defended on a more
modern basis by use of work discussed in this text. Supporters such
as the Catholic based Canadian *Michael* journal continue to accept
the Douglas books as canonical (Even, 1996).

There is also an anti-Semitism in the writings of Douglas and
even Soddy that a modern reader will find astonishing. Douglas is
best known for his support of a Jewish-Finance-One-World-
Government conspiracy theory. Soddy at times leans in such a direction. Martinez-Alier believes that Soddy exhibited only "run-of-

the-mill Eurocentrism and anti-Semitism" (Martinez-Alier, 1993, 142). However in Soddy's *Wealth, Virtual Wealth and Debt*, passages such as the following can be found:

> Hitherto in this field of high finance, the semi-Oriental cradled in the battleground between East and West, has been supreme. Before the development of science, the flood of mystical half-truths that inundated the Western world from this quarter had effectually subjugated it intellectually. The Westerner, in trying to assimilate and digest this exotic spiritual diet, entirely lost and, indeed, counted it well lost – any intellectual independence. He was fascinated and hypnotised by the iridescent bubble of beliefs blown around the world by the Hebraic hierarchy, and even now, long after the lancet of science has pricked the bubble and let in the light, the alleged doings of the chosen people thousands of years ago is still considered an essential part of everyone's education, whatever else of human story and achievement be omitted. It would be unwise to underrate the influence of a dominant force of this magnitude over people's lives in accounting for the inversion of science . . . (Soddy, 1926, 289)

The reader is free to make his/her own assessment of the soundness of Martinez-Alier's defense.

8. According to Clarence Carson in *Basic Economics*: "Inflation is simply an increase in the money supply. It is accomplished by debasing or devaluing if it is paper currency. In 20th Century American political lingo, inflation has been made to mean a general rise in prices. The rise in prices, however, is the effect; the increase in the money-supply – inflation – is the cause" (Carson, 1988, 95–6). By this definition of "inflation" (and we by no means reject the definition of inflation, say "inflation*," that means a general rise in the price level) there is the *potential* for inflation to arise in principle from any credit creation scheme. Whether this occurs in practice will depend upon the operation of a range of countervailing variables (Ormerod, 1995). The Sovereignty Movement argues that most inflation is caused by high interest bearing debt and that the social and environmental crisis facing humanity is far more serious than small potential inflationary trends.

9. A similar problem of logical circularity occurs in the ranking of production alternatives for "the calculation of return or profit involves valuation and, therefore, the ranking of the production alternatives cannot be independent of prices" (Bharadwaj, 1978, 53).

Bibliography

Acampora, R.A. (1994). Using and Abusing Nietzsche for Environmental Ethics. *Environmental Ethics* 16: 187–94.

Ackerman, B. (1980). *Social Justice in the Liberal State*. New Haven: Yale University Press.

Adams, P. (1991). *Odious Debts: Loose Lending, Corruption and the Third World's Environmental Legacy*. Toronto: Energy Probe.

Agassi, J. (1990). Global Responsibility. *Journal of Applied Philosophy* 7: 217–21.

Alexander, R. (1987). *The Biology of Moral Systems*. New York: Aldine De Gruyter.

Allen, D. (1991). *Fear of Strangers – and Its Consequences*. Garnerville, New York: Allen/Bennington.

Allen, G. (1971). *None Dare Call it Conspiracy*. Seal Beach, California: Concord Press.

Allen, G. (1987). *Say "No!" to the New World Order*. Seal Beach, California: Concord Press.

Almond, B. (1992). Philosophy and the Cult of Irrationalism. *Philosophy* 33: 201–17.

Aloni, N. (1991). *Beyond Nihilism: Nietzsche's Healing and Edifying Philosophy*. Lanham: University Press of America.

Anderson, B. (1983). *Imagined Communities: Reflections on the Origin and Spread of Nationalism*. London: Verso/New Left Books.

Anderson, M. (1992). *Imposters in the Temple: American Intellectuals are Destroying Our Universities and Cheating Our Students of Their Future*. New York: Simon and Schuster.

Anonymous. (1996/97). Let's Not Go Down Like New Zealand! *Monetary Reform Magazine*: 31.

Ansell-Pearson, K. (1990). Nietzsche: A Radical Challenge to Political Theory. *Radical Philosophy* 54: 10–18.

Antonsen, F. and Bormann, K. (1995). Problems in Time-Machine Construction Due to Wormhole Evolution. *International Journal of Theoretical Physics* 34: 2061–9.

Appiah, A. (1986). The Uncompleted Argument: Du Bois and the Illusion of Race. In: Gates, H.L. Jr. ed. *"Race", Writing and Difference.* Chicago: University of Chicago Press: 21–37.

Archard, D. (1995). Myths, Lies and Historical Truth: A Defence of Nationalism. *Political Studies* 43: 472–81.

Archer, M.S. (1985). The Myth of Cultural Integration. *British Journal of Sociology* 36: 333–53.

Archer, P. (1992). *The Australian Crisis: What Sort of Country are We Leaving Our Children?* Weston, New South Wales: The Author.

Armstrong, D. (1978a). *Nominalism and Realism: Universals and Scientific Realism.* Volume 1. Cambridge: Cambridge University Press.

Armstrong, D. (1978b). *A Theory of Universals: Universals and Scientific Realism.* Volume II. Cambridge: Cambridge University Press.

Arnason, J.P. (1990). Nationalism, Globalization and Modernity. *Theory, Culture and Society* 7: 207–36.

Arndt, H.W. (1981). National Identity. *Quadrant* 25: 27–30.

Asad, T. (1990). Multiculturalism and British Identity in the Wake of the Rushdie Affair. *Politics and Society* 18: 455–80.

Aschenbrenner, K. (1971). Nietzsche's Triumph Over Nihilism. *Ratio* 13: 103–18.

Aspden, H. (1969). *Physics Without Einstein.* Southampton: Sabberton Publications.

Aspden, H. (1972). *Modern Aether Science.* Southampton: Sabberton Publications.

Associated Press. (1997). Famine Toll Mounts. *The Advertiser* (Adelaide) September 30: 11.

Ayer, A.J. (1989). Someone Might Go Into the Past. *London Review of Books* January 5:6.

Ayittey, G. (1990). Black Tyranny: A Deafening Silence. *Readers Digest* May: 127–8.

Bader, V. (1995). Citizenship and Exclusion: Radical Democracy, Community, and Justice. Or, What is Wrong with Communitarianism? *Political Theory* 23: 211–46.

Bagnall, P. (1996). Where Have All the Time Travellers Gone? *New Scientist* July 6: 45.

Baker, L.R. (1987). *Saving Belief: A Critique of Physicalism.* Princeton: Princeton University Press.

Baker, M. (1997a). Mahathir Slams Currency 'Rogues' *The Age* July 25: B1–B2.

Baker, M. (1997b). Mahathir Compares Soros to 'Drug Dealers.' *The Sydney Morning Herald* July 28: 38.

Baker, R. (1997). Tiger, Tiger, Burning Out. *The Bulletin* October 14: 46.

146   *Bibliography*

Baker, T. (1995). Water Deal is Wrong, Wrong. *The Advertiser* (Adelaide) September 8: 15.

Balogh, T. (1982). *The Irrelevance of Conventional Economics*. London: Weidenfeld and Nicolson.

Bandow, D. (1996). Uncle Sam, International Nanny. *Chronicles* May: 16–18.

Barber, B.R.(1995).*Jihad vs. McWorld*. New York: Times Books/Random House.

Barbó, F.R. (1968). A Philosophical Remark on Gödel's Unprovability of Consistency Proof. *Notre Dame Journal of Formal Logic* 9: 67–74.

Barkan, E.R. (1992). *Asian and Pacific Islander Migration to the United States: A Model of New Global Patterns*. Westport, Connecticut: Greenwood Press.

Barnard, M. (1991). Have We Pushed South Africa Over the Edge? *The Age* March 5: 13.

Barrett, W. (1978). *The Illusion of Technique: A Search for Meaning in a Technological Civilization*. Garden City, New York: Anchor Press/Doubleday.

Barrow, J.D. (1991). *Theories of Everything: The Quest for Ultimate Explanation*. Oxford: Clarendon Press.

Barruel, A.A. (1798). *Memoirs Illustrating the History of Jacobinism*, 4 volumes. London: T. Burton.

Barry, B. (1989). *Democracy, Power and Justice: Essays in Political Theory*. Oxford: Clarendon Press.

Barth, F. (1989). The Analysis of Culture in Complex Societies. *Ethnos*. 54: 120–42.

Bartlett, S.J. and Suber, P. eds. (1987). *Self-Reference: Reflections on Reflexivity*. Dordrecht: Martinus Nijhoff.

Basinski, P.A. (1990). Nihilism and the Impossibility of Political Philosophy. *Journal of Value Inquiry* 24: 269–84.

Bates, S. (1997). Belgian Soldiers Acquitted Over Somali Child 'Roast'. *The Age* July 2: A17.

Batra, R. (1993). *The Myth of Free Trade: A Plan For America's Economic Revival*. New York: Charles Scribner's Sons.

Bauman, Z. (1990). Modernity and Ambivalence. *Theory, Culture and Society* 7: 143–69.

Bauman, Z. (1992). Soil, Blood and Identity. *Sociological Review* 40: 675–701.

Baumeister, R.F. (1997). *Evil: Inside Human Cruelty and Violence*. New York: W.H. Freeman and Company.

Baynes, K., Bohman, J. and McCarthy, T. (1993). *After Philosophy: End or Transformation?* Cambridge, Massachusetts: MIT Press.

Bearn, G.C.F. (1986). Nietzsche, Feyerabend and the Voices of Relativism. *Metaphilosophy* 17: 135–52.

Bechtel, W. (1993). The Case for Connectionism. *Philosophical Studies* 71:119–54.

Beitz, C.R. (1983). Cosmopolitan Ideals and National Sentiment. *Journal of Philosophy* 80: 591–600.

Beitz, C.R. (1994). Cosmopolitan Liberalism and the States System. In: Brown, C. ed. *Political Restructuring in Europe: Ethical Perspectives.* London and New York: Routledge: 123–36.

Bell, D. (1992). The Cultural Wars. *Quadrant* July–August: 8–27.

Bell, E.T. (1987). *Mathematics: Queen and Servant of Science.* Redwood, Washington: Tempus Books.

Bellamy, C. (1996). *Knights in White Armour: The New Art of War and Peace.* London: Hutchinson.

Belloc, H. (1977). *The Servile State.* Indianapolis: Liberty Classics.

Benda, J. (1969). *The Treason of the Intellectuals.* New York: Norton.

Benford, G. (1997). Breaking The Time Limit. *New Scientist* July 26: 54–5.

Bennet, W.J. (1992). *The De-Valuing of America: The Fight for Our Culture and Our Children.* New York: Summit Books.

Beran, H. (1987). *The Consent Theory of Political Obligation.* Beckenham, Kent: Croom Helm.

Beran, H. (1994). The Place of Secession in Liberal Democratic Theory. In: Gilbert, P. and Gregory, P. eds. *Nations, Cultures and Markets.* Aldershot: Avebury: 47–65.

Berkowitz, P. (1995). *Nietzsche: The Ethics of An Immoralist.* Cambridge, Massachusetts: Harvard University Press.

Berman, E. (1997). UNfair Bias. *The Australia/Israel Review* August 8–28: 6.

Berman, P. ed. (1992) *Debating P.C.: The Controversy Over Political Correctness on College Campuses.* New York: Laurel.

Bernal, M. (1987). *Black Athena: The Afroasiatic Roots of Classical Civilization* (Volume 1). London: Free Association Books.

Bernstein, R. (1994). *Dictatorship of Virtue: Multiculturalism and the Battle for America's Future.* New York: Alfred A. Knopf.

Berryhill, D.A. (1994). *The Liberal Contradiction: How Contemporary Liberalism Violates its Own Principles and Endangers Its Own Goals.* Lafayette, Louisiana: Huntington House Publishers.

Beshir, M.O. (1975). *The Southern Sudan: From Conflict to Peace.* London: Hurst.

Bharadwaj, K. (1978). *Classical Political Economy and the Rise to Dominance of Supply and Demand Theories.* New Delhi: Orient Longman.

Bickle, J. (1993). Connectionism, Eliminativism, and the Semantic View of Theories. *Erkenntnis* 39: 359–82.

Billington, J.H. (1980). *Fire in the Minds of Men: The Origins of the Revolutionary Faith*. New York: Basic Books.

Black, R. and Robinson, V. eds, (1993). *Geography and Refugees: Patterns and Processes of Change*. London and New York: Belhaven Press.

Bloom, A. (1987). *The Closing of the American Mind: How Higher Education has Failed Democracy and Impoverished the Souls of Today's Students*. New York: Simon and Schuster.

Bloom, H. (1995). *The Lucifer Principle: A Scientific Expedition into the Forces of History*. St. Leonards, New South Wales: Allen and Unwin.

Boulding, K.E. (1978). *Ecodynamics: A New Theory of Societal Evolution*. Beverly Hills: Sage Publications.

Boyle, T.C. (1995).*The Tortilla Curtain*. London: Bloomsbury Publishing.

Breuilly, J. (1985). Reflections on Nationalism. *Philosophy of the Social Sciences* 15: 65–75.

Brillouin, L. (1970). *Relativity Reexamined*. New York and London: Academic Press.

Brimelow, P. (1993). The National Question. *Chronicles* June: 19–20.

Broderick, D. (1996). The Lore of Nature. *The Australian* (Weekend Review) April 6–7: 8.

Broin,V.E. (1994). Separatism: A Political Strategy for Building Alliances. *Journal of Social Philosophy* 25: 228–40.

Bronner, M.E. (1997). The Mother of Battles: Confronting the Implications of Automobile Dependence in the United States. *Population and Environment* 18: 489–507.

Brown, G.B. (1976). Experiment Versus Thought-Experiment. *American Journal of Physics* 44: 801–2.

Brown, L.R. (1963). *The Might of the West*. New York: Ivan Obolensky Inc.

Browne, D. (1990). Ethics Without Morality. *Australasian Journal of Philosophy* 68: 395–412.

Bub, J. (1981). Hidden Variables and Quantum Logic – A Sceptical View. *Erkenntnis* 16: 275–93.

Buchanan, A. (1989). Assessing the Communitarian Critique of Liberalism. *Ethics* 99: 852–82.

Buchanan, A. (1991a). *Secession: The Morality of Political Divorce from Fort Sumter to Lithuania and Quebec*. Boulder: Westview Press.

Buchanan, A. (1991b). Toward a Theory of Secession. *Ethics* 101: 322–42.

Buchanan, M. (1997). Crossing the Quantum Frontier. *New Scientist* April 26: 38–41.

Buchheit, L.C. (1978). *Secession: The Legitimacy of Self-Determination.* New Haven: Yale University Press.

Bunge, M. (1985). *Treatise on Basic Philosophy* vol. 7, *Epistemology and Methodology* III: *Philosophy of Science and Technology* Part II, *Life Science, Social Science and Technology.* Dordrecht: D. Reidel.

Burgess, J.A. (1990). The Sorites Paradox and Higher-Order Vagueness. *Synthese* 85: 417–74.

Burgi, E.L. (1994). *Money Creation: The Great Confidence Trick.* Wandin: The Author.

Burnham, J. (1941). *The Managerial Revolution.* New York: John Day.

Burns, L.C. (1991). *Vagueness: An Investigation into Natural Languages and the Sorites Paradox.* Dordrecht: Kluwer Academic.

Butrick, R. (1965). The Gödel Formula: Some Reservations. *Mind* 74: 411–14.

Caiazza, J. (1997). The Paralysis of Science. *Chronicles* February: 28–29.

Cameron, D. and Finn, E. (1996). *10 Deficit Myths.* Ottawa: Canadian Centre for Policy Alternatives.

Cantell, T. and Pedersen, P.P. (1992). Modernity, Postmodernity and Ethics – An Interview with Zygmunt Bauman. *Telos* 93: 133–44.

Carey, G.W. (1996).Circumventions and Subversions.*Chronicles* February: 34–6.

Carroll, J. (1993). *Humanism: The Wreck of Western Culture.* London: Fontana Press/HarperCollins Publishers.

Carson, C. (1988). *Basic Economics.* Wadley: American Textbook Committee.

Casati, R. and Varzi, A.C. (1994). *Holes and Other Superficialities.* Cambridge, Massachusetts: MIT Press/Bradford.

Casti, J.L. and Karlqvist, A. eds. (1996) *Boundaries and Barriers.* Reading, Massachusetts: Addison-Wesley.

Castles, S., Kalantzis, M., Cope, B., and Morrissey, M. (1988). *Mistaken Identity: Multiculturalism and the Demise of Nationalism in Australia.* Sydney: Pluto Press.

Catley, B. (1997). Repicturing the World. *Quadrant* May: 75–6.

Cattell, R.B. (1972). *A New Morality from Science: Beyondism.* New York: Pergamon Press.

Chaitin, G.J. (1987a). *Algorithmic Information Theory.* Cambridge:Cambridge University Press.

Chaitin, G.J. (1987b). *Information, Randomness and Incompleteness: Papers on Algorithmic Information Theory.* Singapore: World Scientific.

Charlesworth, M. (1993). *Bioethics in a Liberal Society.* Cambridge: Cambridge Unversity Press.

150 *Bibliography*

Chatham, R.E. (1976). Consistency in Relativity. *Foundations of Physics* 6: 681–5.
Chihara, C.S. (1984). Priest, The Liar, and Gödel. *Journal of Philosophical Logic* 13: 117–24.
Chomsky, N. (1993). *Year 501: The Conquest Continues*. London: Verso.
Chomsky, N. (1994). *World Orders, Old and New*. London: Pluto Press.
Chown, M. (1992). Time Travel Without the Paradoxes. *New Scientist* March 28: 15.
Christensen, P. (1991). Driving Forces, Increasing Returns and Ecological Sustainability. In: Costanza, R. ed. *Ecological Economics: The Science and Management of Sustainability*. New York: Columbia University Press: 75–87.
Christie,D.(1993).Comments on Bechtel's "The Case for Connectionism". *Philosophical Studies* 71: 155–62.
Churchland, P.M. (1984). *Matter and Consciousness*. Cambridge, Massachusetts: MIT/Bradford.
Clark, G.L., Forbes, D. and Francis, R. eds. (1993) *Multiculturalism, Difference and Postmodernism*. Melbourne: Longman Cheshire.
Clark, M. (1987). The Truth About Heaps. *Analysis* 47: 177–9.
Clarke, T. and Tigue, J.J. (1975). *Dirty Money: Swiss Banks, The Mafia, Money Laundering and White Collar Crime*. New York: Simon and Schuster.
Cling, A.D. (1990). Disappearance and Knowledge. *Philosophy of Science*. 57: 226–47.
Cockett, R. (1994). *Thinking the Unthinkable: Think-Tanks and the Economic Counter-Revolution — 1931–83*. London: HarperCollins.
Cohen, A. and Dascal, M. eds. (1989). *The Institution of Philosophy: A Discipline in Crisis?* La Salle, Illinois: Open Court.
Cohen, J.E. (1995). *How Many People Can the Earth Support?* New York and London: W.W. Norton and Company.
Cohen, M. (1984). Moral Skepticism and International Relations. *Philosophy and Public Affairs* 13: 299–346.
Cohen, M. (1989). Simultaneity and Einstein's Gedankenexperiment. *Philosophy* 64:391–6.
Cohen, M. (1992). Einstein on Simultaneity. *Philosophy* 67:543–8.
Cohen, M. (1995). Simultaneity: A Composite Rejoinder. *Philosophy* 70: 587–9.
Cohn, N. (1970). *The Pursuit of the Millennium*. New York: Oxford University press.
Cohn, N. (1993). *Cosmos, Chaos and the World to Come*. New Haven and London: Yale University Press.
Colebatch, H. (1932). *Douglas Credit, Currency and Purchasing Power*. Sydney: The Sane Democracy League.

Commission on Global Governance (1995). *Our Global Neighbourhood.* Oxford: Oxford University Press.

Connelly, M. and Kennedy, P. (1994). Must it be the Rest Against the West? *The Atlantic Monthly* December: 61–84.

Connor, W. (1984). *The National Question in Marxist-Leninist Thought and Strategy.* Princeton, New Jersey: Princeton University Press.

Connor, W. (1994). *Ethnonationalism: The Quest for Understanding.* Princeton, New Jersey: Princeton University Press.

Conway, R. (1992). *The Rage for Utopia.* St. Leonards, New South Wales: Allen and Unwin.

Coon, C.S. (1939). *The Races of Europe.* New York: Macmillan.

Cooray, L.J.M. (1989). Warning on Child Abuse Rights. *The Australian* December: 10.

Cowen, T. (1993). The Scope and Limits of Preference Sovereignty. *Economics and Philosophy* 9: 253–69.

Crabb, A. (1997). Water Supply Under Threat of Salinity. *The Advertiser* (Adelaide) April 4: 7.

Crittenden, P.J. (1988). Perspectivism: The Nietzschean Point of View. *Dialectic* 31: 52–66.

Crouch, B. (1994). Gay Ruling New Can of Worms. *Sunday Mail.* (Adelaide) April 17: 46.

Crozier, B. (1993). *Free Agent: The Unseen War, 1941–1991.* London: HarperCollins.

Cullwick, E.G. (1981). Einstein and Special Relativity: Some Inconsistencies in his Electrodynamics. *British Journal for the Philosophy of Science* 32: 167–76.

Curry, H.B. (1942). The Inconsistency of Certain Formal Logics. *Journal of Symbolic Logic* 7: 115–17.

Daly, H.E. (1980). The Economic Thought of Frederick Soddy. *History of Political Economy* 12: 469–88.

Daly, H.E. and Cobb, J.B. (1989). *For the Common Good: Redirecting the Economy Toward Community, the Environment, and a Sustainable Future.* Boston: Beacon Press.

Danielson, P.(1992). *Artificial Morality: Virtuous Robots for Virtual Games.* London and New York: Routledge.

Dauncey, G. (1988). *After The Crash.* London: Green Print.

Davidson, J.D. and Rees-Mogg, W. (1992). *The Great Reckoning.* London: Sidgwick and Jackson.

Davidson, J.D. and Rees-Mogg, W. (1994). *The Great Reckoning: How the World Will Change Before the Year 2000.* London: Pan Books.

Davies, P. (1980). Why Pick on Einstein? *New Scientist* August 7: 463–5.

Davies, P. (1984). *Quantum Mechanics.* London: Routledge and Kegan Paul.

Davies, P. (1990). Time Travel: The Fact in the Science Fiction. *The Weekend Australian* July 21–22: 21–22.

Davies, P. (1995). *About Time: Einstein's Unfinished Revolution*. London: Penguin Books.

Davies, S. (1992). *Big Brother*. East Roseville, New South Wales: Simon and Schuster.

Davis, D.B. ed. (1971). *The Fear of Conspiracy*. Ithaca and London: Cornell University Press.

Davis, P.J. and Hersh, R. (1986). *Descartes' Dream: The World According to Mathematics*. London: Penguin Books.

De Alva, J.K., Shorris, E., and West, C. (1996). Our Next Race Question. *Harper's Magazine* April: 55–63.

Deas, R. (1989). Sorensen's Sorites. *Analysis* 49: 26–31.

De Lacey, P. and Moens, G. (1990). *The Decline of the University*. Tahmoor, New South Wales: Law Press.

Delgado, R. (1996). *The Coming Race War? And Other Apocalyptic Tales of America After Affirmative Action and Welfare*. New York and London: New York University Press.

Dench, G. (1986). *Minorities in the Open Society: Prisoners of Ambivalence*. London and New York: Routledge and Kegan Paul.

Dennett, D.C. (1981). *Brainstorms: Philosophical Essays on Mind and Psychology*. Sussex: Harvester Press.

Dennett, D.C. (1993). *Consciousness Explained*. London: Penguin Books.

Denyer, N. (1995). Priest's Paraconsistent Arithmetic. *Mind* 104: 567–75.

Derrida, J. (1982). *Margins of Philosophy*. Chicago: University of Chicago Press.

Derrida, J. (1988). *Limited Inc.* Chicago: Northwestern University Press.

De Silva, K.M. (1986). *Managing Ethnic Tensions in Multi-Ethnic Societies: Sri Lanka 1880–1985*. Lanham: University Press of America.

De Silva, K.M. and May, R.J. eds. (1991). *Internationalization of Ethnic Conflict.* London: Pinter Publishers.

Deutsch, D. (1997). *The Fabric of Reality*. London: Allan Lane/The Penguin Press.

Devlin, K. (1991). *Logic and Information*. Cambridge: Cambridge University Press.

Devlin, K. (1997). *Goodbye Descartes: The End of Logic and the Search for a New Cosmology of the Mind.* New York: John Wiley and Sons.

Dewald, W.G. (1969). Multiple Expansion of Bank Deposits Under Australian Institutional Conditions: Comment. *The Economic Record* 45: 293–6.

DeWitt, R. (1992). Remarks on the Current Status of the Sorites Paradox. *Journal of Philosophical Research* 17: 93–118.

Diamond, J. (1991). *The Rise and Fall of the Third Chimpanzee*. London: Vintage.

Dieks, D. (1988) Discussion: Special Relativity and the Flow of Time. *Philosophy of Science* 55:456–60.

Dingle, H. (1972). *Science at the Crossroads*. London: Martin Brian and O'Keefe.

Dixon, N.F. (1987). *Our Own Worst Enemy*. London: Jonathan Cape.

Douglas, C.H. (1974). *Economic Democracy*. Surrey: Bloomfield Publishing.

Douglas, C.H. (1979a). *The Monopoly of Credit*. Suffolk: Bloomfield Books.

Douglas, C.H. (1979b). *Social Credit*. Vancouver: Institute of Economic Democracy.

Douthwaite, R. (1992). *The Growth Illusion*. Bideford. Devon: Resurgence.

Douthwaite, R. (1996). *Short Circuit: Strengthening Local Economies for Security in an Unstable World*. Devon: A Resurgence Book/Green Books.

Dow, S. (1994). UN Gay Stance Will Reform Other Countries Too: Judge. *The Australian* April 11: 3.

Drange, T.M. (1990). Liar Syllogisms. *Analysis* 50: 1–7.

Dreyfus, H.L. (1979). *What Computers Can't Do: The Limits of Artificial Intelligence* (Revised edition). New York: Harper Colophon Books, Harper and Row Publishers.

D'Souza, D. (1991). *Illiberal Education: The Politics of Race and Sex on Campus*. New York: The Free Press.

D'Souza, D. (1995). *The End of Racism: Principles for a Multiracial Society*. New York: The Free Press.

Du Bois, W.E.B. (1992). The Conservation of Races. In: Brotz, H. ed. *African-American Social and Political Thought, 1850–1920*. New Brunswick, New Jersey: Transaction Publishers: 483–92.

Dunn, J. (1985). *Rethinking Modern Political Theory*. Cambridge: Cambridge University Press.

Dunn, T. L. (1994). Strangers and Liberals. *Political Theory* 22: 167–75.

Dyson, F. (1997). *Imagined Worlds*. Cambridge, Massachusetts: Harvard University Press.

Earle, S.A. (1997). Roll On, Deep Blue. *Time* (Special Edition) November: 34–7.

Earman, J. (1995). Outlawing Time Machines: Chronology Protection Theorems. *Erkenntnis* 42: 125–39.

Economic and Social Council, Commission on Crime Prevention and Criminal Justice (1996a). Measures to Regulate Firearms – Report of the Secretary-General. Vienna: Economic and Social Council. April 16: E/CN.15/1996/14.

Economic and Social Council, Commission on Crime Prevention and Criminal Justice (1996b). *Criminal Justice Reform and Strengthening of Legal Institutions – Measures to Regulate Firearms.* Vienna: Economic and Social Council. April 28–May 9: E/CN.15/1997/L.19.

Einstein, A. (1982). Aphorisms for Leo Baek. In: *Ideas and Opinions.* New York: Three Rivers Press: 27–8.

Ekins, P. ed. (1986). *The Living Economy: A New Economics in the Making.* London: Routledge and Kegan Paul.

Ekins, P. (1989). Trade and Self-Reliance. *The Ecologist* 19, September/October: 186–90.

Ellis, B. (1997). Rationalism? No, Lunacy. *The Sydney Morning Herald* July 7: 15.

Ellul, J. (1990). *The Technological Bluff.* Grand Rapids, Michigan: William B. Eerdmans Publishing Company.

Emerson, R.W. (1911). Self-Reliance. In: *Essays and Other Writings.* London: Cassell and Company: 43–66.

Environment South Australia. (1997). Greenhouse Debate Hots Up. *Environment South Australia* 6, 2: 35.

Epstein, B. R. and Forster, A. (1967). *The Radical Right: Report on the John Birch Society and Its Allies.* New York: Random House.

Eringer, R. (1980). *The Global Manipulators.* Bristol: Pentacle Books.

Esman, M. ed. (1976). *Ethnic Conflict in the Western World.* Ithaca, New York: Cornell University Press.

Essen, L. (1971). *The Special Theory of Relativity: A Critical Analysis.* Oxford: Clarendon Press.

Etchemendy, J. (1990). *The Concept of Logical Consequence.* Cambridge, Massachusetts: Harvard University Press.

Evans, G. (1993). *Cooperating for Peace: The Global Agenda for the 1990s and Beyond.* St. Leonards, New South Wales: Allen and Unwin.

Even, L. (1996). *In this Age of Plenty: A New Conception of Economics: Social Credit.* Rougemont, Quebec: The Pilgrims of Saint Michael.

Ewin, R.E. (1995). Can There be a Right to Secede? *Philosophy* 70:341–62.

Fairchild, H. P. (1947). *Race and Nationality as Factors in American Life.* New York: Ronald Press.

Ferguson, M. (1980). *The Aquarian Conspiracy.* Los Angeles: J.P. Tarcher.

Fetzer, J.H. (1990). *Artificial Intelligence: Its Scope and Limits.* Dordrecht: Kluwer.

Feyerabend, P. (1991). *Three Dialogues on Knowledge.* Oxford: Basil Blackwell.

Feynman, R. (1985). *QED: The Strange Theory of Light and Matter.* London: Penguin Books.

Field, H.H. (1980). *Science Without Numbers: A Defense of Nominalism.* Oxford: Basil Blackwell.

Figgie, H.E. and Swanson, G.J. (1993). *Bankruptcy 1995: The Coming Collapse of America and How to Stop It.* Boston: Little Brown and Company.

Finkielkraut, A. (1988). *The Undoing of Thought.* (Translated by Denis O'Keeffe). London and Lexington: The Claridge Press.

Fischer, S., Dornbusch, R. and Schmalensee, R. (1988). *Economics* 2nd edition. New York: McGraw-Hill.

Fisher, J. (1936). *100% Money.* New York: Adelphi Company.

Fleming, T. (1996). Treason Against the New Order. *Chronicles* August: 8–11.

Fleming, T. (1997). Other People. *Chronicles* March: 8–11.

Flew, A. (1994). The Terrors of Islam. In: Kurtz, P. and Madigan, T.J. eds. *Challenges to the Enlightenment: In Defense of Reason and Science.* Buffalo, New York: Prometheus Books: 272–83.

Fodor, E.V. (1997). The Real Cost of Growth in Oregon. *Population and Environment* 18: 373–88.

Fowler, M. (1990). Nietzschean Perspectivism: "How Could Such a Philosophy – Dominate?" *Social Theory and Practice* 16: 119–62.

Francis, S. (1992). The Growth of a U.N. Superpower is a Threat to Us. *Tennessean* (Nashville) December: 17: 15A.

Francis, S. (1993). *Beautiful Losers: Essays on the Failure of American Conservatism.* Columbia and London: University of Missouri Press.

Frankel, B. (1987). *The Post-Industrial Utopians.* Cambridge: Polity Press.

Frankel, B. (1988). National Chauvinism and Abstract Internationalism. *Arena* 82: 136–44.

Freedman, D.H. (1989). Cosmic Time Travel. *Discover* June: 58–64.

Freeman, D.A. (1988). Nietzsche: Will to Power as a Foundation of a Theory of Knowledge. *International Studies in Philosophy.* 20: 3–14.

Friedman, M. (1995). *What Went Wrong? The Creation and Collapse of the Black-Jewish Alliance.* New York: The Free Press.

Fuchs, W.W. (1988). Philosophy – Nietzsche – Philosophy. *Man and World* 21: 127–43.

Galbraith, J.K. (1975). *Money: Whence It Came, Where It Went.* Boston: Houghton Mifflin.

Galtung, J. (1979). *Development, Environment and Technology: Towards a Technology for Self-Reliance.* New York: United Nations.

Galtung, J. (1982). *Environment, Development and Military Activity.* Oslo: Norwegian Universities Press.

Galtung, J. (1986). Towards a New Economics: On the Theory and Practice of Self-Reliance. In: Ekins, P. ed. *The Living Economy*. London: Routledge and Kegan Paul: 97–109.

Galtung, J., O'Brien, P. and Preiswerk, R. (1980). *Self-Reliance: A Strategy For Development*. London: Bogle-L'Ouverture Publications Ltd.

Gardner, R.A., Gardner, B.T., Chiarelli, B. and Plooij, F.X. eds. (1994). *The Ethological Roots of Culture*. Dordrecht: Kluwer Academic Publishers.

Gardner, R.N. (1974). The Hard Road to World Order. *Foreign Affairs*. 52: 556–76.

Gare, A.E. (1996). *Postmodernism and the Environmental Crisis*. London: Routledge.

Gates, H.L. and West, C. (1996). *The Future of the Race*. New York: Alfred A. Knopf.

Gauthier, D. (1994). Breaking Up: An Essay on Secession. *Canadian Journal of Philosophy* 24: 357–72.

Gazard, D. (1996). UN Backs Aussie Sell-Outs. *The Advertiser* (Adelaide) January 3: 4.

Geach, P. (1954). On *Insolubilia. Analysis* 15: 71–2.

Geach, P. (1976). *Reason and Argument*. Oxford: Basil Blackwell.

Gellner, E. (1983). *Nations and Nationalism*. Oxford: Basil Blackwell.

George, S. (1990). *A Fate Worse than Debt: The World Financial Crisis and the Poor*. New York: Grove/Weidenfeld.

Georgescu-Roegen, N. (1971). *The Entropy Law and the Economic Process*. Cambridge, Massachusetts: Harvard University Press.

Gewirth, A. (1988). Ethical Universalism and Particularism. *Journal of Philosophy* 85: 283–302.

Geyer, G.A. (1985). Our Disintegrating World: The Menace of Global Anarchy. *Encyclopaedia Britannica, Book of the Year*. Chicago: University of Chicago Press: 10–25.

Gibbins, P. (1987). *Particles and Paradoxes: The Limits of Quantum Logic*. Cambridge: Cambridge University Press.

Giddings, F.H. (1898). *The Element of Sociology*. London: Macmillan.

Giddings, F.H. (1906). *Reading in Descriptive and Historical Sociology*. London: Macmillan.

Gilbert, P. (1990). Community and Civil Strife. *Journal of Applied Philosophy* 7: 3–14.

Gilbert, P. and Gregory, P. eds. (1994). *Nations, Cultures and Markets*. Aldershot: Avebury.

Gilding, P. (1997). The Corporate Environment – Pragmatism of Greening. *Environment South Australia* 6, 2: 6.

Gilfedder, P. (1986). Self-Refuting Self-Reflection: The Case Against Nietzsche. *Dialectic* 28: 33–56.

Gill, S. (1990). *American Hegemony and the Trilateral Commission.* Cambridge: Cambridge University Press.

Ginsberg, A. (1984). On a Paradox in Quantum Mechanics. *Synthese* 61: 325–50.

Glazer, N. (1994). Golden Door Closes on the Tired, Huddled Masses. *The Australian* January 11: 9.

Glazer, N. (1997). *We are All Multiculturalists Now.* Cambridge, Massachusetts: Harvard University Press.

Glazer, N. and Moynihan, D.P. (1970). *Beyond the Melting Pot* (2nd edition). Cambridge, Massachusetts: MIT Press.

Gödel, K. (1949). An Example of a New Type of Cosmological Solution of Einstein's Field Equations of Gravitation. *Reviews of Modern Physics* 21: 447–50.

Goldberg, D.T. ed. (1994). *Multiculturalism: A Critical Reader.* Oxford: Blackwell.

Goldman, A. (1988). *Empirical Knowledge.* Berkeley: University of California Press.

Goldsmith, E. (1996a). The Last Word: Family, Community, Democracy. In: Mander, J. and Goldsmith, E. eds. *The Case Against the Global Economy and For a Turn Toward the Local.* San Francisco: Sierra Club Books: 501–14.

Goldsmith, M. (1996b). *Political Incorrectness: Defying the Thought Police.* Rydalmere, New South Wales: Hodder and Stoughton.

Goldstein, L. (1988). The Sorites as a Lesson in Semantics. *Mind* 97: 447–55.

Gomberg, P (1994). Universalism and Optimism. *Ethics* 104: 536–557.

Gonella, F. (1994). Time Machine, Self-Consistency and The Foundations of Quantum Mechanics. *Foundations of Physics Letters* 7: 161–66.

Goodin, R.E. (1988). What Is So Special About Our Fellow Countrymen? *Ethics* 98: 663–686.

Goodship, L. (1996). On Dialethism. *Australasian Journal of Philosophy* 74: 153–61.

Gore, A. (1997). Respect the Land. *Time* (Special Edition) November: 8–9.

Gott, R. (1994). Death of a Dinosaur. *New Internationalist* December: 26.

Graubard, S.R. ed., (1988) *The Artificial Intelligence Debate: False Starts, Real Foundations.* Cambridge, Massachusetts: MIT Press.

Gray, A. (1946). *The Socialist Tradition.* London: Longmans, Green.

Gray, J. (1986). *Liberalism.* Minneapolis: University of Minnesota Press.

Gray, J. (1995). *Enlightenment's Wake: Politics and Culture at the Close of The Modern Age.* London and New York: Routledge.

Gray, J. (1996). If the Fez Fits. *The Guardian* January 8: 13.

Greider, W. (1987). *Secrets of the Temple: How the Federal Reserve Runs the Country*. New York: Simon and Schuster.

Greider, W. (1997). *One World, Ready or Not: The Manic Logic of Global Capitalism*. New York: Simon and Schuster.

Grim, P. (1991). *The Incomplete Universe: Totality, Knowledge, and Truth*. Cambridge, Massachusetts: MIT Press.

Grøn, Ø. and Nicola, M. (1976). The Consistency of the Postulates of Special Relativity. *Foundations of Physics* 6: 677–80.

Guardian/Reuter. (1997). UN's 'Quiet Revolution'. *The Age* July 18: A13.

Gurr, N. (1997). Return to Darkness. *New Scientist* July 26: 65.

Guyatt, D.G. (1996). The Pinay Circle: An Invisible Power Network. *Nexus* August-September: 11–14.

Haack, S. (1976). The Justification of Deduction. *Mind* 85: 112–19.

Haack, S. (1982). Dummett's Justification of Deduction. *Mind* 91: 216–39.

Hacker, A. (1992). *Two Nations: Black and White, Separate, Hostile, Unequal*. New York: Scribner's.

Hajari, N. (1997). Bursting at the Seams. *Time* (Special Edition) November: 31–3.

Hallowell, C. (1997). Will the World Go Hungry? *Time* (Special Edition) November: 22–6.

Handlin, L. and Handlin, O. (1995). America and Its Discontents: A Great Society Legacy. *The American Scholar* Winter: 15–37.

Hannerz, U. (1990). Cosmopolitans and Locals in World Culture. *Theory, Culture and Society* 7: 237–51.

Hardin, G. (1974). Living on a Lifeboat. *BioScience* 24: 561–68.

Hardin, G. (1976). Carrying Capacity as an Ethical Concept. In: Lucas Jr., G.R. and Ogletree, T.W. eds. *Lifeboat Ethics: The Moral Dilemmas of World Hunger*. New York: Harper and Row: 120–37.

Hardin, G. (1977a). *The Limits of Altruism: An Ecologist's View of Survival*. Bloomington, Indiana: Indiana University Press.

Hardin, G. (1977b). Lifeboat Ethics: The Case Against Helping the Poor. In: Aiken, A. and LaFollette, H. eds., *World Hunger and Moral Obligation*. Englewood Cliffs, New Jersey: Prentice-Hall Inc: 12–21.

Hardin, G. (1978a). *Stalking the Wild Taboo*. Los Altos: William Kaufmann.

Hardin, G. (1978b). The Limits of Sharing. *World Issues* February/March: 5–10.

Hardin, G. (1979). Heeding the Ancient Wisdom of *Primum Non Nocere*. In: Finnin, W.M. and Smith, G.A. *The Morality of Scarcity: Limited Resources and Social Policy*. Baton Rouge and London: Louisiana State University Press: 25–35.

Hardin, G. (1980a). Limited World, Limited Rights. *Society* May/June: 5–8.

Hardin, G. (1980b). *Promethean Ethics: Living With Death, Competition, and Triage.* Seattle and London: University of Washington Press.

Hardin, G. (1982) Discriminating Altruisms. *Zygon.* 17: 163–86.

Hardin, G. (1985). *Filters Against Folly.* New York: Viking.

Hardin, G. (1986). Carrying Capacity: A Biological Approach to Human Problems. *BioScience* 36: 599–606.

Hardin, G. (1993). *Living Within Limits: Ecology, Economics, and Population Taboos.* New York and Oxford: Oxford University Press.

Hardin, G. (1994). Three Essays. *Population and Environment* 16: 191–95.

Hardin, G. (1995). *The Immigration Dilemma: Avoiding the Tragedy of the Commons.* Washington DC: Federation for American Immigration Reform.

Harries, O. (1993). Clash of Civilisations. *The Weekend Australian* April 3–4: 19.

Harris, J. (1982). A Paradox of Multicultural Societies. *Journal of Philosophy of Education* 16: 223–33.

Harvey, D. (1989). *The Conditions of Postmodernity: An Enquiry into the Origins of Cultural Change.* Oxford: Basil Blackwell.

Hattersley, J.M. (1988). Frederick Soddy and the Doctrine of "Virtual Wealth." A Paper Presented to the 14th Annual Convention of the Eastern Economics Association, Boston, Massachusetts, March 1988. 19 pages.

Havas, R. (1995). *Nietzsche's Genealogy: Nihilism and the Will to Knowledge.* Ithaca: Cornell Univerity Press.

Hawken, P. (1993). *The Ecology of Commerce: A Declaration of Sustainability.* New York: HarperBusiness.

Hawking, S.W. and Ellis, G.F.R. (1973). *The Large-Scale Structure of Space-Time.* Cambridge: Cambridge University Press.

Hawkins, W.R. (1996). Social Engineering in the Balkans: Building a "New World" State. *Chronicles* May: 12–14.

Hayek, F.A. (1976a). *Denationalisation of Money: An Analysis of the Theory and Practice of Concurrent Currencies.* London: The Institute of Economic Affairs.

Hayek, F.A. (1976b). *Choice in Currency: A Way to Stop Inflation.* London: The Institutue of Economic Affairs.

Hayek, F.A. (1986). *The Road to Serfdom.* London: Ark Paperbacks.

Hazelett, R. and Turner, D. eds. (1979). *The Einstein Myth and the Ives Papers: A Counter-Revolution in Physics.* Old Greenwich, Connecticut, Devin-Adair Company.

Hazen, A. (1990). A Variation on a Paradox. *Analysis* 50: 7–8.

Hazzard, S. (1995). Three Jeers for the U.N. *The Weekend Australian* July 1–2: 27.

Heason, H.W. (1963). *Beyond Relativity*. London: Regency Press.

Heck, R.G. (1993). A Note on the Logic of (Higher-Order) Vagueness. *Analysis*. 53: 201–8.

Heffernan, J.D. (1978). Some Doubts About "Turing Machine Arguments". *Philosophy of Science* 45: 638–47.

Heller, M. (1998). Vagueness and the Standard Ontology. *Nous* 22: 109–31.

Hellyer, P. (1994). *Funny Money: A Common Sense Alternative to Mainline Economics*. Toronto: Chimo Media Limited.

Helms, J. (1996). Saving the U.N. *Foreign Affairs* September/October: 2–7.

Hems, J.M. (1971). The Limits of Decision. *Philosophy and Phenomenological Research*. 31: 527–39.

Henderson, G. (1997a). (Tzadik Column). *The Australia/Israel Review* August 8–28: 24

Henderson, G. (1997b). Ideologies of a Desert Island. *The Sydney Morning Herald* July 29:15.

Henderson, G. (1997c). Inventing the Enemy. *The Sydney Morning Herald*. July 8: 15.

Herald Sun (1997). Chilling Future for Earth. *Herald Sun* September 12: 35.

Herbert, R.T. (1987). The Relativity of Simultaneity. *Philosophy* 62: 455–71.

Hersh, S.M. (1994). The Wild East. *The Atlantic Monthly* June: 61–86.

Herzberger, H.G. (1982). Notes on Naive Semantics. *Journal of Philosophical Logic* 11: 61–102.

Hilton, H.C. (1994). *The Nature of Money and Banking: A Historical Perspective*. Master of Philosophy Thesis, Faculty of Commerce and Administration, Griffith University, Queensland.

Hinckfuss, I. (1987). *The Moral Society: Its Structure and Effects*. Discussion Papers in Environmental Philosophy, No 16. Canberra: Department of Philosophy, Research School of Social Sciences, Australian National University.

Hirsh, M. (1994). Capital Wars. *The Bulletin* (Australia) October 25: 66–70.

Hirst, P. and Thompson, G. (1992). The Problem of 'Globalization': International Economic Relations, National Economic Management and the Formation of Trading Blocs. *Economy and Society* 21: 357–96.

Hirst, P. and Thompson, G. (1996). *Globalization in Question: The International Economy and the Possibilities of Governance*. Cambridge: Polity Press.

Hiskett, W.R. and Franklin, J.A. (1939). *Searchlight on Social Credit*. Westminster: P.S. King and Son.

Hixon, W.F. (1991). *A Matter of Interest: Reexamining Money, Debt, and Real Economic Growth.* Westport, Connecticut and London: Praeger.

Hobsbawn, E.J. (1992). Ethnicity and Nationalism in Europe Today. *Anthropology Today* 8: 3–8.

Hoey, L. (1990). The Scourge of Nationalism in the Modern World: Is There a Non-Hierarchical Solution? *Social Alternatives* 8: 54–6.

Hofstadter, D.R. (1980). *Gödel, Escher, Bach: An Eternal Golden Braid.* Harmondsworth: Penguin Books.

Hofstadter, D.R. (1986). *Metamagical Themas: Questing for the Essence of Mind and Pattern.* Harmondsworth: Penguin Books.

Hofstadter, D.R. and Dennett, D.C. eds. (1981). *The Mind's I: Fantasies and Reflections on Self and Soul.* Sussex: Harvester Press.

Holbrook, P.E. (1988). Metaphor and the Will to Power. *International Studies in Philosophy* 20: 19–28.

Honderich, T. (1988a). *Mind and Brain: A Theory of Determinism* Volume 1. Oxford: Clarendon Press.

Honderich, T. (1988b). *The Consequences of Determinism: A Theory of Determinism* Volume 2. Oxford: Clarendon Press.

Hook, S. (1989). Is Teaching "Western Culture" Racist or Sexist? *Encounter* September–October: 14–19.

Hooker, C. and Penfold, B. (1995). Artificial Versus Natural Intelligence: What Role for the Brain? *Search* 26: 281–84.

Hoppe, H–H. (1996). Small is Beautiful and Efficient: The Case for Secession. *Telos* 107: 95–101.

Horgan, J. (1996). *The End of Science: Facing the Limits of Knowledge in the Twilight of the Scientific Age.* Reading, Massachusetts: Helix Books, Addison-Wesley Publishing Company Inc.

Horgan, T. and Woodward, J. (1985). Folk Psychology is Here to Stay. *Philosophical Review* 94: 197–226.

Horowitz, I.L. (1993). *The Decomposition of Sociology.* New York: Oxford University Press.

Horwich, P. (1975). On Some Alleged Paradoxes of Time Travel. *Journal of Philosophy* 72: 432–44.

Hoskin, M. (1991). *New Immigrants and Democratic Society: Minority Integration in Western Democracies.* New York: Praeger.

Hotson, J.H. (1993). Financing Sustainable Development. In: Hotson, J.H. and Good, R. eds. *The COMER Paper* Volume 3. Ontario: Committee On Monetary and Economic Reform, University of Waterloo: 171–75.

Hoyle, F. (1964). *Of Men and Galaxies.* Seattle: University of Washington Press.

Huck, S. (1997). *Why Do We Americans Submit to This?* McLean, Virginia: Newcomb Publishers.

Hughes, R. (1992). The Fraying of America. *Time* (Australia) February 3: 82–7.

Hughes, R. (1993). *Culture of Complaint: The Fraying of America*. New York: Oxford University Press.

Hughes, R. (1997a). *American Visions:The Epic History of Art in America*. London: Harvill Press.

Hughes, R. (1997b). The Cult of Identity. *The Weekend Australian Review* May 24–25: 3.

Hugly, P. and Sayward, C. (1989). Can There be a Proof that Some Unprovable Arithmetic Sentence is True? *Dialectica* 43: 289–92.

Hull, E. (1983). The Rights of Aliens: National and International Issues. In: Papademetriou, D.G. and Miller, M.J. eds. *The Unavoidable Issue: U.S. Immigration Policy in the 1980s*. Philadelphia: Institute for the Study of Human Issues: 215–49.

Hunter, G. (1988). What Computers Can't Do. *Philosophy* 63: 175–89.

Huntington, S.P. (1993). If Not Civilizations, What? Paradigms of the Post-Cold War World. *Foreign Affairs* 72, November/December: 186–94.

Huntington, S.P. (1996). *The Clash of Civilizations and the Remaking of World Order*. New York: Simon and Schuster.

Hyde, D. (1994). Why Higher-Order Vagueness is a Pseudo-Problem. *Mind* 103: 35–41.

Hylton, P. (1990). *Russell, Idealism, and the Emergence of Analytic Philosophy*. Oxford: Clarendon Press.

Ibanez-Noe, J.A. (1994). Truth and Ethos: The Philosophical Foundations of Nietzsche's Ethics. *Philosophy Today* 38: 70–87.

Icke, D. (1996) . . . *And the Truth Shall Set You Free* (2nd edition). London: Bridge of Love.

Ideström, A. (1948). *The Relativity Theories of Einstein—Untenable*. Uppsala: Almqvist and Wiksells Boktryckeri.

Iggulden, J. (1988). *How Things are Wrong and How to Fix Them* (Volume 2: *The Promised Land Papers*). Sydney: Cobham Publishers.

Ignatieff, M. (1995a). Nationalism and the Narcissism of Minor Differences. *Queens Quarterly* 102: 13–25.

Ignatieff, M. (1995b). The Seductiveness of Moral Disgust. *Index on Censorship*. 5: 22–38.

Irvine, A.R. (1992). Gaps, Gluts and Paradox. *Canadian Journal of Philosophy*. (Supplementary) 18: 273–99.

Isaacs, H.R. (1989). *Idols of the Tribe: Group Identity and Political Change*. Cambridge, Massachusetts: Harvard University Press.

Iseminger, G.I. (1980). Is Relevance Necessary for Validity? *Mind* 89: 196–213.

Isham, C. (1992). Quantum Gravity. In: Davies, P. eds. *The New Physics.* Cambridge: Cambridge University Press: 70–93.

James, P. (1984). The Nation and Its Post-Modern Critics. *Arena* 69: 159–74.

James, P. (1989). National Formation and the 'Rise of the Cultural': A Critique of Orthodoxy. *Philosophy of the Social Sciences* 19: 273–90.

Janover, M. (1986). Two Perspectives on Perspective in Nietzsche. *Dialectic.* 26: 46–60.

Jauch, J.M. (1989). *Are Quanta Real? A Galilean Dialogue.* Bloomington, Indianapolis: Indiana University Press.

Jenkins, P. (1996). Affirmative Action and the Academy. *Chronicles* September: 38–41.

Jenkins, R. (1995). Nations and Nationalisms: Towards More Open Models. *Nations and Nationalism* 1: 369–90.

Jenkins, S. (1990). Home Fires Will Always be Burning. *The Australian* January 8: 11.

Johnson, L.E. (1992). *Focusing on Truth.* London and New York: Routledge.

Johnson, P. (1991) Universities? We'd Be Better Off Without Them. *The Australian* September 18: 21.

Johnson, P. (1995). The Logical End of Black Racism is a Return to Africa. *The Spectator* December 30: 20.

Johnstone, A. (1981). Self-Reference, The Double Life and Gödel. *Logique et Analyse* 24: 35–47.

Kaplan, R.D. (1997). *The Ends of the Earth: A Journey at the Dawn of the 21st Century.* London: Papermac, Macmillan.

Karlov, L. (1981). Fact and Illusion in the Speed-of-Light Determinations of the Römer Type. *American Journal of Physics* 49: 64–6.

Kauffman, B. (1997). World Citizens on Main Street. *Chronicles* March: 12–14.

Kauffman, G.B. ed., (1986). *Frederick Soddy, 1877–1956.* Dordrecht: D. Reidel.

Kelly, C. (1969). *Conspiracy Against God and Man.* Boston: Western Islands.

Kelton, G. (1995). World Bank Backs Govt Water Plan. *The Advertiser* (Adelaide) September 8: 2.

Kemp, R. (1994). UN's Right to Meddle Stifles Nation's Voice. *The Australian* April 8: 13.

Kennedy, M. (1990). *Interest and Inflation Free Money: How to Create an Exchange Medium that Works for Everybody.* Ginsterweg Steyerberg, West Germany: Permakultur Publikationen.

Kennedy, P. (1993). *Preparing for the Twenty-first Century.* New York: Random House.

Kimball, R. (1990). *Tenured Radicals: How Politics has Corrupted Our Higher Education*. New York: Harper and Row.

Kingsley, J.M. (1975). On the Consistency of the Postulates of Special Relativity. *Foundations of Physics* 5:295–300.

Kirkpatrick, J. (1994). Clinton's Real Mistake in Somalia. *Reader's Digest* February: 67–70.

Kitcher, P. (1983). *The Nature of Mathematical Knowledge*. New York and Oxford: Oxford University Press.

Kitcher, P. (1993). *The Advancement of Science: Science Without Legend, Objectivity Without Illusions*. Oxford: Oxford University Press.

Kleinberg, S. (1991). *Politics and Philosophy: The Necessity and Limitations of Rational Argument*. Oxford: Blackwell.

Kline, M. (1980). *Mathematics: The Loss of Certainty*. Oxford: Oxford University Press.

Knelman, F. (1978). *Anti-nation: Transition to Sustainability*. Oakville, Ontario: Mosaic Press.

Knight, S. (1983). *The Brotherhood: The Secret World of the Freemasons*. London: Grafton Books.

Koelb, C. ed. (1990). *Nietzsche as Postmodernist.* Albany: State University of New York Press.

Kohr, L. (1976). *The Overdeveloped Nations: The Diseconomies of Scale*. Swansea: Christopher Davies.

Kohr, L. (1978). *The Breakdown of Nations*. New York: E.P. Dutton.

Kohr, L. (1992). Disunion Now: A Plea for a Society Based Upon Small Autonomous Units (1941). *Telos* 91: 94–8.

Koons, R.C. (1994). A New Solution to the Sorites Problem. *Mind* 103: 439–49.

Korten, D.C. (1990). *Getting to the 21st Century: Voluntary Action and the Global Agenda*. West Hartford, Connecticut: Kumarian Press.

Korten, D.C. (1995). *When Corporations Rule the World*. London: Earthscan.

Kosko, B. (1994). *Fuzzy Thinking: The New Science of Fuzzy Logic*. New York: Flamingo/HarperCollins Publishers.

Kuhse, H. and Singer, P. (1985). *Should the Baby Live?* Oxford: Oxford University Press.

Kvanvig, J.L. (1994). Review of Patrick Grim *The Incomplete Universe*. *Philosophical Books* 35: 117–19.

Lang, T. and Hines, C. (1993). *The New Protectionism: Protecting the Future Against Free Trade*. New York: New Press.

Laraudogoitia, J.P. (1989). On Paradoxes in Naive Set Theory. *Logique and Analyse* 32: 241–5.

Larson, D.B. (1963). *The Case Against the Nuclear Atom*. Portland, Oregon: North Pacific Publishers.

Larson, D.B. (1964). *Beyond Newton:An Explanation of Gravitation.* Portland, Oregon: North Pacific Publishers.

Larson, D.B. (1965). *New Light on Space and Time.* Portland, Oregon: North Pacific Publishers.

Lasch, C. (1991). Conservatism Against Itself. *Australia and World Affairs* 7: 5–17.

Lee, J. (1991). *The New World Order and the Destruction of Australian Industry.* Cranbrook, Western Australia: Veritas Publishing.

Lefkowitz, M.R. and MacLean Rogers, G. eds (1996). *Black Athena Revisited.* Chapel Hill and London: University of North Carolina Press.

Lehrer, K. (1990). *Theory of Knowledge.* Boulder, Colorado: Westview Press.

Leslie, J. (1989). *Universes.* London and New York: Routledge.

Leslie, J. (1996). *The End of the World: The Science and Ethics of Human Extinction.* London and New York: Routledge.

Levin, M. (1997). *Why Race Matters: Race Differences and What They Mean.* Westport: Praeger.

Levine, L.W. (1996). *The Opening of the American Mind: Canons, Culture, and History.* Boston: Beacon Press.

Lewis, B. (1990). The Roots of Muslim Rage. *The Atlantic Monthly* September: 47–54.

Lewis, D. (1973). *Counterfactuals.* Oxford: Basil Blackwell.

Lewis, D. (1976). The Paradoxes of Time Travel. *American Philosophical Quarterly* 13: 145–52.

Lewis, J. (1935). *Douglas Fallacies: A Critique of Social Credit.* London: Chapman and Hall.

Lewis, M.W. (1992) *Green Delusions: An Environmentalist Critique of Radical Environmentalism.* Durham and London: Duke University Press.

Lind, M. (1991). National Disinterest. *IPA Review* 44: 39–41.

Lind, M. (1995). Twilight of the U.N. *The New Republic.* October 30: 25–33.

Linden, E. (1997). What Have We Wrought? *Time* (Special Edition) November: 10–13.

Linsky, L. ed. (1971). *Reference and Modality.* Oxford: Oxford University Press.

Lipsey, R.G. (1969). *An Introduction to Positive Economics.* London: Weidenfeld and Nicolson.

Littman, G. (1992). The Irrationalist's Paradox. Paper Read at the Annual Conference of the Australasian Association of Philosophy, University of Queensland.

Löb, M.H. (1955). Solution of a Problem of Leon Henkin. *Journal of Symbolic Logic* 20: 115–18.

Loescher, G. ed. (1992). *Refugees and the Asylum Dilemma in the West.* University Park, Pennsylvania: Pennsylvania State University Press.

Lohrey, A. (1984). Australian Nationalism as a Myth. *Arena* 68: 107–23.

Lormand, E. (1990). Framing the Frame Problem. *Synthese* 82: 353–74.

Loux, M.J. ed., (1970). *Universals and Particulars: Readings in Ontology.* Notre Dame and London: University of Notre Dame Press.

Lowe, D.A. (1995). The Planckian Conspiracy: String Theory and the Black Hole Information Paradox. *Nuclear Physics* B 456: 257–68.

Lukacs, J. (1970). *The Passing of the Modern Age.* New York: Harper and Row.

Lukacs, J. (1993). *The End of the Twentieth Century and the End of the Modern Age.* New York: Ticknor and Fields.

Luntley, M. (1991). *Language, Logic and Experience: The Case for Anti-Realism.* La Salle, Illinois: Open Court.

Lustick, I.S. (1995). What Gives a People Rights to a Land? *Queen's Quarterly* 102: 53–68.

Luttwak, E., Tough, P., Blackwell, R., Dunlap, A., Gilder, G. and Reich, R. (1996). Does America Still Work? *Harper's Magazine* May: 36–47.

Lynch, A. (1997). Millennium Bug Legal Bills More Costly Than Cure: Expert. *The Australian* August 19: 36.

Lynch, F.R. and Beer, W.R. (1990). "You Ain't the Right Color, Pal." White Resentment of Affirmative Action. *Policy Review.* Winter: 64–7.

Lyons, G., Moore, E. and Smith, J.W. (1995). *Is the End Nigh? Internationalism, Global Chaos and the Destruction of the Earth.* Aldershot: Avebury.

Lyotard, J-F. (1988). *The Postmodern Condition: A Report on Knowledge.* Minneapolis: University of Minnesota Press.

MacIntyre, A. (1981). *After Virtue.* London: Duckworth.

MacIntyre, A. (1988). *Whose Justice? Which Rationality?* Notre Dame: University of Notre Dame Press.

MacIntyre, A. (1990). *Three Rival Versions of Moral Inquiry: Encyclopaedia, Genealogy and Tradition.* London: Duckworth.

Mackie, J.L. (1973). *Truth, Probability and Paradox.* Oxford: Clarendon Press.

Macrae, N. (1984). *The 2025 Report: A Concise History of the Future.* New York: Macmillan.

Magarey, J. (1994). UN Takes on Tassie Over Gays. *The Advertiser* (Adelaide) April 14: 11.

Magnus, B. (1983). Perfectibility and Attitude in Nietzsche's Ubermensch. *Review of Metaphysics* 36: 633–60.

Malament, D. (1985). Minimal Acceleration Requirements for Time Travel in Gödel Space-Time. *Journal of Mathematical Physics* 26: 774–77.

Maloney, C.J. (1987). The Right Stuff. *Synthese* 70: 349–72.

Mander, J. and Goldsmith, E. eds. (1996). *The Case Against the Global Economy and For a Turn Toward the Local.* San Francisco: Sierra Club Books.

Manning, R.C. (1987). Why Sherlock Holmes Can't be Replaced by an Expert System. *Philosophical Studies* 51: 19–28.

Marquand, D. (1997). Free Market and Free Society: Are They Really Compatible? *News Weekly* October 18: 14–17.

Martin, E.P. and Meyer, R.K. (1982). Solution ot the P-W Problem. *Journal of Symbolic Logic* 47: 869–87.

Martin, G.T. (1989). *From Nietzsche to Wittgenstein: The Problem of Truth and Nihilism in the Modern World.* New York: Lang.

Martin, H-P. and Schumann, H. (1997). *The Global Trap: Globalization and the Assault on Democracy and Prosperity.* New York: Zed Books.

Martinez-Alier, J. (1993). *Ecological Economics: Energy, Environment and Society.* Oxford: Blackwell.

Marx, K. (1972). Economic and Philosophic Manuscripts of 1844. In: Tucker, R. ed. *The Marx-Engels Reader.* New York: W.W. Norton: 52–103.

Matthews, R. (1997). Beyond Space and Time. *New Scientist* May 17:38–42.

Matustik, M.J. (1993). *Postnational Identity.* New York and London: Guilford Press.

Maxwell, M. (1990) *Morality Among Nations: An Evolutionary View.* New York: State University of New York Press.

Maxwell, M. (1995). A Reply: The Future of International Morality. *Biology and Philosophy* 10: 459–63.

Maxwell, N. (1985). Are Probabilism and Special Relativity Incompatible? *Philosophy of Science* 52: 23–43.

Maxwell, N. (1988). Are Probabilism and Special Relativity Compatible? *Philosophy of Science* 55: 640–45.

Maxwell, N. (1993). Discussion: On Relativity Theory and Openness of the Future. *Philosophy of Science* 60: 341–48.

McCall, S. (1966). Connexive Implication. *Journal of Symbolic Logic* 31: 415–33.

McCall, S. (1967). Connexive Implication and the Syllogism. *Mind* 76, 1967, 346–56.

McClintock, A. (1995). *The Convergence of Machine and Human Nature: A Critique of the Computer Metaphor of Mind and Artificial Intelligence.* Aldershot: Avebury.

McCormack, D. (1996). The Overseas Chinese: Ever the Golden Venture (Book Review). *The Social Contract* 7, Winter: 144–6.

McGee, V. (1992). Two Problems With Tarski's Theory of Consequence. *Proceedings of the Aristotelian Society* XCII: 273–92.

McGuinness, P.P. (1995). Left and Right Combine in Attack on International Financial Institutions Policy. *The Sydney Morning Herald* October: 19: 30.

McLaughlin, A.C. (1993). The Connectionism/Classical Battle to Win Souls. *Philosophical Studies* 71: 163–90.

McLean, P. and Renton, J. (1992). *Bankers and Bastards*. Hawthorn: Hudson Publishing.

McMurtry, J. (1997). The Value Crisis of the Global Market. *Economic Reform* 9, February: 4–5.

Meadwell, H. (1989). Ethnic Nationalism and Collective Choice Theory. *Comparative Political Studies* 22: 139–54.

Meiland,J.W. (1974). A Two Dimensional Passage Model of Time for Time Travel. *Philosophical Studies* 26: 153–73.

Menand, L. (1991). What are Universities For? *Harper's Magazine* December 1991: 47–56.

Mendus, S. (1989). *Toleration and the Limits of Liberalism*. Macmillan: London.

Meyer, R.K. and Abraham, A. (1984). A Model for the Modern Malaise. *Philosophia* 14: 25–40.

Meyer, R.K., Routley, R. and Dunn, J. (1979). Curry's Paradox. *Analysis* 39: 124–8.

Mickunas, A. (1988). Nietzsche and Rhetorical Aesthetics. *International Studies in Philosophy* 20: 35–46.

Midgley, M. (1984). *Wickedness: A Philosophical Essay*. London: Routledge and Kegan Paul.

Mikesell, R.F. (1995). The Limits to Growth: A Reappraisal. *Resources Policy* 21: 127–31.

Milbrath, L.W. (1989). *Envisioning a Sustainable Society: Learning Our Way Out*. Albany, New York: State University of New York Press.

Mill, J.S. (1958). *Considerations on Representative Government*, C.V. Shields ed. Indianapolis: Bobbs-Merrill Company.

Miller, D. (1988). The Ethical Significance of Nationality. *Ethics* 98: 647–62.

Miller, D. (1995). Citizenship and Pluralism. *Political Studies* 43: 432–50.

Milne, A. (1996). Has 'Liberalism' Become Despotic? *Right NOW!* April/June: 16–17.

Milne, F. (1993). Overcoming the Illusion of Monetary Scarcity. In: Rees, R., Rodley, G. and Stilwell, F. eds. *Beyond the Market: Alternatives to Economic Rationalism*. Leichhardt, New South Wales: Pluto Press: 203–21.

Milner, A. (1987). Cringing and Whinging: Imperialism, Nationalism and Cultural Critique. *Arena* 81: 57–74.

Minogue, K. (1985). *Alien Powers: The Pure Theory of Ideology*. London Weidenfeld and Nicolson.

Mitchell, B. (1997). UN Told Wik Proposal Is Divisive. *The Age* July 31: A2.

Mittelstaedt, P. (1991). An Inconsistency between Quantum Mechanics and Its Interpretation: The "Disaster" of Objectification. In: Schurz, G. and Dorn, G.J.W. eds. *Advances in Scientific Philosophy*. Amsterdam: Rodopi: 203–14.

Monahan, B.W. (1967). *An Introduction to Social Credit*. London: K.R.P. Publications.

Moorhouse, F. (1996). The Grand Days are Over: Time to Quit the UN. In: Coleman, P. ed. *Double Take: Six Incorrect Essays*. Port Melbourne: Mandarin/Reed Books Australia: 163–94.

Morris, R. (1990). *The Edges of Science: Crossing the Boundary from Physics to Metaphysics*. New York: Prentice Hall Press.

Morris-Jones, W.H. (1972). Pakistan Post-Mortem and the Roots of Bangladesh. *Political Quarterly* 18:187–200.

Mortensen, C. (1981). A Plea for Model Theory. *Philosophical Quarterly* 31: 152–57.

Mortensen, C. (1989). Anything is Possible. *Erkenntnis* 30: 319–37.

Mortensen, C. (1995). *Inconsistent Mathematics*. Dordrecht: Kluwer Academic Publishers.

Mortimer, J. (1990). Blasphemers Must Die. *The Spectator* September 22: 18–20.

Mosley, G. (1993). National Self-Sufficiency: An Alternative Environmentally Based Policy for the Australian Economy. Australian Conservation Foundation Council Discussion Paper May 25, 14 pages.

Mosley, G. (1994). Goodbye Global Trade – Hello National Self-Sufficiency. *Enveco* 1: 4–5, 7.

Moynihan, D.P. (1993). *Pandaemonium: Ethnicity in International Politics*. Oxford: Oxford University Press.

Mühlhölzer, F. (1995). Science Without Reference. *Erkenntnis* 42: 203–22.

Mumford, L. (1972). *The Transformations of Man*. New York: Harper and Row.

Myers, N. (1993). Population, Environment, and Development. *Environmental Conservation* 20: 205–16.

Myhill, J. (1960). Some Remarks on the Notion of Proof. *Journal of Philosophy* 57: 461–71.

Napoli, E. (1985). Is Vagueness a Logical Enigma? *Erkenntnis* 23: 115–21.

Nathanson, S. (1989). In Defense of "Moderate Patriotism". *Ethics* 99: 535–52.

National Australia Bank Limited (1992). *Yearbook 1992*. Sydney: National Australia Bank Limited.

Neale, S. (1990). *Descriptions*. Cambridge, Massachusetts: MIT Press/ Bradford.

Nehamas, A. (1985). *Nietzsche: Life as Literature*. Cambridge, Massachusetts: Harvard University Press.

Nelson, B.A. (1994). *America Balkanized: Immigration's Challenge to Government*. Monterey, Virginia: The American Immigration Control Foundation.

Nelson, R.H. (1991). *Reaching for Heaven on Earth: The Theological Meaning of Economics*. Savage, Marylands: Rowman and Littlefield.

Nelson, R.J. (1982). *The Logic of Mind*. Dordrecht: D. Reidel.

Neuberger, B. (1995). National Self-Determination: Dilemmas of a Concept. *Nations and Nationalism* 1: 297–325.

Newman, E.G. (1982). The Meta-Moralism of Nietzsche. *Journal of Value Inquiry*. 16: 207–22.

Nielsen, K. (1983). Global Justice and the Imperatives of Capitalism. *Journal of Philosophy* 80: 608–610.

Nielsen, K. (1986). How to be Sceptical about Philosophy. *Philosophy* 61: 83–93.

Nielsen, K. (1993). Secession: The Case of Quebec. *Journal of Applied Philosophy* 10: 29–43.

Nordenson, H. (1969). *Relativity, Time and Reality: A Critical Investigation of the Einstein Theory of Relativity from a Logical Point of View*. London: George Allen and Unwin.

Norris, C. (1989). *Deconstruction and the Interests of Theory*. Norman: University of Oklahoma Press.

Noyes, P. (1975). The Abandonment of Simultaneity. *Theoria to Theory* 9: 23–32.

Nozick, R. (1981). *Philosophical Explanations*. Oxford: Clarendon Press.

O'Brien, C.C. (1995). *On the Eve of the Millennium*. New York: Free Press.

O'Leary-Hawthorne, J. and Cortens, A. (1995). Towards Ontological Nihilism. *Philosophical Studies* 79: 143–65.

O'Loughlin, E. (1997). Winnie Cover-Up Claimed. *The Sydney Morning Herald* September 11:9.

O'Neill, J. (1994). Should Communitarians be Nationalists? *Journal of Applied Philosophy* 11: 135–43.

Ormerod, P. (1995). *The Death of Economics*. London: Faber and Faber.

Outlaw, L. (1992). Against the Grain of Modernity: The Politics of Difference and the Conservation of "Race". *Man and World* 25: 443–68.

Owen, D. (1994). *Maturity and Modernity: Nietzsche, Weber, Foucault and the Ambivalence of Reason.* London and New York: Routledge.

Palaver, W. (1992). Leopold Kohr: Prophet of a Federal Europe? *Telos* 91: 87–93.

Parker-Rhodes, A.F. (1981). *The Theory of Indistinguishables: A Search For Explanatory Principles Below the Level of Physics.* Dordrecht: D. Reidel.

Parsons, T. (1979). Referring to Nonexistent Objects. *Theory and Decision* 11: 95–110.

Parsons, T. (1980). *Nonexistent Objects.* New Haven: Yale University Press.

Payer, C. (1991). *Lent and Loss: Foreign Credit and Third World Development.* London and New York: Zed Books.

Peacocke, C. (1981). Are Vague Predicates Incoherent? *Synthese* 46: 121–41.

Peat, F.D. (1991). *Superstrings and the Search for the Theory of Everything.* London: Cardinal.

Penrose, R. (1989). *The Emperor's New Mind: Concerning Computers, Minds, and the Laws of Physics.* New York and Oxford: Oxford University Press.

Penrose, R. (1994). *Shadows of the Mind: A Search for the Missing Science of Consciousness.* Oxford: Oxford University Press.

Penrose, R. (et al) (1997). *The Large, the Small and the Human Mind.* New York: Cambridge University Press.

Perelman, L.J. (1980). Speculations on the Transition to Sustainable Energy. *Ethics* 90: 392–416.

Perloff, J. (1988). *The Shadows of Power: The Council on Foreign Relations and the American Decline.* Appleton: Western Islands.

Perrings, C. (1995). Ecology, Economics and Ecological Economics. *Ambio* 24: 60–4.

Pfeffer, R. (1965). Eternal Recurrence in Nietzsche's Philosophy. *Review of Metaphysics* 19: 276–300.

Philpott, D. (1995). Sovereignty: An Introduction and Brief History. *Journal of International Affairs* 48: 353–68.

Pigden, C. (1995). Popper Revisited, or What Is Wrong With Conspiracy Theories? *Philosophy of the Social Sciences* 25: 3–34.

Piotrowicz, R. (1997). The Soldier as Sadist. *The Age* July 7: A13.

Platts, M. ed., (1980). *Reference, Truth and Reality: Essays on the Philosophy of Language.* London: Routledge and Kegan Paul.

Pogge, T.W. (1992). Cosmopolitanism and Sovereignty. *Ethics* 103: 48–75.

Pogge, T.W. (1994). Cosmopolitanism and Sovereignty. In: Brown, C. ed. *Political Restructuring in Europe: Ethical Perspectives*. London and New York: Routledge: 89–122.

Poole, R. (1990) Nietzsche: The Subject of Morality. *Radical Philosophy* 54: 2–18.

Poole, R. (1991). *Morality and Modernity*. London: Routledge.

Popper, K. (1966). *The Open Society and Its Enemies*. London: Routledge and Kegan Paul.

Post, J.F. (1970). The Possible Liar. *Nous* 4: 405–9.

Post, J.F. (1978–79). Presupposition, Bivalence and the Possible Liar. *Philosophia* 8: 645–650.

Premdas, R. (1990). Secessionist Movements in Comparative Perspective. In: Premdas, R., De A. Samarasinghe, S.W.R. and Anderson, A.B. *Secessionist Movements in Comparative Perspective*. London: Pinter Publishers: 12–29.

Premdas, R., De A. Samarasinghe, S.W.R. and Anderson, A.B. (1990). *Secessionist Movements in Comparative Perspective*. London: Pinter Publishers.

Preston, B. (1995). The Ontological Argument Against the Mind-Machine Hypothesis. *Philosophical Studies* 80: 131–57.

Price, H. (1996). *Time's Arrow and Archimedes' Point: New Directions for the Physics of Time*. New York: Oxford University Press.

Priest, G. (1979). The Logic of Paradox. *Journal of Philosophical Logic* 8: 219–41.

Priest, G. (1984). Logic of Paradox Revisited. *Journal of Philosophical Logic* 13: 153–79.

Priest, G. and Routley, R. (1984). *On Paraconsistency*. Canberra: Department of Philosophy, Research School of Social Sciences, Australian National University.

Priest, G. (1987a). Unstable Solutions to the Liar Paradox. In: Bartlett, S.J. and Suber, P.eds. *Self-Reference: Reflections on Reflexivity*. Dordrecht: Martinus Nijhoff: 145–75.

Priest, G. (1987b). *In Contradiction: A Study of the Transconsistent*. Dordrecht: Martinus Nijhoff.

Priest, G. (1991). Sorites and Identity. *Logique and Analyse* 34: 293–96.

Priest, G. (1992). What is a Non-Normal World? *Logique and Analyse* 35: 291–302.

Priest, G. (1994a). Is Arithmetic Consistent? *Mind* 103: 337–49.

Priest, G. (1994b) What Could the Least Inconsistent Number Be? *Logique and Analyse* 37: 3–12.

Priest, G. (1995a). Etchemendy and Logical Consequence. *Canadian Journal of Philosophy* 25: 283–92.

Priest, G. (1995b). *Beyond the Limits of Thought*. Cambridge: Cambridge University Press.

Priest, G. (1996). On Inconsistent Arithmetics: A Reply to Denyer. *Mind* 105: 649–59.

Pylyshyn, Z.W. ed., (1987). *The Robot's Dilemma: The Frame Problem in Artificial Intelligence*. Norwood, New Jersey: Ablex Publishing Corporation.

Quigley, C. (1966). *Tragedy and Hope: A History of the World in Our Time*. New York: Macmillan.

Quine, W.V. (1963). *From a Logical Point of View: 9 Logico-Philosophical Essays*. New York: Harper Torchbooks, Harper and Row.

Radnitzky, G. and Bartley III, W.W., eds. (1987). *Evolutionary Epistemology, Rationality, and the Sociology of Knowledge*. La Salle, Illinois: Open Court.

Randle, R. (1970) From National Self-Determination to National Self-Development. *Journal of the History of Ideas* 31: 49–68.

Rasmussen, D. ed. (1990). *Universalism Versus Communitarianism: Contemporary Debates in Ethics*. Cambridge: Cambridge University Press.

Rawls, J. (1972). *A Theory of Justice*. Cambridge, Massachusetts: Belknap Press/Harvard University Press.

Ray, C. (1991). *Time, Space and Philosophy*. London and New York: Routledge.

Rea, G. (1989). Degrees of Truth Versus Intuitionism. *Analysis* 49: 31–2.

Read, S. (1979). Self-Reference and Validity. *Synthese* 42: 265–74.

Read, S. (1988). *Relevant Logic: A Philosophical Examination of Inference*. Oxford: Basil Blackwell.

Read, S. (1995). *Thinking About Logic: An Introduction to the Philosophy of Logic*. Oxford: Oxford University Press.

Readings, B. (1996) *The University in Ruins*. Cambridge, Massachusetts: Harvard University Press.

Redmount, I. (1990). Wormholes, Time Travel and Quantum Gravity. *New Scientist* April 28: 33–7.

Reinecke, I. (1988). *The Money Masters: Banks, Power and Economic Control*. Richmond, Victoria (Australia): William Heinemann.

Rescher, N. (1973). *The Coherence Theory of Truth*. Oxford: Clarendon Press.

Rescher, N. (1979). *Cognitive Systematization*. Oxford: Basil Blackwell.

Rescher, N. (1985). *The Strife of Systems:An Essay on the Grounds and Implications of Philosophical Diversity*. Pittsburgh: University of Pittsburgh Press.

Reuter, Associated Press. (1997). Graveyard Theft Fear in Korean Famine. *The Age* April 30: A13.

Reuters. (1991). Winnie 'Hummed, Danced During Whipping'. *The Australian* March 8: 6.

Reynolds, V., Falger, V., and Vine, I. eds. (1987). *The Sociobiology of Ethnocentrism*. London and Sydney: Croom Helm.

Rickard, M. (1994). Liberalism, Multiculturalism, and Minority Protection. *Social Theory and Practice* 20: 143–70.

Rieff, D. (1993). Multiculturalism's Silent Partner. *Harper's Magazine* August: 62–72.

Rietdijk, C.W. (1966). A Rigorous Proof of Determinism Derived from the Special Theory of Relativity. *Philosophy of Science* 33: 341–4.

Rietdijk, C.W. (1976). Special Relativity and Determinism. *Philosophy of Science* 43:598–609.

Roberts, A. (1989). Migration and a Sense of Place. *Arena* 87: 151–5.

Roberts, P.C. and Stratton, L.M. (1995). *The New Color Line: How Quotas and Privilege Destroy Democracy*. Washington D.C.: Regnery Publishing Inc.

Robertson, G. (1991). *Hypotheticals*. Crows Nest, New South Wales: Australian Broadcasting Corporation.

Robins, N. and Pye-Smith, C. (1997). The Ecology of Violence. *New Scientist* March 8: 12–13.

Robinson, W.S. (1992). Penrose and Mathematical Ability. *Analysis* 52: 80–7.

Robison, J. (1798). *Proofs of a Conspiracy*. New York: George Forman.

Roche, G. (1994). *The Fall of the Ivory Tower: Government Funding, Corruption, and the Bankrupting of American Higher Education*. Washington D.C.: Regnery Gateway.

Rodewald, R. (1985). Does Liberalism Rest on a Mistake? *Canadian Journal of Philosophy* 15: 231–52.

Rodrik, D. (1997). *Has Globalization Gone Too Far?* Washington DC: Institute for International Economics.

Roediger, D. (1992). The Racial Crisis of American Liberalism. *New Left Review* 196: 114–19.

Ronen, D. (1979). *The Quest for Self-Determination*. New Haven and London: Yale University Press.

Rorty, A. O. (1994). The Hidden Politics of Cultural Identification. *Political Theory* 22: 152–66.

Rorty, R. (1982).*Consequences of Pragmatism*.Brighton,Sussex: Harvester Press.

Rorty, R. (1989). *Contingency, Irony and Solidarity*. Cambridge: Cambridge University Press.

Rorty, R. (1991a). *Objectivity, Relativism and Truth: Philosophical Papers*, vol. 1. Cambridge: Cambridge University Press.

Rorty, R. (1991b). *Essays on Heidegger and Others: Philosophical Papers,* vol. 2. Cambridge: Cambridge University Press.

Rosas, A. (1995). State Sovereignty and Human Rights: Towards a Global Constitutional Project. *Political Studies* 43: 61–78.

Rosen, J. (1994). Is Affirmative Action Doomed? *The New Republic* October 17: 25–35.

Routley, R. (1980). *Exploring Meinong's Jungle and Beyond.* Canberra: Department of Philosophy, Research School of Social Sciences, Australian National University.

Routley, R., Plumwood, V., Meyer, R.K. and Brady, R.T. (1982). *Relevant Logics and their Rivals I.* Atascadero,California: Ridgeview Publishing Company.

Rowan, C.T. (1996). *The Coming Race War in America: A Wake-up Call.* Boston: Little, Brown and Company.

Rucker, R. (1982). *Infinity and The Mind: The Science and Philosophy of the Infinite.* Sussex: Harvester Press.

Rushdie, S. (1990). There is No Belief, Thus No Blasphemy. *The Age* February 12: 8.

Rushdie, S. (1997). Let Us Return to Civilisation. *The Australian* February 14: 15.

Rushdoony, R.J. (1970). *The Politics of Guilt and Pity.* New Jersey: The Craig Press.

Russell, B. (1897). *An Essay on the Foundations of Geometry.* Cambridge: Cambridge University Press.

Russell, B. (1919). *Introduction to Mathematical Philosophy.* London: George Allen and Unwin.

Russell, B. (1923). Vagueness. *Australasian Journal of Philosophy and Psychology* 1: 84–92.

Russell, B. (1946). The Atomic Bomb and the Prevention of War. *Bulletin of the Atomic Scientists* 2: 19–21.

Russell, B. (1975). *Power: A New Social Analysis.* London: Unwin Books.

Ruthven, M. (1990). *A Satanic Affair: Salman Rushdie and the Rage of Islam.* London: Chatto and Windus.

Ryn, C.G. (1993). Cultural Diversity and Unity. *Chronicles* June: 21–4.

Sachs, M. (1982). On the Incompatibility of the Quantum and Relativity Theories and a Possible Resolution. *Hadronic Journal* 5:1781–801.

Sachs, W. (1986). Delinking from the World Market. In Ekins, P. ed. *The Living Economy.* London: Routledge and Kegan Paul: 333–44.

Safir, O. (1976). Concrete Forms – Their Application to the Logical Paradoxes and Gödel's Theorem. *Journal of Philosophical Logic* 5: 133–54.

Sainsbury, M. (1991). Is There Higher-Order Vagueness? *Philosophical Quarterly* 41: 167–82.

Sale, K. (1980). *Human Scale*. London: Secker and Warburg.

Salmon, N.U. (1981). *Reference and Essence*. Princeton: Princeton University Press.

Samuelson, P.A., Hancock, K. and Wallace, R. (1975). *Economics* 2nd edition. Sydney: McGraw-Hill.

Sanford, D.H. (1975a). Borderline Logic. *American Philosophical Quarterly* 12: 29–39.

Sanford, D.H. (1975b). Infinity and Vagueness. *Philosophical Review* 84: 520–35.

Santamaria, B.A. (1994). Sin of Usury Escapes Capital Punishment. *The Weekend Australian* July 2–3: 24.

Santamaria, B.A. (1995). Who Rules Australia Anyway? *The Weekend Australian* (Focus) December 30–31: 9–10.

Santamaria, B.A. (1996a). Saving *Our* Sovereignty. *The Weekend Australian* January 6–7: 22.

Santamaria, B.A. (1996b). Working Capital. *The Australian* June 24: 33.

Santamaria, B.A. (1996c). Australia's Economic Problem: The Issue of Sovereignty. *Australia and World Affairs* 27: 13–25.

Santamaria, B.A. (1996d). The Politics of Financing. *The Weekend Australian* February 3–4: 26.

Santamaria, B.A. (1997a). The National Economy: How to Get Australia Working. *News Weekly* (Special Edition): 3–16

Santamaria, B.A. (1997b). Market Must be Put in Its Place. *The Weekend Australian* July 12–13: 22.

Santamaria, B.A. (1997c). Benefits Go to the Few. *The Sydney Morning Herald* August 4: 23.

Santamaria, B.A. (1997d). How to Spend Our Way Out of Trouble. *The Weekend Australian* August 2–3: 23.

Santilli, R.M. (1984). *Ethical Probe on Einstein's Followers in the U.S.A.* Newtonville: Alpha Publishing.

Sauer-Thompson, G. and Smith, J.W. (1996). *Beyond Economics: Postmodernity, Globalization and National Sustainability*. Aldershot: Avebury.

Sauer-Thompson, G. and Smith, J.W. (1997). *The Unreasonable Silence of the World: Universal Reason and the Wreck of the Enlightenment Project*. Aldershot: Avebury/Ashgate.

Saul, J.R. (1997). *The Unconscious Civilisation*. London: Penguin.

Schacht, R. (1973). Nietzsche and Nihilism. *Journal of the History of Philosophy* 11: 65–90.

Schacht, R. (1983). *Nietzsche*. London: Routledge and Kegan Paul.

Schlegel, R. (1980). *Superposition and Interaction: Coherence in Physics*. Chicago and London: University of Chicago Press.

Schock, R. (1981). The Inconsistency of the Theory of Relativity. *Zeitschrift Fuer Allgemeine Wissenschaftstheorie* 12: 285–96.

Schumacher, E.F. (1973). *Small is Beautiful*. New York: Harper and Row.

Schumpeter, J.A. (1976). *History of Economic Analysis*. New York: Oxford University Press.

Schutte, O. (1984). *Beyond Nihilism: Nietzsche Without Masks*. Chicago: University of Chicago Press.

Schwartz, S.P. and Throop, W. (1991). Intuitionism and Vagueness. *Erkenntnis* 34: 347–56.

Schwartzchild, L. (1947). *Karl Marx: The Red Prussian*. New York: Grosset and Dunlap.

Scruton, R. (1982). *A Dictionary of Political Thought*.London: Macmillan.

Scruton, R. (1985). *Thinkers of the New Left*. Essex: Longman.

Scruton, R. (1990). *The Philosopher on Dover Beach*. Manchester: Carcanet.

Scully, M.O., Englert, B-G. and Walther, H. (1991). Quantum Optical Tests for Complementarity. *Nature* 351: 111–16.

Searle, J. (1990). The Storm Over the University. *The New York Review of Books* December 6: 34–42.

Segal, R. (1967). *The Race War: The World-Wide Conflict of Races*. Harmondsworth: Penguin Books.

Seigfried, H. (1992). Nietzsche's Natural Morality. *Journal of Value Inquiry* 26: 423–31.

Sellars, W. (1979). *Naturalism and Ontology*. Reseda, California: Ridgeview Publishing Company.

Sen, A. (1993). Money and Value: On the Ethics and Economics of Finance. *Economics and Philosophy*. 9: 203–27.

Serrill, M.S. (1997).Wells Running Dry. *Time* (Special Edition) November: 16–21.

Shafer, B.C. (1972). *Faces of Nationalism: New Realities and Old Myths*. New York: Harcourt Brace Jovanovich.

Shafer, B.C. (1982). *Nationalism and Internationalism: Belonging in Human Experience*. Malabar, Florida: R.E. Krieger.

Shapiro, D. (1995). Recent Work on Liberalism and Communitarianism. *Philosophical Books* 36: 145–55.

Shaw, P. (1989). *The War Against the Intellect: Episodes in the Decline of Discourse*. Iowa City: University of Iowa Press.

Sheridan, G. (1993). 'Culture Wars': A Product of the Conspiracy Junkies. *The Australian* April 7: 9.

Sheridan, G. (1996). Time to Make Cultural Diversity a Winner. *The Australian* December 18: 13.

Sheridan, M. (1997). Bankers Blast Ballots. *The Australian* April 16: 25.

Shue, H. (1983). The Burdens of Justice. *Journal of Philosophy* 80: 600–608.

Shue, H. (1988). Mediating Duties. *Ethics* 98: 687–704.

Silverstein, J. (1980). *Burmese Politics: The Dilemma of National Unity.* New Brunswick, New Jersey: Rutgers University.

Simon, J.L. ed. (1995). *The State of Humanity.* Oxford and Cambridge, Massachusetts: Blackwell.

Singer, P. (1990). *Animal Liberation.* 2nd edition. New York: New York Review of Books/Random House.

Singer, P. (1993). *How Are We to Live? Ethics in An Age of Self-Interest.* Melbourne: Text Publishing Company.

Singer, P. (1994). *Rethinking Life and Death: The Collapse of Our Traditional Ethics.* Melbourne: Text Publishing Company.

Sklar, H. ed. (1980). *Trilateralism: The Trilateral Commission and Elite Planning For World Management.* Boston: South End Press.

Skousen, W.C. (1958). *The Naked Communist.* Salt Lake City: Ensing Publishing Co.

Skousen, W.C. (1970). *The Naked Capitalist.* Salt Lake City: The Author.

Slater, B.H. (1984). Sensible Self-Containment. *Philosophical Quarterly* 34: 163–64.

Sleeper, J. (1990). *The Closest of Strangers: Liberalism and the Politics of Race in New York.* New York: W.W. Norton.

Smith, A. (1976). *The Theory of Moral Sentiments.* Oxford: Clarendon Press.

Smith, A.D. (1983). Ethnic Identity and Nationalism. *History Today* 33: 47–50.

Smith, A.D. (1988). The Myth of the 'Modern Nation' and the Myths of Nations. *Ethnic and Racial Studies* 11: 1–26.

Smith, A.D. (1990). Towards a Global Culture? *Theory, Culture and Society* 7: 171–91.

Smith, A.D. (1994a). The Problem of National Identity: Ancient, Medieval and Modern. *Ethnic and Racial Studies* 17: 375–99.

Smith, B. (1994b). Global Competition Challenges the Socio-Economic Structure of Europe and North America. *Journal of Social, Political and Economic Studies* 19: 447–79.

Smith, C.L. (1995). Assessing the Limits to Growth. *BioScience* 45: 478–83.

Smith, J.W. (1986a). *Reason, Science and Paradox: Against Received Opinion in Science and Philosophy.* London: Croom Helm.

Smith, J.W. (1986b). Time Travel and Backward Causation. In: Smith, J.W., *Reason, Science and Paradox.* Kent: Croom Helm: 49–58.

Smith, J.W. (1988a). *Essays on Ultimate Questions: Critical Discussions on the Limits of Contemporary Philosophical Inquiry.* Aldershot: Avebury.

Smith, J.W. (1988b). *The Progress and Rationality of Philosophy as a Cognitive Enterprise: An Essay on Metaphilosophy.* Aldershot: Avebury.

Smith, J.W. (1991a). *AIDS, Philosophy and Beyond.* Aldershot: Avebury.

Smith, J.W. (1991b). *The High Tech Fix: Sustainable Ecology or Technocratic Megaprojects for the 21st Century?* Aldershot: Avebury.

Smith, J.W. (1991c). The Number 0.999 . . . . *Explorations in Knowledge* 8: 45–67.

Smith, J.W. ed. (1991). *Immigration, Population and Sustainable Environments: The Limits to Australia's Growth.* Bedford Park, South Australia: Flinders Press.

Smith, J.W., Lyons, G. and Sauer-Thompson, G. (1997). *Healing a Wounded World: Economics, Ecology, and Health for a Sustainable Life.* Westport, Connecticut and London: Praeger.

Smith, J.W., Lyons, G. and Sauer-Thompson, G. (1998a). *The Bankruptcy of Economics: Ecology, Economics and the Sustainability of the Earth.* London: Macmillan.

Smith, J.W., Lyons, G. and Moore, E. (1998b). *Global Meltdown: Immigration, Multiculturalism and National Breakdown in the New World Disorder.* Westport, Connecticut and London: Praeger.

Smith, P. (1990). *Killing the Spirit: Higher Education in America.* New York: Viking.

Smock, D.R. and Smock, A.C. (1975). *The Politics of Pluralism.* New York: Elsevier.

Smyth, W.F. (1991). Multiculturalism and Racism: Cause and Effect. In Smith J.W. ed. *Immigration, Population and Sustainable Environments: The Limits to Australia's Growth.* Adelaide: Flinders Press: 421–35.

Soddy, F. (1926). *Wealth, Virtual Wealth and Debt: The Solution of the Economic Paradox.* London: George Routledge and Sons.

Soddy, F. (1931). *Money Versus Man: A Statement of the World Problem from the Standpoint of the New Economics.* London: Elkin Mathews and Marrot.

Soddy, F. (1934). *The Role of Money.* London: George Routledge and Sons.

Solomon, S. (1995). *The Confidence Game: How Unelected Central Bankers are Governing the Changed World Economy.* New York: Simon and Schuster.

Sorensen, R. (1986). *Blindspots.* Oxford: Oxford University Press.

Sorensen, R. (1988). Vagueness, Measurement, and Blurriness. *Synthese* 75: 45–82.

Soros, G. (1997). The Capitalist Threat. *The Atlantic Monthly* February: 45–58.

Sporting Shooters Association of Australia. (1997). Who's Driving the Gun Grab? *Australian Shooters Journal* September (Special Edition) 15 pages.

Sprigge, T.L.S. (1990). The Satanic Novel: A Philosophical Dialogue on Blasphemy and Censorship. *Inquiry* 33: 377–400.

Sprigge, T.L.S. (1993). Is Dennett a Disillusioned Zimbo? *Inquiry* 36: 33–57.

Sraffa, P. (1926). The Laws of Returns Under Competitive Conditions. *Economic Journal* 36: 535–50.

Stack, G.J. (1982). Nietzsche's Myth of the Will to Power. *Dialogos* 17: 27–50.

Stalin, J. (1945). *Marxism and the National Question*. Moscow: Foreign Languages Publishing House.

Stanford, J.D. (1968). Multiple Expansion of Bank Deposits Under Australian Institutional Conditions. *The Economics Record* 44: 249–51.

Stanford, J.D. (1969). Multiple Expansion of Bank Deposits Under Australian Institutional Conditions: A Reply. *The Economic Record* 45: 297–8.

Stein, H. (1970). On the Paradoxical Time-Structures of Gödel. *Philosophy of Science* 37: 589–601.

Stein, H. (1991). On Relativity Theory and Openness of the Future. *Philosophy of Science* 58:147–67.

Stent, G. (1969). *The Coming of the Golden Age: A View of the End of Progress*. Garden City, New York: Natural History Press.

Stent, G. (1978). *The Paradoxes of Progress*. San Francisco: W.H. Freeman.

Stewart, D. (1988). Democratic Sovereignty. *Dialogue* 27: 579–89.

Stewart, R.M. (1986). Nietzsche's Perspectivism and the Autonomy of the Master Type. *Nous* 20: 371–89.

Stiles, G. (1994). The "Genius" of Einstein – Versus – A *Simple* Problem Reflecting Newtonian Laws of Motion. *Explorations in Knowledge* 11: 1–11.

Still, W.T. (1990). *New World Order: The Ancient Plan of Secret Societies*. Lafayette, Louisiana: Huntington House of Publishers.

Stix, N. (1997). The War on White Teachers. *Chronicles* March: 39–41.

Stocker, M. (1976). Agent and Other: Against Ethical Universalism. *Australasian Journal of Philosophy* 54: 206–7.

Stone, J. (1985). *Racial Conflict in Contemporary Society*. London: Fontana Press/Collins.

Stove, D. (1986). *The Rationality of Induction.* Oxford: Clarendon Press.

Stove, D. (1995). Racial and Other Antagonisms. In: *Cricket Versus Republicanism and Other Essays.* Sydney: Quakers Hill Press: 91–105.

Streeck, W. (1992). Inclusion and Secession: Questions on the Boundaries of Associative Democracy. *Politics and Society* 20: 513–20.

Stuart, J.G. (1983). *The Money Bomb.* Glasgow: William MacLellan (Embryo) Limited.

Stuart, J.G. (1992). *Economics of the Green Renaissance.* Glasgow: Ossian Publishers.

Stumph, J. (1997). Secession and the New American Constitution. *Chronicles* May: 48–50.

Sturgess, G. (1996). Who Rules a World Without Boundaries? *The Australian* October 3: 13.

Sun Yat-Sen. (1932). *San Min Chu I: The Three Principles of the People.* Shanghai: Commercial Press.

Sunstein, C.R. (1994). Approaching Democracy: A New Legal Order for Eastern Europe: Constitutionalism and Secession. In: Brown, C. ed. *Political Restructuring in Europe: Ethical Perspectives.* London and New York: Routledge: 11–49.

Suter, K. (1992). *Global Change: Armageddon and the New World Order.* Sutherland, New South Wales: Albatross Books.

Sutton, A.C. (1985). *How the Order Creates War and Revolution.* Bullsbrook, Western Australia: Veritas Publishing.

Sykes, C.J. (1988). *Profscam: Professors and the Demise of Higher Education.* New York: Kampmann and Co.

Sykes, C.J. (1990). *The Hollow Men: Politics and Corruption in Higher Education.* Washington D.C.: Regnary Gateway.

Sylvan, R. (1984). *Philosophy, Politics and Pluralism I. Relevant Modellings and Arguments.* Research Series in Logic and Metaphysics No. 2. Canberra: Department of Philosophy, Research School of Social Sciences, Australian National University.

Sylvan, R. (1988). Radical Pluralism – An alternative to Realism, Anti-Realism and Relativism. In: Nola, R. ed. *Relativism and Realism in Science.* Dordrecht: Kluwer Academic Publishers: 253–91.

Sylvan, R. (1989a). *Idealism and Coherence: One Rehabilitation Attempt.* Research Series in Unfashionable Philosophy No. 3. Canberra: Department of Philosophy, Research School of Social Sciences, Australian National University.

Sylvan, R. (1989b). *Bystanders' Guide to Sociative Logics.* (No. 4: Research Series in Logic and Metaphysics). Canberra: Department of Philosophy, Research School of Social Sciences, Australian National University.

Sylvan, R. (1992). Grim Tales Retold: How to Maintain Ordinary Discourse About – And Despite – Logically Embarrassing Notations and Totalities. *Logique and Analyse* 35: 349–74.

Sylvan, R. (n.d.) Item-Theory Further Liberalized. Unpublished manuscript.

Sylvan, R., Goddard, L. and da Costa, N. (1989). *Reason, Cause and Relevant Containment With an Application to Frame Problems.* Canberra: Department of Philosophy, Research School of Social Sciences, Australian National University.

Tamedly, E.L. (1969). *Socialism and International Economic Order.* Caldwell and Idaho: Caxton Printers Ltd.

Tamir, Y. (1995). The Enigma of Nationalism. *World Politics* 47: 418–40.

Tanton, J., McCormack, D. and Smith, J.W. eds. (1996). *Immigration and the Social Contract: The Implosion of Western Societies.* Aldershot: Avebury.

Tarski, A. (1956). *Logic, Semantic, Metamathematics.* Oxford: Clarendon Press.

Taylor, C. (1989a). *Sources of the Self: The Making of the Modern Identity.* Cambridge, Massachusetts: Harvard University Press.

Taylor, C. (1989b). The Rushdie Controversy. *Public Culture* 2: 118–22.

Taylor, C. (1992). *Multiculturalism and "The Politics of Recognition"* (with commentary by Gutmann, A., Rockefeller, S.C., Walzer, M., and Wolf, S.). Princeton, New Jersey: Princeton University Press.

Taylor, J. (1991). Up Against the New McCarthyism. *The Sydney Morning Herald* April 2: 13.

The 46 Civilian Doctors of Elisabethville (1962). *46 Angry Men.* Belmont, MA: American Opinion.

The Economist (London) (1997a). Second Thoughts About Globalisation. *The Economist* June 21: 90.

The Economist (London). (1997b). UN Soldiers of Mercy Murdered and Tortured Somalis. *The Weekend Australian.* July 5–6: 18.

Thomas, G.B. (1966). *Calculus and Analytic Geometry* (3rd edition). Reading, Massachusetts: Addison-Wesley.

Thompson, D. (1997). Melt Away Future. *Time* (Special Edition) November: 38–40.

Thompson, D.W. (1942). *On Growth and Form.* Cambridge: Cambridge University Press.

Thompson, J. (1992). *Justice and World Order: A Philosophical Inquiry.* London and New York: Routledge.

Thorne, K.S. (1995). *Black Holes and Time Warps: Einstein's Outrageous Legacy.* London: Papermac/Macmillan.

Thornton, A.P. (1995). Rights as a European Export. *Queen's Quarterly* 102: 85–99.

Thorp, J. (1980). *Free Will: A Defence Against Neurophysiological Determinism.* London: Routledge and Kegan Paul.

Thurow, L. (1996). *The Future of Capitalism: How Today's Economic Forces Shape Tomorrow's World.* St. Leonard's, New South Wales: Allen and Unwin.

Tobin, J. (1971). Commercial Banks as Creators of "Money." In: *Essays in Economics Volume 1: Macroeconomics.* Amsterdam: North-Holland Publishing Company: 272–82.

Toynbee, A.J. (1960). *A Study of History.* Oxford: Oxford University Press.

Toynbee, A.J. (1969). *Experiences.* London: Oxford University Press.

Trainer, T. (1995). *The Conserver Society: Alternatives for Sustainability.* London and New Jersey: Zed Books.

Trainer, T. (1996). *Towards a Sustainable Economy: The Need for Fundamental Change.* Sydney: Envirobook.

Trainer, T. (1997). Economic Rationalism is *Not* a Mistake. *Economic Reform Australia Newsletter* March/April: 4–5.

Travis, C. (1985). Vagueness, Observation, and Sorites. *Mind* 94: 345–66.

Tsung, S. (1980). The Process of Credit Creation in Non-Bank Financial Institutions. Macquarie University, Centre for Studies in Money, Banking and Finance, Working Paper No. 8020, September.

Tully, J. ed. (1994). *Philosophy in an Age of Pluralism: The Philosophy of Charles Taylor in Question.* Cambridge: Cambridge University Press.

Turnbull, C.S.S. (1986). Financing World Development Through Decentralized Banking. In: Mtewa, M. ed. *Perspectives in International Development.* New Delhi: Allied Publishers: 93–6.

Turner, B.S. ed. (1990) *Theories of Modernity and Postmodernity.* London: Sage.

Twinning, W. ed. (1991). *Issues of Self-Determination.* Aberdeen: Aberdeen University Press.

Tye, M. (1994). Why the Vague Need Not be Higher-Order Vague. *Mind* 103: 43–5.

Unger, P. (1979a). There Are No Ordinary Things. *Synthese* 41: 117–54.

Unger, P. (1979b). Why There Are No People. *Midwest Studies in Philosophy* 4: 177–222.

United Nations Industrial Development Organization. (1975). *Lima Declaration and Plan of Action on Industrial Development and Co-Operation.* Lima, Peru: Second General Conference of the United Nations Industrial Development Organization, March 12–26.

Van Atta, D. (1995a). The Folly of U.N. Peacekeeping. *Reader's Digest* November: 53–8.

Van Atta, D. (1995b). The United Nations is Out of Control. *Reader's Digest* December: 112–17.

Van Benthem, J.F.A.K. (1978). Four Paradoxes. *Journal of Philosophical Logic* 7: 49–72.

Verdery, K. (1994). Beyond the Nation in Eastern Europe. *Social Text* 38: 1–19.

Von Borzeszkowski, H-H. and Treder, H.J. (1988). *The Meaning of Quantum Gravity*. Dordrecht: Kluwer.

Vulliamy, E. (1996). Battle Joined on Britain's Streets. *Guardian Weekly* January 7: 23.

Walker, M.U. (1987). Moral Particularity. *Metaphilosophy* 18: 171–85.

Wallerstein, I. (1990). Culture as the Ideological Battleground of the Modern World-System. *Theory, Culture and Society* 7: 31–55.

Walsh, J. (1995). The U.N. at 50: Who Needs It? *Time* (Australia) October 23: 28–35.

Walter, I. (1989). *Secret Money: The World of International Financial Secrecy*. London: Unwin Paperbacks.

Walton, G. (1995). Cohen on Einstein and Simultaneity. *Philosophy* 70: 114–18.

Walzer, M. (1980a). The Moral Standing of States: A Response to Four Critics. *Philosophy and Public Affairs* 9: 209–29.

Walzer, M. (1980b). *Just and Unjust Wars*. Harmondsworth: Penguin.

Walzer, M. (1990). The Communitarian Critique of Liberalism. *Political Theory* 18: 6–23.

Walzer, M. (1994). Notes on the New Tribalism. In: Brown, C. ed. *Political Restructuring in Europe: Ethical Perspectives*. London and New York: Routledge: 187–200.

Warby, M. (1997). A Rational Dream for Economic Tolerance. *The Age* August 28: A17.

Ward, D.V. (1989). Human Rights and National Self-Determination. In: Peden, C. and Sterba, J.P. eds., *Freedom, Equality, and Social Change*. Lewiston: Edwin Mellen Press: 51–67.

Warren, M. (1991). *Nietzsche and Political Thought*. Cambridge, Massachusetts: MIT Press.

Watson, G. (1996). Don't Give Us India: The Multiculturalist Case. *Chronicles* September: 14–17.

Watson, G. ed. (1982). *Free Will*. Oxford: Oxford University Press.

Watson, J. (1994). *Between Auschwitz and Tradition: Postmodern Reflections on the Task of Thinking*. Amsterdam: Rodopi.

Watson, L. (1995). *Dark Nature: A Natural History of Evil*. London: Hodder and Stoughton.

Webster, N.H. (1919). *The French Revolution: A Study in Democracy*. London: Constable.

Webster, N.H. (1921). *World Revolution: The Plot Against Civilization*. London: Constable.

Webster, N.H. (1924). *Secret Societies and Subversive Movements*. London: Boswell.

Weingard, R. (1979). General Relativity and The Conceivability of Time Travel. *Philosophy of Science* 46:328–32.

Weizenbaum, J. (1987). *Computer Power and Human Reason: From Judgement to Calculation*. London: Penguin Books.

Wellman, C.H. (1995). A Defence of Secession and Political Self-Determination. *Philosophy and Public Affairs* 24: 142–71.

Wells, H.G. (1940). *The New World Order*. London: Secker and Warburg.

White, A.R. (1975). *Modal Thinking*. Oxford: Basil Blackwell.

White, V.A. (1991). Cohen on Einstein's Simultaneity Gedankenexperiment. *Philosophy* 66: 244–5.

White, V.A. (1993). Relativity and Simultaneity Redux. *Philosophy* 68: 401–4.

Wicker, T. (1996). *Tragic Failure: Racial Integration in America*. New York: William Morrow and Company, Inc.

Wilcox, J.T. (1972). Elements of Irrationalism in Nietzsche's Metaethics. *Philosophy and Phenomenological Research* 33: 227–40.

Will, C.M. (1995). *Was Einstein Right? Putting General Relativity to the Test*. Oxford: Oxford University Press.

Williams, B. (1989). A Class Act: Anthropology and the Race to Nation Across Ethnic Terrain. *Annual Review of Anthropology* 18: 401–44.

Williams, C.H. (1987). The Question of National Congruence. In: Johnston, R.J. and Taylor, P.J. eds. *A World in Crisis? Geographical Perspectives*. Oxford: Basil Blackwell: 196–230.

Williams, M. (1988). Transcendence and Return: The Overcoming of Philosophy in Nietzsche and Wittgenstein. *International Philosophical Quarterly* 28: 403–19.

Williamson, D. (1996). Men, Women and Human Nature. In: Coleman, P. ed. *Double Take: Six Incorrect Essays*. Port Melbourne: Mandarin: 9–33.

Williamson, T. (1992). Inexact Knowledge. *Mind* 101: 217–42.

Williamson, T. (1994). *Vagueness*. London and New York: Routledge.

Willkie, W.L. (1943). *One World*. New York: Simon and Schuster.

Wilson, A.J. (1988). *Break-Up of Sri Lanka: Tamil-Sinhalese Conflict*. London: Hurst.

Wilson, E.O. (1993). Is Humanity Suicidal? *New York Times Magazine* May 30: 25–28.

Wilson, J.K. (1995). *The Myth of Political Correctness: The Conservative Attack on Higher Education*. Durham and London: Duke University Press.

Windt, P.Y. (1973). The Liar in the Prediction Paradox. *American Philosophical Quarterly* 10: 65–68.

Winner, L. (1986). *The Whale and the Reactor: A Search for Limits in an Age of High Technology*. Chicago and London: University of Chicago Press.

Wood, A. (1997). The Crisis in Jobs. *The Australian* June 21: 21.

Wood, D. (1990). *Philosophy at the Limit: Problems of Modern European Thought*. Scranton: Unwin Hyman.

Woodward, B. (1994). *The Agenda*. New York: Simon and Schuster.

Woodward, J.F. (1995). Making the Universe Safe for Historians – Time Travel and the Laws of Physics. *Foundations of Physics Letters* 8: 1–39.

Woolcott, R. (1993).We Must be the Odd Man In. *The Weekend Australian* April 17–18: 8.

Woollacott, M. (1996). Old Habits Die Hard in the Deep South. *Guardian Weekly* June 30: 13.

World Constitution and Parliament Association. (1991). *Constitution for the Federation of Earth*. Lakewood, Colorado: World Constitution and Parliament Association.

Wrangham, R. and Peterson, D. (1996). *Demonic Males: Apes and the Origins of Human Violence*. London: Bloomsbury.

Wright, C. (1992). Is Higher-Order Vagueness Coherent? *Analysis* 52: 129–39.

Wurmbrand, R. (1986). *Marx and Satan*. Westchester, Illinois: Crossway Books.

Yallop, R. (1997). Austrian Writer Sees Hansons Everywhere. *The Weekend Australian* July 19–20: 4.

Yates, S. (1992). Multiculturalism and Epistemology. *Public Affairs Quarterly* 6: 435–56.

Yuting, S. (1995). Two Semantical Paradoxes. *Journal of Symbolic Logic* 20: 119–20.

Zalta, E.N. (1983). *Abstract Objects: An Introduction to Axiomatic Metaphysics*. Dordrecht: D. Reidel.

Zangari, M. (1994). Zeno, Zero and Indeterminate Forms: Instants in the Logic of Motion. *Australasian Journal of Philosophy* 72: 187–204.

Zarlenga, S. (1996a). Early U.S. History: Bankers Seize Money Supply. *The Barnes Review* April: 31–4.

Zarlenga, S. (1996b). Money Systems of the World – How We Got Where We Are. *The Barnes Review* June: 9–13.

Index